Gewirthian Perspectives on Human Rights

Gewirth's theory of human rights has made a major contribution to philosophy. In this edited collection, contributors from a broad range of disciplines discuss the theoretical and practical application of Gewirthian theory to current world issues. The case studies highlight mental health, the LGBT community, intellectual disabilities, global economic inequality, and market instability to provide a truly interdisciplinary study. This important contribution to human rights scholarship provides a platform for further discussion of Gewirthian theory. It will be of interest to those researching moral, legal, and political philosophy, as well as policy makers, social workers, and medical staff.

Per Bauhn is a Professor of Practical Philosophy at Linnaeus University, Sweden. He has previously applied Alan Gewirth's moral theory to problems relating to political terrorism and nationalism (*Ethical Aspects of Political Terrorism*, 1989, *Nationalism and Morality*, 1995, both Lund University Press) as well as to the virtue of courage (*The Value of Courage*, Nordic Academic Press, 2003). He has published several articles in international philosophical journals on the duty to rescue.

Routledge Studies in American Philosophy

Edited by Willem deVries, *University of New Hampshire, USA*
and Henry Jackman, *York University, Canada*

1 **Intentionality and the Myths of the Given**
Between Pragmatism and Phenomenology
Carl B. Sachs

2 **Richard Rorty, Liberalism and Cosmopolitanism**
David E. McClean

3 **Pragmatic Encounters**
Richard J. Bernstein

4 **Toward a Metaphysics of Culture**
Joseph Margolis

5 **Gewirthian Perspectives on Human Rights**
Edited by Per Bauhn

Gewirthian Perspectives on Human Rights

Edited by Per Bauhn

NEW YORK AND LONDON

First published 2016
by Routledge
711 Third Avenue, New York, NY 10017

and by Routledge
2 Park Square, Milton Park, Abingdon, Oxon OX14 4RN

Routledge is an imprint of the Taylor & Francis Group, an informa business

© 2016 Per Bauhn

The right of the editor to be identified as the author of the editorial material, and of the authors for their individual chapters, has been asserted in accordance with sections 77 and 78 of the Copyright, Designs and Patents Act 1988.

All rights reserved. No part of this book may be reprinted or reproduced or utilized in any form or by any electronic, mechanical, or other means, now known or hereafter invented, including photocopying and recording, or in any information storage or retrieval system, without permission in writing from the publishers.

Trademark notice: Product or corporate names may be trademarks or registered trademarks, and are used only for identification and explanation without intent to infringe.

Library of Congress Cataloging-in-Publication Data
Names: Bauhn, Per, editor.
Title: Gewirthian perspectives on human rights / edited by Per Bauhn.
Description: 1 [edition]. | New York : Routledge, 2016. | Series: Routledge studies in American philosophy ; 5 | Includes bibliographical references and index.
Identifiers: LCCN 2015044961 | ISBN 9781138649866 (alk. paper)
Subjects: LCSH: Gewirth, Alan. Human rights. | Civil rights. | Civil rights—Moral and ethical aspects. | Human rights. | Human rights—Moral and ethical aspects.
Classification: LCC JC571.G443 G49 2016 | DDC 323.01—dc23
LC record available at http://lccn.loc.gov/2015044961

ISBN: 978-1-138-64986-6 (hbk)
ISBN: 978-1-315-62564-5 (ebk)

Typeset in Sabon
by Apex CoVantage, LLC

Printed and bound in Great Britain by
TJ International Ltd, Padstow, Cornwall

Alan Gewirth 1912–2004

Source: Photo courtesy of the University of Chicago News Office

Contents

List of Figures and Table	ix
Introduction PER BAUHN	1

PART I
Gewirthian Theory

1 Gewirth Versus Kant on Kant's Maxim of Reason:
Towards a Gewirthian Philosophical Anthropology   13
DERYCK BEYLEVELD

2 Is Alan Gewirth's Moral Philosophy Neo-Stoic?   30
EDWARD SPENCE

3 'On Pain of Contradiction': A Key Moment in Deductive
Agency Arguments   47
MICHAEL BOYLAN

4 Dialectical Necessity and the 'Is-Ought' Problem   63
STUART TODDINGTON

PART II
Gewirthian Contributions

5 A Dialectically Necessary Approach to the Sociological
Understanding of Power and Real Interests   81
STEPHEN A. BROWN

6 Gewirth's Moral Philosophy and the Foundation
of Catholic Social Thought   96
CHRISTOPH HÜBENTHAL

viii *Contents*

7 Confucianism and Gewirthian Human Rights in a
Taiwanese Context 111
SHU-MEI TANG AND SHANG-YUNG YEN

8 The Gewirthian Ideal of Self-Fulfillment: Enhancing the
Moral Foundations of International Law 125
ROBERT A. MONTAÑA

9 Thomas Piketty and Alan Gewirth: Is a Global Community
of Rights Possible in the Twenty-First Century? 140
GREGORY J. WALTERS AND MARIE CONSTANCE MORLEY

PART III
Gewirthian Applications

10 A Gewirthian Framework for Protecting the Basic Human
Rights of Lesbian, Gay, Bisexual, and Transgender
(LGBT) People 157
VINCENT J. SAMAR

11 Justifying Mental Health Rights From a Gewirthian Perspective 174
PHIL BIELBY

12 Gewirthian Philosophy and Young Adults Who Have Down
Syndrome: Towards a Human Rights-Based Model of
Community Engagement for Young People Living With
an Intellectual Disability 191
MIRIAM STEVENSON

13 The Gewirthian Duty to Rescue 212
PER BAUHN

Contributors 227
Index 231

Figures and Table

FIGURES

12.1	The theoretical framework of the research	195
12.2	Global themes and organizing themes as dynamic and interconnected citizenship processes	201
12.3	Framework of social citizenship theory for young people involved in the research	202
12.4	The foundation and practice domains of the Citizen Engagement Model	204

TABLE

12.1	Action research project aims for the community engagement of young people who have Down syndrome	193

Introduction

Per Bauhn

ALAN GEWIRTH: A SHORT BIOGRAPHY[1]

Alan Gewirth was born in Union City, New Jersey, on November 28, 1912, as Isidore Gewirtz. His parents, Hyman Gewirtz and Rose Lees Gewirtz, were immigrants from what was then Tsarist Russia, where the anti-semitic pogroms of the early twentieth century forced many people to cross the Atlantic in the hopes of a new beginning and a better life for themselves. Gewirth was later to dedicate his 1982 book *Human Rights*, 'To the memory of my Mother and Father and to Aunt Rebecca and Cousin Libby who as young emigrants from Czarist Russia knew the importance of human rights'.[2] At age eleven, after having been teased by playmates on the schoolyard as 'Dizzy Izzy', he announced to his parents that from now on, his first name was to be Alan. The source of inspiration here was a character in Robert Louis Stevenson's historical adventure novel *Kidnapped*, Alan Breck Stewart, an eighteenth-century Scottish Jacobite, whom the young boy Gewirtz admired as a fearless man of the people. Later, in 1942, at the time of his first marriage, he changed his last name from Gewirtz to Gewirth. At a time when anti-semitism was rife also in the US, many Jewish Americans found it necessary to anglicize their names. In this way, Isidore Gewirtz became Alan Gewirth.

His father, who once had entertained a dream of becoming a concert violinist, gave him violin lessons when Alan was just four or five years old, and later had him take professional lessons. At around age eleven or twelve, Alan himself started to give violin lessons to younger children in the family's apartment. After entering Columbia University in 1930, he joined the Columbia University Orchestra as a violinist, becoming concertmaster in 1934.

At Columbia, Gewirth was encouraged to pursue philosophical studies by his teacher Richard McKeon. In 1937, he became McKeon's assistant at the University of Chicago. Gewirth served in the US Army 1942–46, moving up the ranks from private to captain, after which time he spent the 1946–47 academic year at Columbia on the GI Bill, completing his doctorate in philosophy with a dissertation on Marsilius of Padua and medieval political

2 Bauhn

philosophy (published as a book in 1951). From 1947 onwards, he was a regular member of the faculty of the University of Chicago, from 1960 as a full professor of philosophy. Gewirth was elected a Fellow of the American Academy of Arts and Sciences in 1975, and served as president of the American Philosophical Association Western Division (1973–74), as well as president of the American Society for Political and Legal Philosophy (1983–84). He was the recipient of several prizes and awards, including the Gordon J. Laing Prize for *Reason and Morality*. He was appointed the Edward Carson Waller Distinguished Service Professor of Philosophy at the University of Chicago in 1975. He continued to teach well into his eighties, teaching a course on the philosophical foundations of human rights within the newly constituted Human Rights Program at the University of Chicago as late as 1997–2000. His last public lecture was given in August 2003 at the XXI World Congress of Philosophy in Istanbul, Turkey. Alan Gewirth died on May 9, 2004.

MORAL PHILOSOPHY IN THE TWENTIETH CENTURY

The twentieth century was not a very hospitable age for philosophers trying to provide an objectivist foundation for moral principles. In the first half of the century, the dominant mode of philosophical thinking about ethics was emotivist and non-cognitivist. Emotivism regarded moral statements about what is right and wrong as mere expressions of the speaker's attitudes and of her desire to make us share these attitudes. Like other emotive statements, they could be neither true nor false, and there could be no way of proving them. Moral pronouncements came to be thought of as similar to claims made in advertising or in various forms of propaganda. Taking its point of departure in the works of philosophers such as Alfred Jules Ayer in the UK and Charles Leslie Stevenson in the US, emotivism maintained a dominant presence in analytic philosophy throughout the Cold War years.

The later years of the twentieth century instead witnessed the rise of postmodernism and a return of pre-modernist cultural relativism. Now there was room for moral values in public debate, but these values were regarded as relative to various traditions or cultures. Once again, belief in objective and universally justified moral values, such as human rights, was rejected as a kind of culturally produced superstition. This time there was also the additional suspicion that any talk of universal moral values was in reality a disguised attempt by the specific culture of Western Enlightenment to impersonate global reason. Hence, the discourse of universal human rights could either be dismissed as a form of cultural imperialism, or find itself compared with a belief in witches and unicorns. The latter claim was made by Alasdair MacIntyre, one of the leading proponents of a communitarian form of relativism.

Against this rather hostile background, Alan Gewirth took it upon himself to prove that there could indeed be given a rational foundation for normative ethics, a foundation that would be valid for all rational agents

Introduction 3

regardless of their subjective preferences or cultural context. Over a period of twenty years, Gewirth published four books[3] and more than sixty journal articles, developing and defending his argument that we, as rational agents who want to realize our goals, logically must claim rights to freedom and well-being, these being the necessary conditions of all successful action. In addition to his own work, two collections of essays by other philosophers, concerning theoretical and practical aspects of his theory and commented on by Gewirth himself, were published during his lifetime.[4] Here, we should also note the impressive task undertaken by Deryck Beyleveld to show that all the objections raised against Gewirth's theory so far (that is, up to the time of the publication of Beyleveld's book in 1991), either had already been successfully resolved by Gewirth himself, or could be so resolved with the help of the theoretical framework created by him.[5]

GEWIRTH'S MORAL THEORY

Gewirth described his theory as 'a modified naturalism'.[6] He wanted to anchor morality in the empirical world of agents and in the canons of deductive and inductive logic, rather than relegating it to a series of intuitions that could be arbitrarily accepted or rejected by different persons. However, any kind of naturalism in ethics will face the formidable obstacle known as Hume's Law, saying that we cannot derive an 'ought' from an 'is'. According to Hume's Law, descriptive and prescriptive statements inhabit different logical domains. For instance, from the descriptive observation that, as a matter of fact, most people in a particular society *are* in favour of a criminalization of blasphemy, we are not allowed to derive the prescriptive conclusion that blasphemy indeed *should* be criminalized (in this or in any other society).

However, Gewirth argues that agency provides a context in which it is indeed possible to escape the obstacle presented by Hume's Law. This is so, since agency, although it applies to empirically existing phenomena (persons acting to achieve their goals), also has a *normative structure*, involving evaluative and prescriptive claims made at least implicitly by every rational agent. To begin with, every agent can be assumed to consider the purpose of her action as something *good*. Gewirth takes this as a conceptual truth of agency. We involve ourselves in agency for the sake of something that we *want* to achieve by our action, and in this sense, our action reveals a positive evaluation of its purpose. This does not mean that we necessarily find the goals of our actions pleasant or agreeable. My goal could be to have a bad tooth extracted, and there is nothing enjoyable about this at all. Still, once I have made up my mind that I need to have my bad tooth extracted, this is my goal and purpose, and I want to achieve it, at least in the sense that I *intend* to achieve it. This means that I prefer a situation in which my bad tooth is extracted over one in which it is not extracted, and that I would

4   *Bauhn*

object to being prevented from having it extracted. In this sense, I consider the purpose of having my bad tooth extracted as something good.

Different agents have, of course, different purposes or ends of action that they consider good in this sense. Some want to climb mountains, others want to complete their stamp collection, and so on. However, since all agents want to successfully achieve their various ends, all agents must also accept that the conditions and capacities that are generally necessary for such successful action are *necessary goods*. These necessary goods of agency are *freedom* and *well-being*. Freedom refers to the agent's control of her behaviour in accordance with her informed and unforced choice, while well-being refers to the agent's capacity for agency as well as her second-order capacities to maintain and expand this capacity. Well-being hence comes in three levels. *Basic well-being* includes life, health, physical integrity, and mental equilibrium, as well as objects necessary to maintain life and health, such as food, shelter, and clothing. *Nonsubtractive* well-being includes whatever is necessary to an agent's maintaining her capacity for agency undiminished, such as not being the victim of theft, broken promises, malicious slander, or generally unsafe conditions of life and work. *Additive well-being*, finally, includes whatever is necessary to an agent's expanding her capacity for agency, such as having self-esteem and the virtues of prudence, temperance, and courage, but also goods such as education and an employment whereby one can earn an income and acquire some wealth for oneself.

Since all agents necessarily want to be successful in their actions, and since freedom and well-being are necessary to all successful action, all rational agents must find it unacceptable to be deprived of or prevented from having freedom and well-being. Consequently, '[s]ince the agent regards as necessary goods the freedom and well-being that constitute the generic features of his successful action, he logically must also hold that he has rights to these generic features'.[7] For an agent not to claim rights to freedom and well-being would be for her to hold that it is acceptable that she is left without freedom and well-being. But this she cannot hold, since she, simply by being an agent, must view freedom and well-being as indispensable and necessary goods. Hence, any agent who were to deny that she has rights to freedom and well-being would thereby also involve herself in a contradiction, since she would both hold (as an agent) that she must have freedom and well-being and at the same time deny that she must have freedom and well-being.

Now, so far the agent has not yet made a *moral* rights-claim. She has only made a *prudential* rights-claim, that is, a rights-claim that is intended to protect the agent's own interest in being a successful and efficient agent. However, since the sufficient ground for her rights-claim is simply the fact that she is an agent with purposes that she wants to fulfill, she must also recognize that the same rights-claim can be made by any other agent as well. Hence, every rational agent must accept the normative conclusion, 'All agents have rights to freedom and well-being'. Now *this* is a moral rights-claim, since it refers to the important interests not only of the individual agent, but of all agents, or, to be more exact, *all prospective purposive agents*, since the claim applies not only to persons who are presently involved in agency, but also to persons who have purposes that they would want to realize through action.

Here it is important to note that Gewirth does not derive moral rights from facts *about* agency. His argument is not of the form '*A* is an agent and hence *A* has moral rights to freedom and well-being'. Instead, he argues that each and every rational agent, from *within her own perspective* as such an agent, must *claim* rights to freedom and well-being. That is, from within her own perspective, the agent moves from 'The end of my action is good' to 'I have rights to freedom and well-being'. This is to derive moral rights in accordance with the *Dialectically Necessary Method* (DNM). The DNM enables us to avoid a conflict with Hume's Law, since it does not derive a prescriptive conclusion directly from a descriptive premise. Instead, it moves from an evaluative claim that the agent logically must make concerning the goodness of the end of her action to a normative claim that she has rights to freedom and well-being. Hence, the DNM operates within the domain of values and norms all the time and there is no attempt to derive norms or values directly from natural facts. In this way, the normative structure of agency in combination with the DNM provides Gewirth with the means necessary to justify a theory of moral rights without offending against Hume's Law.

The outcome of Gewirth's argument is that agents in their dealings with each other must respect each other's rights to freedom and well-being, since these rights are generic to agency itself, being the objects of claims that necessarily must be made by each and every agent. Hence, every rational agent must accept the *Principle of Generic Consistency* (PGC): '*Act in accord with the generic rights of your recipients as well as of yourself*'.[8]

The rights prescribed by the PGC are both negative and positive. Agents are required both not to interfere with their recipients' possession of freedom and well-being, and to help them have freedom and well-being when they are unable to secure these necessary goods by their own efforts, and when help can be given at no comparable cost to the helping agent. Conflicts between rights are to be resolved in accordance with the *Criterion of Degrees of Needfulness for Action*, which gives priority to the right whose object is most needed for successful agency. For instance, the right to life (basic well-being) is more important to successful agency than is the right not to have one's property interfered with (nonsubtractive well-being), which justifies that I use your boat without your consent if this is necessary to save a drowning person.

IMPLICATIONS OF GEWIRTH'S THEORY FOR POLITICAL AND PERSONAL MORALITY

However, the PGC applies not only to the domain of interpersonal agency, but also to political institutions, including the state. While the negative right to well-being justifies the minimal state protecting persons from attacks on

6 Bauhn

their life and property, the right to freedom makes a democratic constitution mandatory, and the positive right to well-being justifies a supportive state, providing its citizens with additive goods, such as education and healthcare. In his later work, *The Community of Rights*, Gewirth developed a radical conception of the supportive state justified by the PGC. Given the importance of having a job and an income to successful agency, he argued that all agents have a positive right to employment, and that '[i]t is the state, acting through the government, that has the correlative duty to take the steps required to provide work for unemployed persons who are able and willing to work'.[9] Moreover, applying the right to freedom to the workplace, Gewirth went on to defend a system of economic democracy 'in which products are put out to be sold in competitive markets and the workers themselves control the productive organization and process', which in turn may involve 'aspects of ownership either by the workers themselves or by the state'.[10] However, economic democracy is subordinated to political democracy, in the sense that civil liberties must not be sacrificed for the sake of securing economic rights.[11]

In his last published book, *Self-Fulfillment*, Gewirth demonstrated that the necessary goods of agency are central not only to interpersonal and social morality, but also to personal morality and to the quest for a fulfilling and meaningful life. For a person to fulfill herself is 'to make maximally effective use of her practical capacities of freedom and well-being'.[12] Freedom here involves cultivating a sense of personal responsibility, implying, among other things, that '[o]ne should avoid regarding oneself solely as a victim, even if one's external circumstances, genetic or environmental, may warrant such a description'.[13] As for the importance of well-being to personal morality, a good life requires that the agent maintains healthy habits of life (basic well-being), that the agent takes care to protect herself against fraud and deceit and to avoid self-defeating behaviour (nonsubtractive well-being), and that she develops in herself an ability to critically reflect on her purposes and to act on purposes that widen her horizons of value and enable her to become all that she can become (additive well-being). This latter development requires 'such virtues as being open to new experiences, new challenges, and new values, both personal and social'.[14] All the time, however, the agent's striving for a good life must be consistent with the requirements of universalist morality. Her self-fulfilment must not be achieved at the expense of other persons' generic rights.

In the decade following Gewirth's death, many scholars all over the globe have continued to analyse aspects of his theoretical framework and to apply his argument to new fields of study. His ideas are certainly much needed by all who strive to give human rights a solid foundation. As Gewirth himself once pointed out, '[i]n a century when the evils that man can do to man have reached unparalleled extremes of barbarism and tragedy, the philosophical concern with rational justification in ethics is more than a quest for certainty.'[15] Referring to the twentieth century, with its two world wars and

Introduction 7

the Holocaust, these words have certainly not lost their relevance in the early years of the twenty-first century, when mankind is tormented by fanaticism and terrorism, as well as by widespread global inequalities between men and women and between those who have and those who have not.

Ours is not a century more suited for relativism than the previous one, if we judge by the conflicts and choices facing us. In fact, the need for a rationally justified morality is as great as ever before in human history, if not greater, given the facts of globalization. Different cultures and moralities are brought in ever closer contact with each other, thereby creating possibilities for conflict as well as for cooperation, while new technologies enable us to affect the lives of people across the globe. Questions of agency, responsibility, and rights hence will be of the utmost importance for how we lead our moral lives. And these are also the areas in which we can benefit from Alan Gewirth's carefully developed arguments.

ABOUT *GEWIRTHIAN PERSPECTIVES ON HUMAN RIGHTS*

The present volume includes important texts written by scholars belonging to many different academic fields, exploring theoretical as well as practical aspects of Alan Gewirth's theory. They contribute to perspectives on human rights and moral theory that can be properly called *Gewirthian*, since they build on Gewirth's theory without necessarily being exact replicas of his own arguments. Sometimes it is a matter of developing his arguments into directions not suggested by himself, but still consistent with the basic framework of his theory. Sometimes it is instead a matter of pointing to possible interpretations of this framework that may differ to some degree from the ones made by Gewirth himself. And sometimes it is a matter of relating his theory to other theories and worldviews as well as to applications not envisaged by himself. But through all the chapters of this volume, an unmistakably Gewirthian approach to morality manifests itself, focusing on rational agency and the rights of human agents.

Gewirthian Perspectives on Human Rights is divided into three parts. In the first part, called *Gewirthian Theory*, we find chapters that deal with questions relating to the philosophical content of Gewirth's theory, its internal structure, and its relationship to other major theories of normative ethics. The second part of the book, called *Gewirthian Contributions*, focuses on how Gewirthian perspectives can contribute to theoretical developments outside the domain of philosophical ethics, like human rights, law, theology, sociology, and economics. In the third and final part, called *Gewirthian Applications*, various applications of Gewirth's moral theory are discussed and developed. These applications concern the protection of the rights of lesbian, gay, bisexual, and transgender people, as well as the rights of people suffering from mental illness and intellectual disability, but they also deal with the Gewirthian duty to rescue.

8   *Bauhn*

Part I, *Gewirthian Theory*, contains four chapters. In the first chapter, Deryck Beyleveld compares Gewirth's argument for the PGC with Kant's argument for the categorical imperative. According to Beyleveld, while Kant and Gewirth share certain methodological assumptions concerning dialectical necessity, Kant's categorical imperative and Gewirth's PGC are, in certain respects, incompatible with each other. The reason for this, Beyleveld argues, is that Gewirth's argument for the PGC implies a different philosophical anthropology from Kant's. Still, on Kant's own methodological premises, the categorical imperative should take the form of the PGC.

In the second chapter, Edward Spence compares Gewirth's ethical theory to stoicism and argues that the concept of self-fulfilment developed by Gewirth in his last published book 'has all the essential characteristics of stoic eudaimonia', or happiness. Especially Gewirth's idea of self-fulfilment as capacity-fulfilment, according to which the agent should try to make the best of herself, comes close to the stoic ethical ideal of a life lived in agreement with both reason and morality.

In the third chapter, Michael Boylan discusses the role played by the law of non-contradiction in the agency-based moral theories of Kant, Gewirth, and Boylan himself. As he points out, the application of this law to ethics not only aims at providing moral philosophizing with a degree of certainty comparable to the one found in the sciences, but it also speaks directly to our nature as rational human beings.

In the fourth and final chapter of Part I, Stuart Toddington discusses Gewirth's moral theory from the point of view of Hume's Law and its prohibition of any move from a descriptive 'is' to a prescriptive 'ought'. Toddington argues that Gewirth's argument both clarifies and provides a valid solution for the is-ought problem.

Part II, *Gewirthian Contributions*, contains five chapters. In the first chapter, Stephen Brown argues that Gewirth's account of the necessary goods of successful agency supplies the concept of real interests with a rationally justified and objective content, which in turn is essential for a sociological analysis of power. Moreover, he defends Gewirthian universalism against charges of being indifferent to the particular circumstances in which concrete human beings live, by arguing that Gewirth's perspective is transhistorical rather than ahistorical and applies to all kinds of social settings.

In the second chapter, Christoph Hübenthal argues that Gewirth's moral and political philosophy, especially as it is developed in *The Community of Rights*, may provide a justificatory framework for the social teaching of the Roman Catholic Church. While Catholic social thought is based on a theological understanding of natural law and hence would fail to convince non-believers, Gewirth's rationalist ethics would be acceptable to both believers and non-believers.

In the third chapter, Shu-Mei Tang and Shang-Yung Yen explore the similarities between the Gewirthian theory of human rights and Confucian natural law. In both doctrines, the ideas of agency and universalizability play an

Introduction 9

important role, making Gewirthian arguments well suited to contribute to the institutionalization of human rights in an East Asian context.

In the fourth chapter, Robert Montaña argues that Gewirthian ethics in general and the Gewirthian ideal of self-fulfilment in particular may provide important contributions to the field of international law. By emphasizing the individual agent's aspirations and dignity, Gewirthian ethics would justify an expansion of the focus of international law to include not only relations and agreements between states, but also the impact of these relations and agreements on the lives of individual human beings.

In the fifth and final chapter of Part II, Gregory Walters and Marie Constance Morley argue, against the background of the 2007–2008 global financial crisis and Thomas Piketty's analysis of contemporary capitalism, that a Gewirthian perspective is very much needed in economic and political decision-making. Such a perspective might help to ensure that the markets serve the freedom and well-being of all instead of just amassing wealth in the hands of a few successful speculators.

Part III, *Gewirthian Applications*, contains four chapters. In the first chapter, Vincent Samar outlines a Gewirthian defence of the rights of lesbian, gay, bisexual, and transgender (LGBT) people. The rights to freedom and well-being prescribed by the PGC, as well as the values of dignity and autonomy that Gewirth relates to self-fulfilment, play an important role in Samar's argument.

In the second chapter, Phil Bielby explores the mental health aspects of the Gewirthian right to well-being. Bielby distinguishes between general mental health rights, focusing on promoting mental health in general, and specific mental health rights, focusing on empowering persons suffering from severe mental illnesses that expose their agency to 'heightened vulnerability'.

In the third chapter, Miriam Stevenson develops an argument that is in certain respects similar to Bielby's, but focusing on the human rights of young persons with an intellectual disability. Using emancipatory research, Stevenson suggests a community engagement model, supported by a Gewirthian human right to social citizenship, to respond to the needs of individuals, families, and communities, locally and globally, whose citizenship rights have been limited or denied. In this way, she argues, the Gewirthian community of rights can be more fully realized.

In the fourth and final chapter of Part III, I explore the Gewirthian duty to rescue. I discuss different interpretations of Gewirth's comparable cost condition, concluding that, in the absence of special circumstances, no agent is required to sacrifice any part of her basic well-being for the sake of maintaining any part of any other agent's basic well-being. Regarding other levels of well-being, a Combined Comparable Cost Condition prescribes that there should be a fair distribution of sacrifices among potential rescuers.

The present collection of works testifies to an ongoing and truly global interest in Alan Gewirth's moral philosophy, with contributors coming from Australia, Asia, Europe, and North America. It also points to the fertility of

10   *Bauhn*

Alan's philosophy, and to its capacity to generate rational and convincing answers to both theoretical and practical aspects of moral life.

Alan was not only a great philosopher, but also a good friend and constant source of inspiration and encouragement. I am grateful for having had the opportunity to know him and to study with him, and I am happy to dedicate this volume to his memory as well as to his moral philosophy.

I also want to express my sincere gratitude to all the contributors who have made this volume possible. It has been an intellectual pleasure and privilege to work with so many talented Gewirthians and to realize this book together with them. Thanks also to Alan Crozier, who checked my English.

Finally, but most importantly, I want to acknowledge my profound gratitude to my beloved wife, Fatma Fulya Tepe, who first convinced me that I should edit a book dedicated to Alan's memory and moral philosophy.

NOTES

1. One prime source for Alan Gewirth's personal life is his wife Jean Laves, with whom the present author had personal communication in 2004.
2. A. Gewirth, Human Rights (Chicago: The University of Chicago Press, 1982), p. v.
3. A. Gewirth, *Reason and Morality* (Chicago: The University of Chicago Press, 1978); A. Gewirth, *Human Rights*; A. Gewirth, *The Community of Rights* (Chicago: The University of Chicago Press, 1996); A. Gewirth, *Self-Fulfillment* (Princeton: Princeton University Press, 1998).
4. E. Regis Jr. (ed), *Gewirth's Ethical Rationalism* (Chicago: The University of Chicago Press, 1984); M. Boylan (ed), *Gewirth* (Lanham: Rowman & Littlefield, 1999).
5. D. Beyleveld, *The Dialectical Necessity of Morality* (Chicago: The University of Chicago Press, 1991).
6. Ibid., p. 363.
7. Ibid., p. 63.
8. Ibid., p. 135 (emphasis in original).
9. Gewirth, *The Community of Rights*, p. 219.
10. Ibid., p. 260.
11. Ibid., pp. 318–24.
12. Gewirth, *Self-Fulfillment*, p. 61.
13. Ibid., p. 114.
14. Ibid., p. 123.
15. Gewirth, *Reason and Morality*, p. ix.

WORKS CITED

Beyleveld, D., *The Dialectical Necessity of Morality* (Chicago: The University of Chicago Press, 1991).
Boylan, M. (ed.), *Gewirth* (Lanham: Rowman & Littlefield, 1999).
Gewirth, A., *Reason and Morality* (Chicago: The University of Chicago Press, 1978).
———, *Human Rights* (Chicago: The University of Chicago Press, 1982).
———, *The Community of Rights* (Chicago: The University of Chicago Press, 1996).
———, *Self-Fulfillment* (Princeton: Princeton University Press, 1998).
Regis Jr., E. (ed.), *Gewirth's Ethical Rationalism* (Chicago: The University of Chicago Press, 1984).

Part I
Gewirthian Theory

1 Gewirth Versus Kant on Kant's Maxim of Reason

Towards a Gewirthian Philosophical Anthropology

Deryck Beyleveld

INTRODUCTION

When Alan Gewirth claims that the Principle of Generic Consistency (PGC)[1] is the supreme principle of morality because its acceptance is dialectically necessary for agents,[2] he assigns it the same status that Kant claims for his Categorical Imperative (KCI)—that it is a synthetic *a priori* principle.[3] But the PGC and the KCI—as Kant interprets it in his Formula of Humanity (FoH),

> *So act that you use humanity, whether in your own person or in the person of any other, always at the same time as an end, never merely as a means*
> *(Groundwork of the Metaphysics of Morals [GMM] 4:429)*[4]

—are incompatible principles. This is because, unlike Kant's FoH, the PGC requires an agent (call her 'Agnes') to respect (not to interfere with and, in certain circumstances, to protect) the generic conditions of agency (GCAs) of all agents *subject to the will of the recipient agent*. The PGC *prohibits* Agnes from voluntarily damaging her own GCAs or permitting others to so harm her *only if* her doing so would damage the GCAs of *other* agents disproportionately against *their* will, whereas Kant's FoH categorically *prohibits* such actions *unless* they are necessary to protect Agnes or others from equivalent or greater harm. This difference[5] is due to the fact that Gewirth's argument for the PGC rests on it being dialectically necessary for Agnes to accept the Principle of Hypothetical Imperatives (PHI):

> 'If doing X or having X is necessary for Agnes to pursue/achieve her chosen purpose E, then Agnes ought to do X or pursue/defend having X, or give up E.'[6]

I argue here that this entails that, while Gewirth and Kant share a methodology of dialectically necessary argumentation, Gewirthians must reject a number of central doctrines of Kant's transcendental philosophy. Kant holds that the dialectical necessity of free will[7] (revealed by the dialectical necessity of the moral law, for which the existence of free will is a necessary

14 *Beyleveld*

condition—its *ratio essendi*) is the keystone that enables Agnes to be certain that agents are immortal and that God exists even though immortality and God are not objects of possible empirical knowledge.[8] But while Gewirth and Kant agree that it is dialectically necessary for Agnes to treat her existence as an agent as the *ratio essendi* of the moral law, if it is dialectically necessary for Agnes to accept the PHI, then it cannot be dialectically necessary for her to consider the essence of agency to reside in her possession of free will (as Kant has it), because it is then merely dialectically necessary for Agnes to hope[9] that she has free will.[10] Hence, my central claim is that Gewirth's argument for the PGC implies a different philosophical anthropology from Kant's, grounded in Kant's own philosophical methodology.

I have presented elements of this argument elsewhere and previously compared Gewirth and Kant.[11] Here, I focus the comparison on the interpretation of Kant's maxims of the common human understanding[12] because I consider that what Kant says about these principles

1. Shows very clearly that his claim that KCI is a synthetic *a priori* proposition,[13] i.e., that it is 'connected (completely *a priori*) with the concept of the will of a rational being as such'[14] but 'not contained in it',[15] is that its acceptance is dialectically necessary for agents;
2. Reveals more clearly than elsewhere what his argument for this claim is; and
3. Shows how Kant thinks that the 'power of judgement' mediates between 'understanding' and 'reason' so as to render possible the harmony between theoretical and practical reason that Kant's view of his philosophy as a system requires.[16]

The argument is broken into four parts. Part I contends that Kant's claim that 'the maxim of reason' is derived by rendering 'the maxim of understanding' consistent with 'the maxim of the power of judgement'[17] reveals that his assertion that the moral law is given to agents as the fact of pure reason[18] amounts to saying that it is required on the basis of its acceptance being dialectical necessity for Agnes (i.e., required by agential self-understanding). The maxim of reason (the acceptance of which is dialectically necessary for Agnes, by the very nature of its derivation) amounts to

'Act in accord with the dialectically necessary commitments of all agents',

which is equivalent to

'Act only on maxims when doing so is consistent with universal laws'.

Part II examines how Kant and Gewirth provide this imperative, which is surely Kant's Formula of Universal Law (FUL) for the KCI:

> [A]ct only in accordance with that maxim which you can at the same time will that it become a universal law

(*GMM* 4:421)

with content. Kant claims that the KCI is grounded in the proposition that rational nature exists as an end in itself,[19] in consequence of which Agnes must consider her existence as an agent to be an end in itself.[20] On this basis, if (as both Kant and Gewirth hold) maxims that are dialectically necessary for Agnes to accept are necessarily universal, it is dialectically necessary for Agnes to accept Kant's FoH. In contrast, Gewirth claims that because it is dialectically for Agnes to accept the PHI, since there are GCAs, it is dialectically necessary for Agnes to accept the prescription SROA (Self-Referring 'Ought', with Agnes as its subject):

> 'I (Agnes) ought to defend my possession of the GCAs unless I am willing to suffer generic damage to my ability to act.'

On this basis, given the universality of dialectically necessary maxims, the maxim of reason requires acceptance of the PGC.

Part III elaborates on the claim that the PGC is the categorical imperative *on Kantian methodological premises.*

Part IV outlines the consequent revisions required to the Kantian transcendental project as a whole (which Kant designates as 'anthropology'),[21] thereby sketching a Gewirthian philosophical anthropology.

PART I: KCI, THE MAXIM OF REASON, AND DIALECTICAL NECESSITY

Kant's three principles of the common human understanding *(sensus communis)* are:

1. To think for oneself;
2. To think in the position of everyone else; and
3. Always to think in accord with oneself.[22]

The *sensus communis* is not what the average person considers to be reasonable or correct. It represents the *a priori* capacity of understanding 'which is the least that can be expected from anyone who lays claim to the name of human being',[23] being

> [a] faculty of judging that in its reflection takes account (*a priori*) of everyone else's way of representing in thought, in order *as it were* to hold its judgment up to human reason as a whole and thereby avoid the illusion which, from subjective private conditions that could easily be held to be objective, would have a detrimental influence on the judgment.[24]

The first maxim is the 'maxim of the understanding, the second that of the power of judgement, the third that of reason'.[25] The maxim of reason is

16 *Beyleveld*

achieved 'by the combination of the first two'.[26] The first maxim is 'the maxim of a reason that is never *passive*';[27] the second reflects on one's own judgements produced by acting in accord with the first maxim 'from a *universal standpoint*'.[28]

In representing *general* rules for the avoidance of error,[29] the *sensus communis* applies to all reasoning, whether theoretical, practical, or aesthetic. Applied practically, the generation of the maxim of reason surely reveals the essence of Kant's argument for the KCI in the form of the FUL.

This is because the first maxim requires Agnes to subject all maxims to the scrutiny of *her own* understanding and not to accept maxims simply on the say so of others, which requires her to give at least some weight to her own personal choices, deliberative reasoning, and associated maxims. The second maxim requires Agnes to adopt any maxims required by virtue of understanding that she is *an* agent. Thus, it exhorts Agnes to adopt maxims that are dialectically necessary for her to accept, the requirements of agential self-understanding. The third maxim commands Agnes to act only in consistency with maxims that are dialectically necessary for her to accept.

I think that Kant, like internalists generally, reasons that for *Agnes* to be given a reason to act, *she* must be given a reason to act *from the standpoint of the particular unique agent she is*. However, unlike Humean internalists, he infers from the observation that exercise of the power of reflective judgment requires Agnes to recognize that she cannot be the particular agent she is unless she is *an* agent (i.e., unless she possesses the powers of understanding necessarily shared by all agents), that for Agnes to think that *she* has *a* personal understanding to oppose the personal understandings of others, she must reason in terms of any maxims she is required to accept simply by virtue of understanding what it is for her to be *an* agent. Since requirements that are dialectically for Agnes to accept are generated by the idea of being *an* agent, and being *an* agent is the same for all agents, any maxim that is dialectically necessary for Agnes to accept will be dialectically necessary for every agent to accept. Hence, maxims that are dialectically necessary for Agnes to accept are universal. Understanding this, consistency requires Agnes to accept the third maxim, to act in consistency with maxims that are dialectically necessary for *any* agent to accept, as itself a maxim that it is dialectically necessary for her to accept. As such, reason requires her to adopt the third maxim as the supreme *criterion* for rational action, which she cannot intelligibly do without treating it as a categorical *imperative* expressed in terms of the FUL, read as:

> 'Act only on maxims that you can act on consistently with universal laws (i.e., consistently with maxims that are dialectically necessary for any agent to accept)'.

Kant's reasoning may also be put as follows. By virtue of being an agent, Agnes possesses the powers of self-understanding. If she uses these powers to achieve agential self-understanding, then she will necessarily be presented with the concept of a categorical imperative (i.e., it is dialectically necessary for Agnes to entertain the idea of a categorical imperative). But a categorical imperative, by its very meaning, is an imperative that all her maxims must be consistent with, which entails that she must accept a categorical imperative, 'Act only on maxims that are consistent with a categorical imperative', which is equivalent to 'Act only on maxims that you can act on consistently with maxims that are dialectically necessary for you to accept'. Therefore, it is dialectically necessary for Agnes to accept the FUL.

In essence, Kant's argument is: It is dialectically necessary for Agnes to accept that the criterion for a permissible maxim is one that is consistent with a categorical imperative. To understand this, however, is to recognize that the FUL is a categorical imperative. Therefore, it is dialectically necessary for Agnes to accept that the FUL is a categorical imperative.

There is much debate on what Kant's argument for the KCI is and dispute over whether or not he changed his mind about this between his *Groundwork of the Metaphysics of Morals (GMM)* and *Critique of Practical Reason (CPrR)*. I believe that Kant's justification for the moral law in *GMM III* and for his contention in *CPrR* that the moral law is given to us as the fact of pure reason[30] both involve the reasoning for the FUL just sketched. Although I cannot justify this claim fully here,[31] I will indicate briefly how *CPrR* and *GMM* can be linked to the maxim of reason of the *Critique of the Power of Judgment (CPoJ)* in this way.

In *CPrR*, after telling us that we become conscious of the moral law as soon as we draw up maxims for ourselves,[32] and that pure reason leads us from consciousness of the moral law to the concept of free will,[33] Kant asks, 'But how is consciousness of that moral law possible?' and answers:

> We can become aware of pure practical laws just as we are aware of pure theoretical principles, by attending to the necessity with which reason prescribes them to us and to the setting aside of all empirical conditions to which reason directs us. The concept of a pure will arises from the first, as consciousness of a pure understanding arises from the latter.[34]

The key parallel statements in *GMM* are that

> a human being really finds in himself a capacity by which he distinguishes himself . . . even from himself insofar as he is affected by objects, and that is *reason*[35]

and that by thinking of oneself

> as an intelligence, that is, as independent of sensible impressions in the use of reason (hence as belonging to the world of understanding) . . .
> . . . [the human being perceives] that pure reason independent of sensibility gives the [moral] law.[36]

18   *Beyleveld*

These statements are not wholly transparent, but I contend that they should be interpreted as making the same claim because: 1) It is possible to do so, *and* Kant says[37] that *CPrR* presupposes *GMM* on the justification of the moral law; 2) the process they refer to is plausibly that involved in generating the maxim of reason by rendering the maxim of understanding consistent with the maxim of the power of judgement;[38] and 3) the three maxims of the *sensus communis* appear as fundamental principles of Kant's philosophy before *GMM* (in *Logic*) and after *CPrR* (in *CPoJ*).

PART II: KANT VERSUS GEWIRTH ON THE CONTENT OF THE MORAL LAW

Whether or not I am right about this, I consider that it is in fact dialectically necessary for agents to accept the FUL on the basis that it is derived by rendering the maxim of understanding and the maxim of the power of judgement *consistent with each other*, and that this renders the FUL a categorical imperative.

I anticipate three objections to this:

1. Even if it is categorically imperative for agents to accept dialectically necessary maxims, these are not intrinsically universal;
2. Even if it is dialectical necessary to accept the FUL, this does not make it categorically binding, because Agnes will not necessarily care whether or not she complies with the requirements of agential self-understanding; and
3. Even if the first two objections can be met, the FUL lacks content.

In essence, my response to the first objection is that if the *ratio cognoscendi* for Agnes to accept any normative claim is that its acceptance is dialectical necessary for her, then it is dialectically necessary for Agnes to regard being *an* agent as the *ratio essendi* for the assertoric validity of the claim, which renders it dialectically necessary for Agnes to treat the dialectically necessary commitments of all agents as assertorically valid, which renders them universal.[39]

The second objection is presented by David Enoch.[40] My short response is that Enoch mistakenly presents Kant and Gewirth as maintaining that normative claims are derived from what constitutes *being* an agent, whereas grounding them in dialectically necessary acceptance constitutes the requirement to accept them as one of agential *self-understanding*. On the latter basis, if Agnes attaches no practical significance to the FUL being dialectically necessary for her to accept, this merely means that she does not care that she categorically ought to act according to the FUL (which circumstance must be possible for it to be intelligible to say that she *ought* to comply with the FUL).

Gewirth Versus Kant on Kant's Maxim of Reason 19

Although more needs to be said about the first and second objections, I will confine my attention here to how Kant and Gewirth deal with objection three, because it is only on this and not on how to respond to objections one and two that I consider them to differ significantly.

Kant's Derivation of the FoH

Kant says that the ground of KCI is '*rational nature exists as an end in itself*'.[41] He surely means that to act rationally (i.e., in accord with the maxim of reason, in consistency with a maxim that it is dialectically necessary for an agent to accept, i.e., in accord with the FUL) is an end in itself. He then says that the 'human being necessarily represents his own existence in this way [i.e., as an end in itself]'.[42] Because he argues that every rational being (human or not) must, on the basis of having to consider that it is an end in itself, consider that the *ratio essendi* for its being an end in itself is its possession of free will (which means that he claims that it is dialectically necessary for Agnes to consider that the essence of agency resides in the possession of free will), he maintains that the FoH is a formula for KCI.[43]

But why must Agnes regard *her existence* as an end in itself? Kant says that it follows from the FUL that the existence of every rational being must be 'the limiting condition of all relative and arbitrary ends'[44] because the FUL requires

> that in the use of means to any end I am to limit my maxim to the condition of its universal validity for every subject [which] is tantamount to saying that the subject of ends, the rational being itself, must be made the basis of all maxims for action, never merely as a means but as the supreme limiting condition in the use of all means, that is, always at the same time as an end.[45]

There is a way of interpreting this that is consistent with the Gewirthian perspective (see Part III). But Kant claims that the FoH, unlike the PGC, prescribes that

> I cannot . . . dispose of a human being in my own person by maiming, damaging or killing him . . .[46]

which statement Kant immediately qualifies by alluding to specific exceptions to save one's own life or the life of another that are more fully dealt with in his *Metaphysics of Morals (MoM)*. If we interpret 'maiming, damaging, or killing' an agent as interfering with the agent's GCAs then, in Gewirthian terms, KCI amounts to

> 'So act that you never interfere with the GCAs of any agent for any relative or arbitrary ends (i.e., as means to your chosen ends) unless to protect the GCAs of an agent.'

20   *Beyleveld*

In this way, Kant's FoH provides the maxim of reason with a content or 'matter'.[47]

Gewirth's Derivation of the PGC

Assuming that dialectically necessary commitments are categorically binding, if the following three propositions are true, then the PGC is the categorical imperative:

1. It is dialectically necessary for Agnes to accept the PHI;
2. There are GCAs; and
3. Maxims that are dialectically necessary for Agnes to accept are universal.

The demonstration of this is as follows:
1 coupled with 2 entails

4. It is dialectically necessary for Agnes to accept 'SROA: "I (Agnes) ought to defend my possession of the GCAs unless I (Agnes) am willing to suffer generic damage to my ability to act"' as a standard for her action.

3 coupled with 4 entails both

5. It is dialectically necessary for any other agent (say, Brian) to accept 'SROB: "I (Brian) ought to defend my possession of the GCAs unless I (Brian) am willing to suffer generic damage to my ability to act"' as a standard for his action;

and

6. It is dialectically necessary for Agnes to accept SROB (as well as SROA) as a standard for her action, and dialectically necessary for Brian to accept SROA (as well as SROB) as a standard for his action.

And 6 is equivalent to 'It is dialectically necessary for all agents to accept the PGC'.

PART III: THE PGC IS THE MORAL LAW ON KANTIAN METHODOLOGICAL PREMISES

Because the PGC is the universalization of SROA (the PHI given content by the GCAs), it does not prohibit Agnes from 'maiming, damaging, or killing' herself, if she does so voluntarily and by so doing does not disproportionately threaten or damage the GCAs of other agents against their will. Thus, if Agnes's humanity consists of her material existence as an agent, then the

PGC does not require Agnes to treat her own humanity as an end in itself. It permits, indeed, requires her *(ceteris paribus)* to treat her own humanity as a means to her own voluntarily chosen ends. On the other hand, if to respect her own humanity is to respect herself as a chooser of ends, then, while she may not treat the humanity *of others* merely as a means, it makes no sense to say that she may not treat *her own* humanity merely as a means because it is *impossible* for her *in acting* to treat her own humanity *merely* as a means. If in treating herself as a means she is acting, she *voluntarily* treats herself as a means, so treats herself as an end *as well as* a means.

Furthermore, if acceptance of the PHI is dialectically necessary for Agnes, then it is a categorical imperative on *Kant's view* about the nature of such an imperative.[48] But Kant recognizes that there can be only one categorical imperative.[49] Consequently, all formulae for the categorical imperative must be consistent with each other and with the PHI. Therefore, Kant's FoH cannot be a formula for KCI. Christine Korsgaard[50] cannot be right that the PHI is merely that aspect of KCI that tells us how to be effective agents. The dialectical necessity of acceptance of the PHI necessarily affects the content of KCI, because no formula for KCI can then be incompatible with the universalization of SROA, which (prior to universalization) only requires Agnes to defend her existence as an agent *if she is unwilling to suffer generic damage to her ability to act.* Gewirthians can agree that it is dialectically necessary for Agnes to make being an agent the supreme limiting condition in the use of all means, but only if this signifies that Agnes must regard being an agent as the *ratio essendi* for her (and others') dialectically necessary commitments. Any further inference depends on what her dialectically necessary commitments are, and given that the dialectical necessity of acceptance of the PHI entails that her dialectically necessary commitment is to SROA, *not* to 'Agnes ought to defend her GCAs *whether or not she is willing to suffer generic damage to her ability to act'* (as Kant maintains), making being an agent the supreme limiting condition in the use of all means requires Agnes to grant every agent a prima facie right to determine what may be done with the agent's own GCAs. It does not require Agnes to recognize any perfect duty *to herself* to defend her material existence as an agent.

PART IV: GEWIRTHIAN REVISIONS TO THE KANTIAN TRANSCENDENTAL PROJECT

However, the dialectical necessity of acceptance of the PHI does not merely require KCI/the FUL to be interpreted in accordance with the PGC rather than Kant's FoH: It requires rejection of the following interlinked Kantian doctrines:

1. The moral law is a law of nature for a being with free will unaffected by heteronomous incentives, and an imperative only for beings with

22   Beyleveld

   free will affected by heteronomous incentives,[51] which implies that KCI cannot apply to all rational beings with a will;

2. The aspect of self-understanding by which Agnes distinguishes herself from herself insofar as she is affected by heteronomous incentives (per *CPoJ*, the reflective power of judgement), reveals her 'proper' self as against merely 'the appearance' of herself;[52]

3. Agnes's 'proper' self, '*homo noumenon*', gives the moral law to her human self—the mere appearance of herself—'*homo phaenomenon*';[53]

4. An agent per se is *homo noumenon*, a being having free will unaffected by heteronomous incentives (implying that the maxim of understanding and the maxim of the power of judgement are rendered consistent with each other *by subordinating the former to the latter*);

5. The moral law and free will are reciprocal[54] in that the dialectical necessity of acceptance of the moral law is the *ratio cognoscendi* for free will correlative to free will being the ratio *essendi* of the moral law;[55] and

6. The dialectical necessity of acceptance of free will renders acceptance of God's existence and the immortality of agents dialectically necessary.[56]

The narrative connecting these propositions runs something like this. In thinking that empirical knowledge is possible, Agnes presupposes that every event has a cause;[57] but she must also believe that her will is free because her possession of free will is necessary for her to be bound by the moral law.[58] If agents have free will, then they are responsible for their actions,[59] and so they ought to receive happiness in proportion to the degree to which they act out of respect for the moral law (this realized state of affairs being the *summum bonum*). But for the *summum bonum* to be possible, for agents to be able to *hope* that the *summum bonum* will be realized, they must be immortal and God must exist. Therefore, the dialectical necessity of acceptance of free will renders belief (faith) in God and immortality dialectically necessary.[60] While actions cannot be products of free will and natural causes in the same aspect,[61] this yields no contradiction, because what Agnes does is only an event subject to the law of nature insofar as it is an object of sense experience, while anything she does as an exercise of her free will is not such an event.[62] While Agnes's perception that she is part of a world that she can know through sense-experience threatens the idea that she has any significance as an end in herself by positing her extinction and an ultimately purposeless cosmos, being subject to the moral law promises that she has such significance by positing her immortality and God's existence.[63] But this threat and this promise do not carry equal weight. Pure practical reason takes priority over pure theoretical reason,[64] because the maxim of reason requires Agnes to subordinate herself as *homo phaenomenon* to herself as *homo noumenon*. Consequently, Agnes ought to be certain that God exists and that her continued existence does not depend on her material existence.

This narrative, quite apart from considerations to do with the dialectical necessity of acceptance of the PHI, is extremely problematic. For example, it is questionable that adherence to a categorical imperative requires Agnes to believe that she has free will as against merely not believing that she does not.[65] It is also questionable that postulation by the moral law of the *summum bonum* and hope that all agents will enjoy happiness in proportion to their virtue requires belief that God exists and that agents are immortal, as against merely not believing that God does not exist, etc., and hoping that God exists, etc.[66] The existence of a categorical imperative does, I think, postulate that agents ought to enjoy happiness in proportion to their virtue. But the fact that they will not necessarily be able to enjoy such happiness unless God exists, etc., only requires belief that God ought to exist, which requires no more than leaving it open that God might exist. And, conversely, the existence of an omnipotent wholly good God (the only being that Kant will recognize as God), surely implies that agents *necessarily will* enjoy happiness in proportion to their virtue, and not merely that they *might* enjoy such happiness, so it is untenable to assign a different epistemic status to the *summum bonum* from that accorded to the existence of free will, immortality, and God.[67]

Furthermore, can the moral law really apply to beings with free will unaffected by heteronomous incentives as a natural law and to those who are affected by such incentives as a categorical imperative? There are several problems here. For example, if immortality is postulated by the moral law through free will, then there is no sense in an imperative that prohibits self-destruction, for self-destruction must be thought to be impossible. It is also difficult to see how a law that governs beings constituted in abstraction *from heteronomy* can be a law of non-natural causality of the behaviour *of heteronomously constituted* beings. As Bernard Williams says, one cannot be a rational agent and no more.[68] So, while Agnes cannot be the particular agent that she is without being *an* agent—which I do not think Williams takes adequate account of[69]—*she* also (as Williams insists) cannot be *an* agent without being the particular agent she is, and she cannot be *a particular* agent without possessing heteronomous properties. Therefore, Kant has difficulty explaining how the ideas of free will and natural causality can apply to the same being. Also, according to Kant, free will is postulated by pure practical reason (the maxim of reason, the faculty of desire). But having *homo noumenon* give the law to *homo phaenomenon* renders free will essentially a postulate of the reflective power of judgement, and only derivatively one of practical reason. This is because negative freedom (absence of heteronomy) is postulated by the power of judgement, while positive freedom (viewed as the *ratio essendi* for the moral law *qua* a law of nature for non-heteronomously affected beings) is generated purely by consistency with negative freedom.

Anyway, the dialectical necessity of acceptance of the PHI renders Kant's picture incoherent because it entails that a *normatively meaningful*

24   *Beyleveld*

abstraction from Agnes's particular self cannot be a conceptual construct that depicts being an agent as something free of all heteronomous qualities. This implies that:

1. The moral law can exist only in the form of a categorical imperative;
2. The maxim of reason is a *synthesis* of the maxim of understanding and the maxim of the power of judgement. Agential self-understanding requires the *unity* of theoretical and practical reason, not the priority of practical reason over theoretical reason,[70] unless such priority signifies merely that all *a priori* rules of understanding/judgment/reason are ultimately rules of agential self-understanding. However, because Agnes cannot be free and determined in the same aspect, *unity* between theoretical and practical reason can only be achieved by suspension of belief in both free will and determinism. Consequently, Agnes may and must entertain only the possibility that she has free will;
3. Being *an* agent, the *ratio essendi* for the moral law, is not having free will in abstraction from having heteronomous incentives, but combining in one's person the heteronomous incentives one has as a particular agent in a particular context with the universal power for choice inherent in all agents. Agnes's agency as the *ratio essendi* for the PGC is a universal *relation*, not a universal *property*, the *relation* between Agnes's heteronomy and her possession of the power of choice, which is the same *relation* as that between Brian's heteronomy and his possession of the power of choice; and
4. Because the same epistemic status must be given to all the ideas linked to the idea of free will, agents may (and must) only hope that God exists and that they are immortal.

Kant's transcendental philosophy is premised, I think correctly, on the view that Agnes cannot know with certainty that there is a world that exists independently of her senses, only that if there is such a world, then every sensible event must have a cause. That she is presented with the idea of a world that exists independently of her senses at all derives from her experience that she is not able to predict or will all her experience, and in this experience, she views herself as *something* independent of what she experiences. However, as Fichte maintains,[71] the ideas of I and not-I are inseparable in this experience. Agnes cannot think of herself as a distinct individual without having the idea of something that is not herself and vice versa. Furthermore, self-reflection also tells her that she cannot be certain that there is anything at all beyond her experience, and the existence of an external world cannot be assessed in probabilistic terms either. Consequently, her powers of pure self-understanding alone cannot secure anything epistemically beyond what is involved in understanding self-understanding.[72] So, Agnes can ascribe certainty only to what she *must* believe in order for self-understanding to be possible for her, which is no more than what she must accept in order to be able to ask questions, to have ideas, etc. Consequently, pure reason places her inescapably in a state of hoping/fearing in relation to all metaphysical matters.

As such, Kant's philosophy is neither a form of metaphysical idealism nor a form of metaphysical realism, but a 'transcendental phenomenology'[73] that requires dubiety on all metaphysical matters and confines *theoretical certainties* to rules governing the operation of the intelligent mind. But, I contend, it is Gewirth, not Kant, who works this out correctly in relation to practical reason.

CONCLUDING REMARKS

The Gewirthian anthropology I have presented is merely a sketch, and some will question my characterization of Kant's position. However, if the PHI is dialectically necessary and dialectically necessary commitments are universal, then Kantians as well as Gewirthians must accept that the PGC is the supreme principle of practical reason and ought to adopt the philosophical anthropology that this entails.[74]

NOTES

1. The PGC requires agents (beings with the capacity and disposition to pursue purposes voluntarily) to act in accord with rights to generic conditions of agency (GCAs), which are necessary means for action and successful action, regardless of the purposes involved. For more on the GCAs, see A. Gewirth, *Reason and Morality* (Chicago: University of Chicago Press, 1978), Chapter 2.
2. To say that the PGC is dialectically necessary for agents to accept is to say that if an agent does not accept the PGC, the agent fails to understand what it is to be an agent, and implicitly denies being an agent.
3. See D. Beyleveld, 'Gewirth and Kant on Justifying the Supreme Principle of Morality', in M. Boylan (ed), *Gewirth: Critical Essays on Action, Rationality, and Community* (Maryland: Rowman and Littlefield, 1999), pp. 97–117; D. Beyleveld, 'Korsgaard *v* Gewirth on Universalization: Why Gewirthians are Kantians and Kantians Ought to be Gewirthians', *Journal of Moral Philosophy*, 12:5 (2015), pp. 573–97.
4. In quoting works from Kant, references to the *Critique of Pure Reason (CPuR)* are given with the A/B-references to the first/second edition. Other works (giving its title/abbreviation) are referred to on the basis of the Academy edition of the *Gesammelte Schriften*, stating volume and page number. Translations are given according to P. Guyer and A. Wood (eds), *Cambridge Edition of the Works of Immanuel Kant* (Cambridge: Cambridge University Press, 1995 sqq).
5. See Beyleveld, 'Korsgaard *v* Gewirth on Universalization'.
6. Kant claims that the proposition

   > Whoever wills the end also wills (insofar as reason has decisive influence on his actions) the indispensably necessary means to it that are within his power (*GMM* 4:417)

   is analytic. This proposition is not the PHI, but a statement of what acting in accord with an hypothetical imperative involves. While 'acceptance of the PHI is dialectically necessary' is analytic, the PHI itself is not analytic.

26 Beyleveld

7. In Kantian terms, 'Agents have free will' is a synthetic *a priori* proposition.
8. See *Critique of Practical Reason (CPrR)* 5:3–4.
9. 'A hopes that X' means 'A has a pro-attitude towards X and (with X in mind) neither believes that X is the case nor that X is not the case'; and 'A fears that X' means 'A hopes that not-X'. See D. Beyleveld, 'Hope and Belief', in R. J. Jenkins and E. Sullivan (eds), *Philosophy of Mind* (New York: Nova Science Publishers Inc., 2012), pp. 1–36.
10. See Beyleveld, 'Hope and Belief'; D. Beyleveld and P. Ziche, 'Towards a Kantian Transcendental Phenomenology of Hope,' *Ethical Theory and Moral Practice*, 18:5 (2015), pp. 927–42. DOI 10.1007/s10677-015-9564. Available at: http://link.springer.com/article/10.1007/s10677-015-9564-x (accessed 25 August 2015).
11. For example: Beyleveld, 'Gewirth and Kant on Justifying the Supreme Principle of Morality'; D. Beyleveld and R. Brownsword, *Human Dignity in Bioethics and Biolaw* (Oxford: Oxford University Press, 2001), Chapter 5; Beyleveld, 'Korsgaard *v* Gewirth on Universalization'.
12. See *Logic* 9:57 and *Critique of the Power of Judgment (CPoJ)* 5:294.
13. E.g., *GMM* 4:420; *CPrR* 5:31.
14. *GMM* 4:426.
15. *GMM* 4:420.
16. According to Kant, the human mind has three faculties: cognition, feeling, and desire. Cognition has three sub-faculties: understanding, power of judgement, and reason, each 'containing' a 'constitutive' a priori principle and sphere of application corresponding to a specific faculty of the mind. 'Understanding' characterizes the faculty of cognition via a principle of lawfulness applied to nature; the power of judgement ('independent of concepts and sensations that are related to the determination of the faculty of desire' (*CPoJ* 5:196–7)) characterizes the faculty of feeling via a principle of purposiveness applied to the experience of beauty and special laws dealing with natural things and events; while 'reason' constitutes the faculty of desire via a principle of the final end applied to freedom (see 5:196–8).

   Kant argues that harmony between theoretical and practical reason is only possible under the concept of a purposiveness of nature, and that the power of (reflective) judgement requires an agent to represent nature as organized in accordance with the purposes of an intelligent cause (God) (*CPoJ* 5:397–404).
17. *CPoJ* 5:295.
18. *CPrR* 5:31.
19. See *GMM* 4:428–9.
20. See *GMM* 4:429; 437–8.
21. Kant says that the field of philosophy may be summed up in the following questions:

   1) What can I know?
   2) What ought I to do?
   3) What may I hope?
   4) What is man?

   Metaphysics answers the first question, *morals* the second, *religion* the third, and *anthropology* the fourth. Fundamentally, however, we could reckon all of this as anthropology, because the first three questions relate to the last one. (*Logic* 9:25; compare *CPuR* A804–5/B832–3)
22. *CPoJ* 5:294. In *Logic*, they are termed 'general rules and conditions for avoiding error' and as '(1) to think (by) oneself, (2) to think in the place of another, and (3) to think consistently with oneself.' (9:57).

23. *CPoJ* 5:293.
24. 5:293. Although Kant is respectful of the insights the 'common man' *can* achieve, he is scathing about the insights that the common man *happens to* achieve being the final court of judgment on philosophical matters. (See, e.g., *GMM* 4:409).
25. *CPoJ* 5:295.
26. 5:295.
27. *CPoJ* 5:294.
28. *CPoJ* 5:295.
29. See note 22 above.
30. See 5:31.
31. I hope to provide it in a future paper.
32. See 5:29.
33. See 5:30.
34. 5:30.
35. *GMM* 4:452.
36. *GMM* 4:457.
37. *CPrR* 5:8.
38. Kant sometimes uses 'understanding' and 'reason' interchangeably to cover all the faculties of the mind, not always in the way stated in note 16 above. This means that Kant's failure to deploy the power of judgement explicitly in *GMM* and *CPrR* is not an insuperable obstacle to my interpretation.
39. See D. Beyleveld, 'Williams' False Dilemma: How to Give Categorical Binding Impartial Reasons to Real Agents', *Journal of Moral Philosophy*, 10 (2013), pp. 204–26 and 'Korsgaard *v* Gewirth on Universalization'. See also, e.g., Gewirth, *Reason and Morality*, p. 110; D. Beyleveld, *The Dialectical Necessity of Morality: An Analysis and Defense of Alan Gewirth's Argument to the Principle of Generic Consistency* (Chicago: University of Chicago Press, 1991), Chapter 8, especially pp. 288–300; D. Beyleveld and G. Bos, 'The Foundational Role of the Principle of Instrumental Reason in Gewirth's Argument for the Principle of Generic Consistency: A Response to Andrew Chitty', *King's Law Journal*, 20 (2009), pp. 1–20.
40. D. Enoch, 'Agency, Shmagency: Why Normativity Won't Come from What Is Constitutive of Action', *Philosophical Review*, 115 (2006), pp. 169–98.
41. *GMM* 4:428–9.
42. *GMM* 4:429.
43. See *GMM* 4:429.
44. *GMM* 4:436.
45. *GMM* 4:438.
46. *GMM* 4:429.
47. *GMM* 4:436.
48. That it is a categorical imperative is accepted by Kantians like C. Korsgaard, *The Constitution of Agency: Essays on Practical Reason and Moral Psychology* (Oxford: Oxford University Press, 2008), p. 68; and J. Hampton, *The Authority of Reason* (Cambridge: Cambridge University Press, 1998), p. 140 note 2.
49. E.g., *GMM* 4:421.
50. Korsgaard, *The Constitution of Agency*, p. 68.
51. E.g., *GMM* 4:454; *CPrR* 5:32.
52. See *GMM* 4:457.
53. 6:239; 335. Kant does claim that *homo noumenon* and *homo phaenomenon* do not refer to two substances, but to different aspects of Agnes. But to hold this consistently, he must relate the maxims of understanding and the power of judgement to each other in a Gewirthian manner (see below).

28 *Beyleveld*

54. See, e.g., *GMM* 4:447; *CPrR* 5:29.
55. See *CPrR* 5:4.
56. See *CPrR* 5:4–5.
57. See *CPuR*.
58. See *CPrR* 5:4.
59. *See CPrR* 5:30.
60. See, e.g., the Canon of Pure Reason in *CPuR*; *CPrR* 5:122–33; *CPoJ* 5:442–84.
61. See, e.g., *GMM* 4:455–6.
62. See, e.g., *GMM* 4:457.
63. See *CPrR* 5:161–2.
64. See *CPrR* 5:119–21.
65. See, e.g., Beyleveld, 'Hope and Belief'.
66. See Beyleveld, 'Hope and Belief'.
67. See, e.g., Beyleveld and Ziche, 'Towards a Kantian Transcendental Phenomenology of Hope'.
68. See B. Williams, *Ethics and the Limits of Philosophy* (Cambridge, MA: Harvard University Press, 1985), p. 63.
69. See Beyleveld, 'Williams' False Dilemma'.
70. It is only because Kant holds that Agnes is categorically required to believe that she has free will that he has to subordinate the maxim of understanding to the maxim of the power of judgment.
71. J. G. Fichte, *Foundations of Natural Right*, M. Baur (trans) and F. Neuhouser (ed) (Cambridge: Cambridge University Press, 2000).
72. In D. Beyleveld and S. Pattinson, 'Defending Moral Precaution as a Solution to the Problem of Other Minds: A Reply to Holm and Coggon', *Ratio Juris*, 23 (2010), pp. 258–73, note 3, it is suggested that precautionary reasoning to avoid violating the PGC requires Agnes to presume that there is a world that exists independently of her senses. As Kant might say, it is 'morally certain' that such a world exists, even though it is merely possible *theoretically* that it does. But the only significance of this is that Agnes may not evade being categorically bound to treat apparent agents as agents (i.e., in accord with the PGC) on the basis of the speculative possibility that they do not really exist. Parallel reasoning does not require Agnes to act as though God exists (as though she believes that God exists) because there is no way in which her actions can affect God's existence if God exists, but they can affect the existence of other agents if they exist.
73. See Beyleveld and Ziche, 'Towards a Kantian Transcendental Phenomenology of Hope' and compare '*a priori* psychology' per W. Waxman, *Kant's Anatomy of the Intelligent Mind* (Oxford: Oxford University Press, 2014).
74. While much of what Kant says about hope in *CPoJ* points to the Gewirthian anthropology I have outlined, Kant doggedly hangs on to 'faith' (rather than 'hope') as the propositional attitude that it is appropriate to have towards the ideas, apart from the *summum bonum*, which he connects with free will. See Beyleveld and Ziche, 'Towards a Kantian Transcendental Phenomenology of Hope'.

WORKS CITED

Beyleveld, D., *The Dialectical Necessity of Morality: An Analysis and Defense of Alan Gewirth's Argument to the Principle of Generic Consistency* (Chicago: University of Chicago Press, 1991).
———, 'Gewirth and Kant on Justifying the Supreme Principle of Morality', in M. Boylan (ed.), *Gewirth: Critical Essays on Action, Rationality, and Community* (Lanham, MD: Rowman and Littlefield, 1999), pp. 97–117.

Gewirth Versus Kant on Kant's Maxim of Reason 29

———, 'Hope and Belief', in R. J. Jenkins and E. Sullivan (eds.), *Philosophy of Mind* (New York: Nova Science Publishers Inc., 2012), pp. 1–36.

———, 'Williams' False Dilemma: How to Give Categorical Binding Impartial Reasons to Real Agents', *Journal of Moral Philosophy*, 10:2 (2013), pp. 204–26.

———, 'Korsgaard *v* Gewirth on Universalization: Why Gewirthians Are Kantians and Kantians Ought to be Gewirthians', *Journal of Moral Philosophy*, 12:5 (2013), pp. 573–97.

Beyleveld, D. and Bos, G., 'The Foundational Role of the Principle of Instrumental Reason in Gewirth's Argument for the Principle of Generic Consistency: A Response to Andrew Chitty', *King's Law Journal*, 20:1 (2009), pp. 1–20.

Beyleveld, D. and Brownsword, R., *Human Dignity in Bioethics and Biolaw* (Oxford: Oxford University Press, 2001).

Beyleveld, D. and Pattinson, S., 'Defending Moral Precaution as a Solution to the Problem of Other Minds: A Reply to Holm and Coggon', *Ratio Juris*, 23:2 (2010), pp. 258–73.

Beyleveld, D. and Ziche, P., 'Towards a Kantian Transcendental Phenomenology of Hope', *Ethical Theory and Moral Practice*, 18:5 (2015), pp. 927–42. Open access: DOI 10.1007/s10677-015-9564-x, available at http://link.springer.com/article/10.1007/s10677-015-9564-x [accessed 25 August 2015].

Enoch, D., 'Agency, Schmagency: Why Normativity Won't Come from What Is Constitutive of Action', *Philosophical Review*, 115:2 (2006), pp. 169–98.

Fichte, J. G., *Foundations of Natural Right*, ed. F. Neuhouser (Cambridge: Cambridge University Press, 2000).

Gewirth, A., *Reason and Morality* (Chicago: University of Chicago Press, 1978).

Hampton, J., *The Authority of Reason* (Cambridge: Cambridge University Press, 1998).

Kant, I., *Cambridge Edition of the Works of Immanuel Kant*, eds. P. Guyer and A. W. Wood (Cambridge: Cambridge University Press, 1995 sqq).

Korsgaard, C., *The Constitution of Agency: Essays on Practical Reason and Moral Psychology* (Oxford: Oxford University Press, 2008).

Waxman, W., *Kant's Anatomy of the Intelligent Mind* (Oxford: Oxford University Press, 2014).

Williams, B., *Ethics and the Limits of Philosophy* (Cambridge, MA: Harvard University Press, 1985).

2 Is Alan Gewirth's Moral Philosophy Neo-Stoic?[1]

Edward Spence

INTRODUCTION

This chapter will attempt to demonstrate that Alan Gewirth's rationalist ethical theory, based on the Principle of Generic Consistency (PGC) is, in all its different facets, paradigmatically and essentially stoic in its structure, scope, and schematically, in its content. To demonstrate the essential stoic features of Gewirth's ethical theory, I will refer extensively to relevant passages in Gewirth's book, *Self-Fulfillment* (1998), which bears close similarities to stoic ethics, especially as regards the stoic views on eudaimonia, or happiness, virtue, and reason. I will argue that Gewirth's notion of 'self-fulfillment' is a neo-stoic version of stoic 'eudaimonia'.

One key doctrine of stoic ethics, which may first appear to be at odds with Gewirth's own views on the matter, is the controversial stoic claim that virtue alone as the only good is both necessary and sufficient for happiness. At the outset, Gewirth appears to be more Aristotelian on this issue. However, there is a neo-stoic way of understanding the necessity and sufficiency of virtue for happiness, one that Laurence Becker convincingly expounds in his book *A New Stoicism* (1998), which I believe accords well with Gewirth's more modest view on the issue.

In the last few years, there has been a notable and steady revival of stoicism. Scholarly works by A. A. Long, Gisela Striker, Julia Annas, Martha Nussbaum, and Laurence Becker,[2] to name but a few, have generated a renewed interest in Stoic philosophy and especially in stoic ethics. Outside academic philosophy, stoicism has also been exerting an indirect and unacknowledged influence. I am referring to the remarkable rise of public philosophy and professional ethics in recent times. Generally Hellenistic in spirit because of their practical orientation, professional ethics and public philosophy have a more specific, stoic pedigree because of the robust professional, political, social, and communal engagement that characterizes them both.[3]

If I am right, the neo-stoic character of Gewirth's ethical theory is at once both surprising and yet not: surprising because Gewirth himself has not consciously or overtly recognized the pronounced and crucial stoic character of his ethical theory.[4] Although frequently making references to the Aristotelian and Kantian elements in his own theory, he rarely if ever makes overt or even indirect references to similarities or differences between his theory and that of the stoics.[5]

METHODOLOGY

First, let me offer some brief explanatory remarks about methodology. In order to demonstrate the essential stoic features of Gewirth's ethical theory, I will juxtapose the main central doctrines of stoic philosophy with similar parallel precepts and principles present in Gewirth's work. I will refer extensively to relevant passages in Gewirth's book, *Self-Fulfillment*,[6] which bears close similarities to stoic ethics, especially as regards the stoic views on eudaimonia, or happiness, virtue, and reason. I will claim, and support this claim with textual analysis of relevant key passages, that the whole tenor of *Self-Fulfillment* is paradigmatically stoic in most if not all of its main features. As we shall see, Gewirth's notion of 'self-fulfillment' is a neo-stoic version of stoic 'eudaimonia'. By the end of the comparative analysis of the central stoic ethical doctrines and Gewirth's ethical principles and precepts, I hope to reach the conclusion, on the basis of that analysis, that Gewirth's ethical theory is essentially neo-stoic, for it shares most if not all of the central doctrines of stoic ethics. I will say more about that later.

A further methodological point is that my references to stoic philosophy will primarily rely on secondary sources, mainly the work of some leading contemporary stoic scholars, such as A.A. Long, Gisela Striker, Julia Annas, Martha Nussbaum, and last but not least, the work of Laurence Becker, especially with regard to neo-stoicism. I will refer to extracts from ancient texts as and when required. I believe that there is sufficient evidence of a general consensus among contemporary stoic scholars of what the central doctrines of stoic ethics are. A consensus that renders any in-depth scholarly exploration of stoic texts in determining what those central doctrines are unnecessary, unnecessary, at least, for my present purposes. I will thus rely primarily on the work of the above-mentioned contemporary stoic scholars in outlining the central stoic doctrines and comparing them to similar principles and precepts in Gewirth's work.

Finally, a related issue to the one above is whether there was a consensus amongst the ancient stoic philosophers themselves as to what constituted the central doctrines of stoicism, specifically, stoic ethics. Were the central doctrines of stoicism common amongst the early stoics, such as Zeno of Citium (342–270 BC) and Chrysippus (280–207 BC) of the early stoa, the stoics of the middle stoa, such as Panaetius (180–109 BC) and Posidonius (135–151 BC), and the much later stoics of the Roman Empire, such as Seneca (4 BC–65 AD) and Epictetus (55–135 AD)? There were indeed some differences between all these stoics, with the later stoics considered to have

32 *Spence*

adopted a more moderate and less stringent ethical doctrine than the early stoics such as Chrysippus. However, as Gisela Striker has pointed out, notwithstanding those differences, there appears to have been a common core of doctrines amongst all those stoic philosophers, corresponding more closely perhaps to the doctrines developed by Chrysippus, generally considered the most important stoic philosopher of antiquity after Zeno of Citium.[7] For the purposes of this chapter, I will follow Striker on this issue and adopt the view that there is in fact a common core of doctrines so fundamental to stoicism that they can be attributed to stoic philosophy as a whole. I will only highlight differences amongst particular stoic philosophers when this is of significant relevance to my comparative analysis of the stoics and Gewirth.

A COMPARATIVE ANALYSIS OF THE CENTRAL DOCTRINES OF STOICISM AND THE CENTRAL PRINCIPLES AND PRECEPTS OF GEWIRTH'S ETHICAL THEORY

Two central doctrines of stoic ethics will be discussed and compared to Gewirthian ethics, namely, those of eudaimonia and virtue. As mentioned earlier, my selection of the central doctrines of stoic ethics is based primarily on a number of representative secondary sources[8] from contemporary stoic scholarship that support a consensus on what constitutes the central doctrines of stoic ethics. This consensus concurs with my own general reading of stoic texts and stoic philosophy. In this regard, I consider that selection to be commonplace and uncontroversial.

For easy comparison, the central doctrines of stoic ethics have been juxtaposed with the parallel and corresponding central features and precepts of Gewirth's rationalist ethics. The comparison is intended to demonstrate the close similarity between stoic and Gewirthian ethics, thus establishing my claim that Gewirth's ethical theory is essentially and paradigmatically neo-stoic.

VIRTUE[9] AND EUDAIMONIA[10]

Stoics

The Stoics' Definition of Virtue

(i) 'Virtue is not defined by the consequences in the world which it succeeds in promoting, but by a pattern of behavior that follows necessarily from a disposition perfectly in tune with Nature's rationality.

(ii) The right thing to do is that which accords with virtue, and this is equivalent to saying that it accords with the nature of a perfect rational being.

Is Alan Gewirth's Moral Philosophy Neo-Stoic? 33

(iii) Virtue accords with nature in the sense that it is the special function or goal of a rational being to be virtuous.'[11]

The Stoic Relationship of Happiness to Virtue

'The life of a stoic sage is filled with such happiness as a consequence of her virtue.'[12]

Another central feature of the stoic conception of happiness is its intrinsic relation to virtue. For as noted earlier, virtue as the primary comprehensive goal of human nature is not only the essential means for the attainment of happiness, but more importantly, it is constitutive of happiness.[13] In being the end or goal of life, virtue is both the means and the end of a happy life. The means, for the development and inculcation of virtue leads to happiness, and the end, because its possession as the only good guarantees a good life, for virtue is constitutive of happiness and its possession as the only good necessarily guarantees one's happiness. Another related characteristic of happiness is its self-sufficiency, for insofar as virtue as the only good is entirely within one's control, and that alone is sufficient for happiness, then happiness results from virtuous self-sufficiency.[14] An important qualification, however, must be made to the view that happiness and virtue in stoic ethics are so intimately and intrinsically connected, that one cannot tell them apart, and as a result, one might then be led to view stoic happiness as nothing more than a life of virtue. This would be a mistake, however, for as Lawrence C. Becker correctly points out, stoic virtue is not the same as, say, Kantian duty.[15] There is joy in stoic ethics over and above the state of just being virtuous and always doing the right thing out of a grudging sense of duty. In stoicism, the possession of virtue fills one's soul with joy similar to how a state of health and fitness fills one with a general sense of well-being, both physically and psychologically. The stoic sage, as the sage in Plato's *Symposium* standing at the top of the ladder of human perfection and gazing at the Form of the Good, is in love with the Good,[16] and that alone fills him with abundant joy.

Julia Annas[17] rightly insists, contrary to the view that stoic eudaimonia is nothing more than a life of virtue, that we must take stoic eudaimonists at their word, for ultimately, what they are offering us is an account of a happy life and not just a virtuous one. And these two things are, though intrinsically connected, conceptually distinct, as are shape and size, for example: Although shape and size are intrinsically connected, they are nevertheless conceptually distinct.

Insofar as virtue is the only good and virtue is entirely within one's control, then possession of the only good is both necessary and sufficient for happiness and potentially within the reach of everyone. Moreover, sages like Socrates and the Buddha are real exemplars that render this view not a mere philosophical abstraction, but a real practical possibility.

34 *Spence*

Stoic Virtue as Both Necessary and Sufficient for Happiness

From the two propositions that human virtue is rational perfection, and that the perfection of one's reason is in agreement with nature, the stoics inferred that virtue is good, the only good, for it alone allows one to live in agreement with nature.[18] Moreover, being a function of human rationality, virtue is within one's rational control and, as the only good, its possession leads to happiness, or eudaimonia. That virtue is the only good follows from the view that only virtue is unconditionally good. For in all circumstances, virtuous conduct is in agreement with nature, which alone determines what is good. Hence, virtue is the only good because it allows one to live in accordance with nature.

Whereas health, wealth, friends, and social status might be 'good' sometimes, they are not always good, as their possession may not only not result in a virtuous life in agreement with nature, but worse, it may lead one to unethical and vicious actions that are bad because such actions are not in agreement with nature; on the contrary, they are in disagreement with nature because, ultimately, they are inconsistent with one's rational nature.

The above analysis is, I believe, in keeping with the general features of stoic ethics concerning the sufficiency of virtue for happiness.[19] What emerges is the following schema:

(1) Virtue is the perfection of one's rational nature.
(2) Virtue as the perfection of one's rational nature allows one to live in agreement with nature.
(3) As the only thing that allows one to live a life in agreement with nature, virtue is the only good.
(4) As such, virtue is unconditionally good.
(5) Only the possession of what is unconditionally is good can render one happy.
(6) Therefore, since only virtue is unconditionally good, only virtue can make one happy.
(7) Virtue is completely within every rational person's control.
(8) Hence, every rational person (because everyone is inherently rational) can potentially become happy and moreover must aim at becoming happy by becoming virtuous.

The above 8-point outline renders, I hope clearly, the intrinsic relationship between the central features of stoic ethics: reason, virtue, nature, and eudaimonia. Moreover, the outline draws attention to both the descriptive as well as the prescriptive characteristics of stoicism. Furthermore, it highlights the ideal and developmental aspects of stoic ethics. However ideal, the status of sagehood, as the only possible state for true and lasting happiness, remains a practical possibility for every rational person. In the *Tusculan Disputations*, Cicero devotes the whole of Book V to a defense of the necessity and

Is Alan Gewirth's Moral Philosophy Neo-Stoic? 35

sufficiency of virtue for happiness. Laurence C. Becker has identified the following premises as the key premises in Cicero's argument:[20]

(1) 'No one can be happy except when good is secure and certain and lasting (V.xiv.40).
(2) The good of virtue is secure and certain and lasting because (a) once achieved, its maintenance is within the agent's control (V.xiv.42), and (b) it is free from the disturbances of the soul that produce wretchedness (V.xv.43).
(3) Moreover, in its affective dimension, a virtuous life is characterized by tranquility and joy, and thus may unproblematically be described as a happy life (V.xv.43)
(4) No form of happiness can be good unless it includes, or is founded upon, virtue, or what is right (V.xv.44–5)'.

Gewirth

Gewirth's Relationship of Happiness to Virtue

Gewirth's attention to the virtues and their relationship to both rationality and morality, mediated through the PGC, is extensive and comprehensive. What will concern us in this section is Gewirth's account of the relationship between virtue and self-fulfillment. The relationship as expressed by Gewirth appears to be as follows: Insofar as morality is intrinsically related to self-fulfillment as capacity-fulfillment,[21] and insofar as the virtues are essential in enabling rational agents to act and live ethically in compliance with the requirements of the PGC,[22] then the virtues are also intrinsically related to self-fulfillment.[23] The above-described relationship between virtue and self-fulfillment appears, in the first instance, to be instrumental. That is, virtues are essential because they are effective means for ethical development, thus enabling one to comply more effectively with both the negative and positive requirements of the PGC.

This instrumental understanding of the virtues is also part of the developmental aspect of stoic ethics. By aiming and attempting to act and live virtuously, one gradually becomes inculcated in virtuous conduct through habituation.[24]

However, there is also, as in stoic ethics, a constitutive aspect of the virtues in Gewirth's model of self-fulfillment. Once one becomes habituated to acting ethically in compliance with the PGC, then virtuous conduct becomes, as it were, one's *second* nature. In the Gewirthian neo-stoic sage, at the limit of virtuous perfection, however, virtue becomes, together with rationality, the sage's *first* and only nature. The perfection of reason and virtue combine and match in the neo-stoic sage, and though remaining conceptually distinct, become, in the sage's actions, *practically* indistinguishable. Thus, the neo-stoic sage acts virtuously not only because his reason demands it, but more importantly, because his reason is attuned to virtuous conduct. Unlike the Kantian 'sage', the Gewirthian neo-stoic sage, like his stoic counterpart, does the right thing

36 Spence

out of love for the good and not out of a joyless sense of duty. The neo-stoic sage, like his stoic predecessor, enjoys being virtuous and this, unlike the Kantian sage, does not in any way diminish his goodness or his happiness.

The *developmental* and the *constitutive* aspects of virtue are illustrated by Gewirth in the following passage:

> There is a difference, however, between one's having a duty to act from a virtue and one's having a duty to try to develop a virtue. It is the latter that is required for capacity-fulfillment.[25]

Once, however, one becomes self-fulfilled, by becoming perfectly virtuous *qua* a rational person, then one's developmental virtue becomes constitutive both of his character and of his happiness or self-fulfillment. Acting out of virtue for a Gewirthian neo-stoic sage, as for the stoic sage of antiquity, is acting out of his perfected rational nature. There is, in contrast to the Kantian 'sage', no separation in the stoic sage between the two distinct thoughts 'this is what I *want* to do' and 'this is what I *ought* to do'. Acting out of desire and acting out of virtue become in the neo-stoic and stoic sage alike are one and the same thing.

The Gewirthian Definition of Virtue

It will be recalled that a stoic definition of virtue is that:

> Virtue is not defined by the consequences in the world which it succeeds in promoting but by a pattern of behavior that follows necessarily from a disposition perfectly in tune with Nature's rationality.[26]

This definition of stoic virtue is very much in keeping with Gewirth's own understanding of virtue: namely, a 'disposition perfectly in tune with human rationality', where *human nature* as rational purposive agency replaces the metaphysical notion of stoic *Nature*. And for Gewirth, so too for the stoics, 'the right thing to do is that which accords with virtue, and this is equivalent to saying that it accords with the *nature of a perfect rational being*' (emphasis added).[27] For Gewirth, the right thing to do accords with the requirements of the PGC, which in turn accords with the natural property of 'rational purposive agency'. And that, in turn, requires the development and inculcation of the virtues as the enabling dispositions for acting and living ethically. And acting and living virtuously then accords, at least for the neo-stoic sage, with the nature of a rational purposive agent.

Gewirthian Virtue as Both Necessary and Sufficient for Happiness

Insofar as health, wealth, fame, and social status, some of the stoic preferred indifferents, are not essential for complying with the requirements of the

PGC, and moreover, under certain circumstances, their possession may result in the violation of those requirements, then virtue would appear to be, as for the stoics so too for Gewirth, the only unconditional good. Unconditional, because only virtue is under all circumstances, at least in principle, *capable* of enabling a rational purposive agent to act in accordance with the negative and positive requirements of the PGC. I say only *capable*, because like rationality, virtue cannot motivate a sociopath or a psychopath to behave ethically. This is partly because the sociopath's and the psychopath's rational nature has, in some way, become dysfunctional.

But even if virtue as the only good, understood as the only unconditional good that is capable of enabling a rational purposive agent to act and live ethically, is necessary for self-fulfillment, is it sufficient? The quick answer is that virtue is not sufficient for the self-fulfillment of the person who has not yet achieved stoic or neo-stoic sagehood, but it is for the person who has attained it. It is not sufficient for the person who falls short of stoic or neo-stoic sagehood, because under adverse circumstances, his happiness or self-fulfillment may be compromised or worse, adversely affected, due to the imperfection of his virtue. A tiny tear in a full sail, that under fair conditions might go unnoticed, may cause the boat serious damage or worse, cause it to sink when a freak storm strikes. Similarly, the partial perfection of virtue in a person who acts and lives ethically under normal favourable conditions may be undermined by a misfortune or extraordinary circumstances, such as war. Under such adverse circumstances, that person may lose both her virtue and happiness. And for the stoics, losing one's virtue is tantamount to losing one's happiness. Hecuba is an illustrative example of such a partially virtuous person who loses both her virtue and happiness by being driven through tragic misfortune to commit terrible deeds. Could Hecuba have remained happy in the face of such overwhelming misfortune if she were a stoic sage? The stoics would give an affirmative answer to that question. Had Hecuba been a stoic sage, she would have retained both her virtue and her happiness. For ultimately, her own virtue, the source of her happiness, was entirely within her control. This may seem preposterous and a reason for rejecting the sufficiency thesis. However, on closer analysis, the sufficiency thesis does not appear preposterous, but reasonable; at least, it ought to appear reasonable to rational agents.

In what follows, I will attempt to construct a Gewirthian neo-stoic version of the sufficiency thesis (premises 1–7):

(1) First, let us distinguish developmental from constitutive virtue. *Developmental* virtue is virtue that enables one to become ethically a good person. Its function is primarily instrumental, as physical fitness is for health. However, once one becomes ethically good, in the sense that one becomes disposed to always act out of virtue, which at this stage of one's development has become identical with one's rational purposive agency, virtue becomes *constitutive* of that person's ethical goodness.

38 *Spence*

To use the same previous analogy, one's physical fitness is no longer merely instrumental for becoming healthy, but it becomes, once one attains and maintains good health, constitutive of one's health and general lifestyle. When constitutive, virtue, like physical fitness, is its own reward—it becomes, together with moral goodness, an end in itself and not merely an instrumental means for ethical conduct.

(2) As regards developmental virtue, rational purposive agents have a duty to develop and inculcate the virtues of character in themselves as an essential means for complying with the PGC's requirements.[28]

(3) However, a purposive agent cannot begin to develop those essential developmental virtues unless he has the minimal material, and other personal and social conditions that are required for the preservation and maintenance of his freedom and well-being. For without the conditions sufficient for preserving and maintaining one's freedom and well-being, as the necessary conditions of one's rational purposive agency, one cannot successfully maintain one's rational purposive agency.

(4) Insofar as agents cannot by their own efforts provide the minimal conditions for the preservation and maintenance of their freedom and well-being, other agents should, both individually and collectively through the various communal and state institutions, assist those agents in procuring and securing those minimal conditions, when they can do so at no comparable cost to themselves. The 'comparable cost' is proportionally minimized when the cost is not borne by individuals, but collectively by the community through its various formal and informal voluntary institutions.[29] This is in keeping with Gewirth's 'community of rights' thesis.[30]

(5) Hence, insofar as agents require some minimal material, personal, and social conditions to function as agents, through the preservation and maintenance of their freedom and well-being, those conditions are essential for the ethical and virtuous development of those agents. Therefore, minimal conditions of health, wealth, education, housing, employment, sufficient for the preservation and maintenance of an agent's rights to freedom and well-being, are essential for the agent's ethical development and ultimately, his self-fulfillment, for without them, he can't function as a purposive agent, let alone an ethical agent.

This interim conclusion may at first appear to undermine the sufficiency thesis. However, on closer reflection we can see that it doesn't, as the premises (2–5) above refer to developmental and not constitutive virtue. It will be recalled that the sufficiency thesis is only intended to refer to constitutive virtue, and in particular, the constitutive virtue of the stoic sage. It is not intended to refer to developmental virtue, and in particular, the developmental virtue of one who does not aspire to become a stoic sage, or if he does so

Is Alan Gewirth's Moral Philosophy Neo-Stoic? 39

aspire, has not made the mark yet. Either way, the developmental virtue of those agents who have not yet acquired constitutive virtue, or who do not aspire to such virtue, is not sufficient for stoic happiness or Gewirthian neo-stoic 'ideal self-fulfillment'.

As for the stoics, so too for Gewirth, such an excellent human agent is a sage—in Gewirth's case, a neo-stoic sage. This ideal second-order understanding of self-fulfillment is evident in the following passage from Gewirth:

> What has emerged from the considerations in this book is that although in important respects self-fulfillment is never completely attainable, it can be approximated in a social context that makes adequate provision for one's efforts as guided by reason.[31]

Importantly, Gewirth's ideal self-fulfillment can best be approached within an egalitarian social context that recognizes everyone's right to first-order self-fulfillment, but in addition, recognizes the desirability for working communally to create a society or a *cosmopolis* in which the optimal conditions for attaining second-order ideal self-fulfillment are available to everyone, a cosmopolis in which Socrates would never again have to drink the hemlock.

As we have seen so far from premises 1–5 above, developmental virtue is not sufficient for stoic eudaimonia or Gewirthian neo-stoic ideal self-fulfillment (henceforth, I will use 'self–fulfillment' to mean second-order ideal self-fulfillment, self-fulfillment *qua* human being, unless otherwise indicated). Is it nevertheless sufficient for constitutive virtue in the case of Gewirthian self-fulfillment? I will answer affirmatively that it is for the reasons expressed in premises 6–7 below:

(6) First, let us assume that our Gewirthian neo-stoic sage has all the creature comforts of contemporary living: a car, a fully equipped house, a well-paid job, a functional and flourishing family, good health, friends, fame, regular holidays to desired destinations, wealth, and a social status to match. Everything a man or woman could ever want or need. Now imagine taking away piecemeal each one of those desirable possessions. Question: At what point exactly would our hypothetical neo-stoic sage stop feeling self-fulfilled? Can we imagine someone like Socrates or the Buddha feeling unhappy or unfilled because they lost any or all of those things? We know that the Buddha gave away all his princely possessions to become poor and homeless but wise. We think of Socrates as someone who felt self-fulfilled in the completeness and self-sufficiency of his virtue. He was uncompromisingly virtuous in both his teachings and his actions. Without laboring the point too much, the question regarding the sufficiency of virtue for happiness becomes the question of how much does a neo-stoic sage need to be happy or self-fulfilled apart from his perfect virtue. In keeping with Gewirth's overall ethical theory

40 *Spence*

and model of self-fulfillment, the answer that is presented to us is that a neo-stoic sage would require the minimal material, personal, and social conditions sufficient for preserving and maintaining his rational purposive agency. Without those conditions he would not be able to preserve and maintain his rational purposive agency, let alone his perfect virtue on which his self-fulfillment or happiness depends. But those minimal conditions, as in the case of Socrates, the Buddha, and possibly stoics such as Zeno or Epictetus, would indeed be the bare minimal conditions sufficient for preserving and maintaining rational purposive agency. Socrates chose the hemlock over exile, perhaps because he thought that the conditions in exile would not have allowed him to preserve and maintain his rational purposive agency in any realistic or meaningful way.

In the Gewirthian sense of ideal self-fulfillment, Socrates was a social sage, one whose self-fulfillment, though within his control, was partly constituted by his cultural and social attachments in the city of Athens. This is not surprising, for as social animals, our identity is at least partly constituted by our social and cultural attachments. Though less attached than normal agents, a sage is also a social being who functions best within a social and communal milieu. A sage is not and need not be a hermit, though a sage could choose to be one. We would then, under my Gewirthian construction of neo-stoicism, allow that, insofar as the neo-stoic sage is a socialized being, a minimal degree of sociability may be part of the minimal conditions sufficient for preserving and maintaining one's rational agency, a social condition that would apply to both a sage and non-sage unlike. If I am right, this is, I believe, a welcome result, for it would otherwise seem unrealistic to maintain that in our contemporary, complex world, a neo-stoic sage could successfully live as a sage in total isolation from any form or content of social or communal interaction. In keeping with the notion of social and political engagement, which was also an important feature of stoicism, a minimal degree of sociability would therefore appear to be one of the minimal conditions for preserving and maintaining rational agency with regard to Gewirth's model of self-fulfillment.

(7) In conclusion, constitutive virtue is sufficient for ideal self-fulfillment so long as rational purposive agency can be preserved and maintained.[32] This will in turn require the presence of the material, personal, and social conditions that are sufficient for the preservation and maintenance of rational agency, nothing more and nothing less. An interesting contrast that seems to support the social dimension of the neo-sagehood I have outlined above is a passage from Julia Annas: '[V]irtue is sufficient for nonunhappiness, but for happiness the person must be able to use, not merely possess, virtue'.[33]

EUDAIMONIA

Stoics[34]

> 'Happiness . . . is the polestar of our ethical theory'.[35]

According to the stoics, eudaimonia, or happiness, is not something that happens to you by chance, like winning the lottery, but rather something that one *achieves* through becoming perfectly rational and virtuous. Only few people can ever achieve eudaimonia, because only a few people can become truly virtuous. At the limit, the sage is viewed by the stoics as an ideal exemplar, someone to be looked upon as a role model for those aspiring to become happy through becoming wise and virtuous. Becoming happy or eudaimon for the stoics was thus considered a *katorthoma*, or supreme achievement. Something earned, not something given. But though difficult, the attainment of happiness through virtue was not only practically possible, but also prescribed by nature, in particular, rational human nature. Insofar as becoming virtuous was within everyone's control, so was happiness.[36]

Gewirth[37]

In *Self-Fulfillment*, Gewirth distinguishes between self-fulfillment as *aspiration-fulfillment* and self-fulfillment as *capacity-fulfillment*. The former he identifies as the satisfaction of one's deepest desires, the latter as the process and goal of making the best of oneself. The difference between the two, as Gewirth claims,

> is that aspirations and their fulfillment are tied more closely to person's actual desires, while capacity-fulfillment bears more on making the best of oneself and thus serves as a normative guide to what desires one ought to have, where this "ought" may (but need not) go beyond person's actual desires.

Gewirth goes on to identify these two distinct conceptions of self-fulfillment with two other conceptions of happiness, thus identifying 'self-fulfillment' with 'happiness'. He goes on to say that the putative connection of his two notions of self-fulfillment as aspiration-fulfillment and capacity-fulfillment with happiness 'brings out further why self-fulfillment is so highly valued as a superlative condition of the self'.[38] Clearly, it is Gewirth's notion of capacity-self-fulfillment that is equivalent to stoic eudaimonia.

From a close examination of *Self-Fulfillment*, it becomes clear that Gewirth's notion of self-fulfillment as capacity-fulfillment has all the essential characteristics of stoic eudaimonia. In claiming this, I take Gewirth's notion of self-fulfillment as capacity-fulfillment to be, with regard to its equivalence

42 *Spence*

to stoic eudaimonia, a *second-order self-fulfillment*. That is, self-fulfillment, *qua* rational human being. A person can attain *first-order self-fulfillment* by becoming the best he can possibly become, given his particular aspirations and capacities, in a certain specific activity, for example, the best tennis player. However, that person may nevertheless fail to become self-fulfilled at the level of second-order self-fulfillment because he does not succeed in becoming the best person, *qua* rational human being, he can possibly become. The attainment of such second-order self-fulfillment, which is equivalent, as I claim, to stoic eudaimonia, would only be possible for a Gewirthian neo-stoic sage and his stoic counterpart. Lesser mortals who do not succeed in becoming perfectly rational and virtuous in all their life plans and activities would be able to attain *first-order self-fulfillment* in their specific activities, but would only be able to attain *second-order self-fulfillment* by first becoming neo-stoic or stoic sages.

For the purpose of this chapter, I will use the term 'happiness' interchangeably with both Gewirth's notion of 'self-fulfillment' and the stoic notion of 'eudaimonia'. Self-fulfillment as capacity-fulfillment is the primary focus of Gewirth in *Self-Fulfillment*. As for the stoics, so too for Gewirth, self-fulfillment as capacity-fulfillment is an achievement, one that requires, as in stoic ethics, a life lived in agreement with both reason and morality. For in both stoic and Gewirthian ethics, human rational nature as an integral part of a rational and divine Universe (as in the case of the stoics), or as rational purposive agency (as in the case of Gewirth), prescribes that one should make the best of oneself. And this in turn requires, at a minimum, living both an ethical and a virtuous life. According to Gewirth:

> Personalist morality . . . gives counsel and precepts for the self's having a good life through personal development of one's capacities whereby one makes the best of oneself.[39]

It is in self-fulfillment, through its relation to purposiveness and the fulfillment of capacities in making the best of oneself, that Gewirth locates the meaning of life. It is not, as in stoicism, a metaphysical meaning that emanates from a divine and rational all-purposeful Universe, but rather a human, all too human, meaning, one that emanates from our own rational purposive nature. It is this inherent purposiveness aligned to our rationality that drives us on to the perfection of our individual selves and not some promise of a metaphysical reward in this life, as in the stoics, or a reward in some other transcendent life, as in Plato. Gewirth's self-fulfillment is wholly naturalistic. For Gewirth,

> the meaning of life . . . consists in the pursuit and attainment of the values of personalist morality as guided by the rational justification of universalist morality and the analysis of freedom and well-being as central

to the highest development of the virtues based upon these necessary goods of action.[40]

However, for practical purposes, both stoic eudaimonia and Gewirthian self-fulfillment amount to the same thing: a quest for making the best of oneself in agreement with one's intrinsic rational human nature that accords with an ethical and virtuous life—one that ultimately leads to eudaimonia, or self-fulfillment. As in stoicism, so to in Gewirth's ethical schema, self-fulfillment is a 'maximalist' concept,[41] for it involves the perfection of oneself through the perfection of one's human rational nature.[42] And as in stoicism, so too in Gewirth's ethical theory, self-fulfillment is something to be aimed at as an ideal, a practically possible target, but one that may never be completely reached. As Gewirth says, 'self-fulfillment is far more a process than a finished product'.[43]

It seems that for Gewirth, as for the stoics before him, self-fulfillment is something that perhaps only a sage can achieve. For mere mortals like the rest of us, the process is all one can hope for. As the Greek poet Constantine Cavafy remarked in a highly suggestive poetic line (*Ithaca*), it is the journey itself that ultimately counts. For in undertaking it, we stand to become wiser, if not completely wise. This perhaps accords with what Gewirth tells us:

> There is no climactic nirvana, but there can be sequences of self-improvement that overcome the effects of alienation and achieve cherished values. One's best is never finalized, but it can be more fully approached.[44]

CONCLUSION

My comparative analysis, if correct, has demonstrated a clear and close parallel between Gewirthian and stoic ethics on the one hand, and a close parallel between Gewirthian ideal self-fulfillment (second-order self-fulfillment) and stoic eudaimonia on the other. In conclusion, Gewirth's ethical theory, including his model of self-fulfillment, bears a strong and striking similarity, methodically and contextually, at least schematically, to stoic ethics and stoic eudaimonia. Insofar as my comparative analysis is correct, Gewirth's ethical theory, including his model of self-fulfillment, is paradigmatically and essentially neo-stoic. I believe this is a significant and welcome result for both contemporary ethics and stoic scholarship.

NOTES

1. An earlier, more extensive, and longer version of this chapter can be found in my book *Ethics with Reason: A Neo-Gewirthian Approach* (2006), Chapter 10.

44 Spence

2. A. A. Long, *Hellenistic Philosophy: Stoics, Epicureans, Skeptics*, second edition (Berkeley and Los Angeles: University of California Press, 1986); G. Striker, *Essays on Hellenistic Epistemology and Ethics* (Cambridge: Cambridge University Press, 1996); J. Annas, *The Morality of Happiness* (New York: Oxford University Press, 1993); M. C. Nussbaum, *The Therapy of Desire* (Princeton, NJ: Princeton University Press, 1994); and L. C. Becker, *A New Stoicism* (Princeton, NJ: Princeton University Press, 1998).

3. For public philosophy, see E. H. Spence, 'Philosophy Plays: A Neo-Stoic Method for Teaching Ethics', *Teaching Ethics*, 5:1, (2004), pp. 41–57; and E. H. Spence, 'The Theatre of Philosophy: A Neo-Socratic Method for Performing Public Philosophy', in Gordon Bull (ed), *Creativity: Brain—Mind—Body: A View into the Future of Australian Art and Design Schools, the 2011 Australian Council of University Art and Design Schools (ACUADS) Conference*, the Australian National University, the University of Canberra, and the Canberra Institute of Technology, 21–23 September 2011 (2012).

4. When in conversation with Gewirth (Chicago, March 2001) I raised the issue of the striking similarity between his ethics and that of the Stoics, he expressed both interest and surprise. I hope to show that the surprise for Gewirth should be a pleasant one and the interest is both warranted and justified.

5. See especially his *Self-Fulfillment* (Princeton, NJ: Princeton University Press, 1998). Although references to Aristotle abound, and the ones to Kant are not infrequent, the references to the Stoics are almost conspicuously scarce, if not entirely absent.

6. Gewirth, *Self-Fulfillment*.

7. G. Striker, 'Stoicism', in Lawrence C. Becker and Charlotte B. Becker (eds), *Encyclopedia of Ethics* (New York: Garland Publishing, 1992), pp. 1208–13.

8. These sources are: J. Annas, *The Morality of Happiness* (New York: Oxford University Press, 1993); abbreviated for reference to MH. J. Annas, *Platonic Ethics, Old and New* (Ithaca: Cornell University Press, 1999); abbreviated for reference to PEON. L. C. Becker, *A New Stoicism* (Princeton, NJ: Princeton University Press, 1998); abbreviated for reference to ANS. A. A. Long, *Hellenistic Philosophy—Stoics, Epicureans, Sceptics*, second edition (Berkeley: University of California Press, 1986); abbreviated for reference to HP. G. Striker, *Essays On Hellenistic Epistemology and Ethics* (Cambridge: Cambridge University Press, 1996); abbreviated for reference to EHEE. G. Striker, 'Stoicism', in Lawrence C. Becker and Charlotte B. Becker (eds), *Encyclopedia of Ethics* (New York: Garland Publishing, 1992); abbreviated for reference to EE.

9. (a) Stoics (EE: 209–10); (ANS: 118–122); (HP: 192, 197–205); (EHEE: 181–2, 240–3, 255, 279, 288); Gewirth (SF: 14, 56–8, 68–9, 79, 87–90, 114–15, 122–3, 126–7, 131, 134–5, 175–7).

10. (b) Stoics. (EE: 2011); (ANS:127–9, 138–149, 150–6); (HP: 197, 134); (EHEE: 182, 194, 224); Gewirth (SF: 14–16, 18, 25, 50, 62, 85, 107, 182–9).

11. (HP: 192).

12. (ANS: 149).

13. (HP: 197).

14. (HP: 234).

15. (ANS: 150–51).

16. In her review of Martha Nussbaum's *Cultivating Humanity: A Classical Defense of Reform in Liberal Education* (1997), Marilyn Friedman points out that the 'idea of love for all humanity' is mentioned by Nussbaum 'no less than fourteen times' (*Cultivating Humanity*, pages 6, 7, 13, 14, 36, 61, 64, 67, 72, 84, 103, 222, 259, 292)—see Marilyn Friedman, 'Educating for World Citizenship', *Ethics*, 110:3 (2000), p. 589. Nussbaum's 'love for all humanity'

seems essentially similar to the 'love of the Good', which, as the primary motivation for doing what is right, I attribute to both the stoic and the neo-stoic.
17. (MH: 329–35).
18. (EE: 1209).
19. In my analysis, I have followed closely Laurence C. Becker's insightful neo-stoic and stoic analysis on the sufficiency thesis of stoic eudaimonia (ANS:108–58).
20. (ANS: 152).
21. (SF: 78–9).
22. (SF: 135).
23. (SF: 87).
24. For a detailed discussion of Stoic *Oikeiosis* and its structural similarity with a similar concept used by Gewirth in his ethical theory, see E. Spence, *Ethics Within Reason: A Neo-Gewirthian Approach* (Maryland: Lexington Books, a division of Rowman and Littlefield, 2006), pp. 433–42.
25. (SF: 135).
26. (HP: 192).
27. (HP: 192).
28. Gewirth argues that 'the PGC shows that . . . virtues are good to have precisely because persons who have them are much more likely to do what the PGC requires and to make more effective use of their freedom and well-being as parts of a good life' (SF: 35). 'More likely' is a probability statement. Insofar as courage, moderation, prudence, and justice, to mention just the cardinal virtues, seem essential for compliance with both the negative and positive requirements of the PGC, I will claim that the value one ascribes to Gewirth's probability statement in the above-quoted passage should be very high. With the progressive inculcation and habituation of the virtues in a rational agent, that value approaches < 1.
29. See E. Spence, 'Positive Rights and the Cosmopolitan Community: Right-Centred Foundations for Global Ethics', *Journal of Global Ethics*, 3:2 (2007), pp. 181–202.
30. See A. Gewirth, *The Community of Rights* (Chicago: University of Chicago Press, 1996).
31. (SF: 226).
32. The necessity of purposive agency as a prerequisite for stoic, and in particular, neo-stoic eudaimonia or happiness is also alluded to by M. Nussbaum in *Symposium on Cosmopolitanism*, 'Duties of Justice, Duties of Material Aid: Cicero's Problematic Legacy', *The Journal of Political Philosophy*, 8:2 (2000), p. 191.
33. J. Annas, *Platonic Ethics, Old and New* (Ithaca: Cornell University Press, 1999), p. 45.
34. (EE: 2011); (ANS: 127; 138–49; 150–6); (HP: 197; 234); (EHEE: 182; 194; 224).
35. (ANS: 138).
36. (EE: 1211).
37. (SF: 14–16; 18; 25; 50; 62; 85; 107; 182–9)
38. (SF: 14–15).
39. (SF: 107).
40. (SF: 189).
41. (SF: 216).
42. When comparing Gewirthian self-fulfillment to Stoic eudaimonia, let it be understood that I am referring specifically to Gewirth's *second-order*, or *ideal* notion *of self-fulfillment*.
43. (SF: 226).
44. (SF: 227).

46 *Spence*

WORKS CITED

Annas, J., *The Morality of Happiness* (New York: Oxford University Press, 1993).
——, *Platonic Ethics, Old and New* (Ithaca: Cornell University Press, 1999).
Becker, L., *A New Stoicism* (Princeton: Princeton University Press, 1998).
Cicero, *Tusculan Disputations* (Loeb Classical Library), 2nd edition, Translated by J. E. King (Cambridge, MA and London: Harvard University Press, 1927).
Friedman, M. 'Educating for World Citizenship', *Ethics*, 110:3 (2000), pp. 586–601.
Gewirth, A., *The Community of Rights* (Chicago: University of Chicago Press, 1996).
——, *Self-Fulfillment* (Princeton: Princeton University Press, 1998).
Long, A. A., *Hellenistic Philosophy—Stoics, Epicureans, Sceptics*, 2nd edition (Berkeley: University of California Press, 1986).
Nussbaum, M., *Cultivating Humanity: A Classical Defense of Reform in Liberal Education* (Cambridge, MA and London: Harvard University Press, 1997).
Spence, E., 'Philosophy Plays: A Neo–Stoic Method for Teaching Ethics', Utah, USA: *Teaching Ethics*, 5:1 (2004), pp. 41–57.
——, *Ethics Within Reason: A Neo–Gewirthian Approach* (Lanham, MD: Lexington Books, a division of Rowman and Littlefield, 2006).
——, 'Positive Rights and the Cosmopolitan Community: Right-Centred Foundations for Global Ethics', *Journal of Global Ethics*, 3:2 (2007), pp. 181–202.
——, 'The Theatre of Philosophy: A Neo–Socratic Method for Performing Public Philosophy', in Gordon Bull (ed.), *Creativity: Brain—Mind—Body: A View Into the Future of Australian Art and Design Schools*, the 2011 Australian Council of University Art and Design Schools (ACUADS) Conference, the Australian National University, the University of Canberra, and the Canberra Institute of Technology, 21–23 September (2011).
Striker, G., 'Stoicism', in Lawrence C. Becker and Charlotte B. Becker (eds.), *Encyclopedia of Ethics* (New York: Garland Publishing, 1992), pp. 1208–13.
——, *Essays on Hellenistic Epistemology and Ethics* (Cambridge: Cambridge University Press, 1996).

3 'On Pain of Contradiction'
A Key Moment in Deductive Agency Arguments

Michael Boylan

There are several ways to ground moral theory and its various sub-categories, such as justice and human rights. I have parsed these categories in the first place into ways to distribute goods and services that are more than just pure procedural justice based upon a thought experiment.[1] What is needed instead is (are) some empirical fact(s) about human existence that can be analysed into its (their) fundamental, primary components.[2] The agency approach to morality, justice, and human rights intends to do just that. This chapter will briefly examine a few popular ways to proceed in this landscape, and then will argue for one position based upon an analysis of the concept of 'logical contradiction', particularly as it has been evaluated in Aristotelian scholarship. The end result aspires to set out advantages and disadvantages in various ways of understanding the fundamental conditions of human action as relevant to morality, justice, and human rights.

THE CONCEPTUAL UNIVERSE FOR JUSTIFICATION

There are two main models that underlie single-principle theories. I have discussed this earlier in the context of theories of morality.[3] Single-principle theories, whether they are about morality, mathematics/logic, or science, require a single touchstone in order to proceed. In the realm of ethics, Kant's first formulation of the categorical imperative fits the bill.[4] In the realm of mathematics, the most famous examples are the axiomatic projects of Euclid and Hilbert.[5] In science, it was the logical empiricist exercise in its attempt to fully axiomatize the presentation of scientific theories. What these projects seek is some fulcrum against which the world might be moved. This is a cornerstone in doing philosophy. Without some point of certainty, an entirely different reality presents itself. This is the reality of Heraclitus and Protagoras: ever-changing principles in which man is the measure of all things true.[6] Whether the practitioner is from the Western or the Eastern tradition, the result is the same. Philosophy works the same in both spheres.[7] On the one

48 *Boylan*

hand, one can adopt some sort of epistemological and ethical relativism, or one can seek for something more solid.

The law of non-contradiction is the cornerstone of those who believe in some sort of realism: moral, epistemological, logical, and metaphysical (which constitute the four principal areas of philosophy). If we can establish a fulcrum, then much is possible in the quest for truth.

So, what's the problem?

HOW THE PRINCIPLE OF NON-CONTRADICTION WORKS IN THE JUSTIFICATION OF THE PRINCIPLE OF GENERIC CONSISTENCY

The law of non-contradiction is especially important in the direct presentation of the Principle of Generic Consistency (PGC). The Principle of Generic Consistency says: 'Act in accord with the generic rights of your recipients as well as of yourself.'[8] The upshot of this has two components: 1. One should act in a reciprocal manner in the world respecting oneself and others;[9] 2. When any particular prospective purposive agent living in the world contemplates the significance of this, the following is a logical result.

THE DIRECT VERSION OF GEWIRTH'S ARGUMENT[10]

Stage I

A Prospective Purposive Agent (PPA) claims:

1. I do (or intend to do) X voluntarily for some purpose, E. By virtue of making this claim, the PPA rationally must consider that (claim) in logical sequence.
2. E is good.
3. My freedom and well-being are generically necessary conditions of my agency.
4. My freedom and well-being are necessary goods.

Stage II

By virtue of having to accept premise #4, the PPA must accept:

5. I (even if no one else) have a claim right (but not necessarily a moral one) to my freedom and well-being.

Stage III

By virtue of having to accept premise #5 on the basis of premise #1, the PPA must accept:

6. Other PPAs have a moral right claim to their freedom and well-being. If this is the case, then every PPA rationally (upon pain of logical contradiction) claims, by virtue of claiming to be a PPA:

7. Every PPA has a moral claim to his or her freedom and well-being. (#7 is a version of the PGC.)

The Indirect Version of Gewirth's Argument

1. Antithesis; 'I' (some possible objector to Gewirth) claim that some PPAs do not have a moral claims right to freedom and well-being—A[ssertion].
2. Action is essential to being human (i.e., is a part of one's human nature)—F[act].
3. In order to act (i.e., to be a PPA), I (or anyone else) must have some modicum of freedom and well-being—F.
4. In order to act effectively (meaning 'at an approximately level starting line'), I (or anyone else) must have a fuller sense of freedom and well-being (beyond biological minimums, relative to the starting line in each society)—F.
5. All people must claim the rights for themselves of that which is essential to their human nature—F.
6. All people, when confronted with acting minimally versus effectively, will choose to act effectively—F.
7. All people must claim for themselves (prudential only) the rights of freedom and well-being (in the fuller sense)—#s 2–6.
8. 'I' or anyone else can recognize the prudential truth of premise #7—F.
9. It is rational to assume that 'I' am no different from anyone else in a relevant sense concerning the foundations of action—F.
10. To deny to others that which I can claim for myself (viz., freedom and well-being), when the basis of the attribution is premise #7, is to assert that I am an exception to the general rule or that others are to be excepted from the general rule, and is to fail to recognize basic facts of deductive and inductive logic, viz., the basic principles of class inclusion (whether seen deductively, as an instance of the universal quantifier, or inductively, as a 'cogent' feature which will allow said attribution)—F.
11. All people, to be fully *homo sapiens*, must accept the dictums of rationality (a minimum sense of deductive and inductive logic (including

50 Boylan

the law of non-contradiction), which includes some informal understanding of the universal quantifier)—A.

12. The universal quantifier does not permit exceptions to a properly constructed generalization, nor does induction allow a special status for any members of a properly described sample space—F.

13. Premise #7 is a properly constructed generalization about what rights must be claimed by everyone—A.

14. To believe in exceptions for myself (or anyone else) from a universal stamen covering all people (when 'I' am no different from others), is to be irrational—#s 7, 13.

15. To deny others the freedom and well-being which I claim for myself is to be irrational—#s 7, 14.

16. I cannot (or anyone cannot) deny to others the freedom and well-being (in the fuller sense) that I claim for myself—#s 15, 11.

17. Moral rights are those rights that apply to every PPA—A.

18. To admit to a universal claims right (which applies to every PPA for freedom and well-being) is to admit to a moral right to freedom and well-being—A.

19. 'I' (or anyone) must claim that all PPAs have a (moral) claims right to freedom and well-being—#s 16–18.

---

20. Thesis: 'I' or anyone else, i.e., every PPA has a (moral) claims right to freedom and well-being—#s 1, 19.

The major difference between the direct and the indirect versions of this argument rests upon these two different styles of logical argument. In the direct form, one is subject to the most stringent laws of deductive-nomological argument (which combines deductive argument along with commonly held inductive principles, such as the laws of science). The move from premise #s 5 to 6 (stage two to stage three) is Universal Generalization, which allows the practitioner to move from the individual, call him John, possessing a property (Fj) to *anyone* possessing that property under a quantifier: $\forall x$ (Fx). There are various hurdles in this move. The first is that one cannot be sure that the trait in question is really a common property of a class in a non-question-begging way. If one were to simply assert that Φ (a general functional ascription) was a property of Σ (a class) just because (j ϵ Σ): j is an element of Σ, and Φj (j possesses Φ), then it would violate the restrictions on Universal Generalization that specifies the condition of j (or any x) possessing Φ, viz., that this is an essential property of class membership (allowing j or any x to belong to Σ). Because Gewirth sets out the move from stage two to stage three (premise #5 to premise #6) in terms of an agent making a claim, some say that he did not spend enough time on restrictions on Universal Generalization. This will be an objection to any author who starts with either a specific agent, John, or a variable for a specific agent, j (above).[11] There are two ways to respond to this first sort of objection:

'On Pain of Contradiction' 51

1. Kant and the first form of the categorical imperative. When queried on whether it is impermissible for John to tell a lie to Sarah, one first has to define what it means to lie (saying that which is contrary to the state of affairs and with a legitimate attempt to deceive the audience). The question at the individual level immediately jumps to the class level, so that we are no longer talking about John and Sarah, but any member (x, y, or z, *et al.*) considered collectively within a general class Σ. The critical dynamics occur within this general realm. Thus, there is no move to $\forall x$ (Fx). Rather, the logical exercise occurs after the general connection is or is not made. Then the move is back to the individual: existential instantiation (non-problematic—simple subsumption). This approach eliminates the necessity of employing the operation of Universal Generalization. These dynamics—particularly in the case of Gewirth—have been a source of some controversy.[12]

2. My own strategy in the argument for the moral status of basic goods (which addresses a similar problem) is to begin in the mode of natural science, which at a general level would specify the requirements for action understood at the species level (beginning at Σ). There is no move to $\forall x$ (Fx). This is because everything begins at the general level with a scientific triage on which goods are necessary for action in order of importance (which I call embeddedness to the principle of action). This is in keeping with Aristotle and modern scientists who think that inductive logic dictates that though we begin our epistemological understanding with particular instances, the relationships are understood generally via statistically based inductive logic and that any laws that influence normative judgements follow these rules first.[13] After the scientifically determined facts are determined about what it means for *homo sapiens* to have the means to commit minimal, intermediate, or optimal conditions for action, e.g., calories—500, 700, 1,000,[14] *et al.*, then I address in scientific triage what is next in the line for *necessity*? I create a two-stage chart for this (with the first stage having two levels and the second stage having three levels) which I call the Table of Embeddedness.[15] Thus, the proximate question is what do science and social science say about the conditions necessary to commit purposive action? After this is determined according to the best sources available at the moment, then the relative triage rank of claim rights is determined at the general level. Once this is agreed upon, then all that is left is logical subsumption, akin to existential instantiation.

The second major logical objection that can be made against this sort of approach is defeasibility, in which there are good reasons for the conclusion to a deductive argument except that the conclusion does not reach the highest standards of validity because the generating premises can be burdened with unacceptable side conditions that renders the argument invalid (according to those side conditions). This is the hurdle that the direct argument for the PGC has to face, as well as all arguments that seek to connect the groundwork of agency to normative judgements. The essence of this objection is that according to the *way one views agents* or *their connection*

52 Boylan

to *rationality, agency,* and the *teleological directions of the same,* one may have a myriad of objections—some of which are true and some of which are false. In fact, in this way, one needs to present only one sort of boundary condition that is invalid to make the whole enterprise invalid (though not necessarily false).

There are several responses to make to these two fronts (I-A and I-B and II). First, one might say that the move to Universal Generalization works just the way Gewirth presented it. But sceptics demur. Or, one might modify the way that the agency argument works so that the agency approach is altered by moving in a different direction. Two such approaches to make the agency approach different can be achieved by moving toward the positions of Kant and Boylan: 1. From Kant's point of view, one starts at the individual level and then instantly moves to the general level (the generic description of the action in question) to solve the general problem and then apply it back again individually; 2. from my (Boylan's) point of view, one starts at the species (general) level as a scientific exercise to determine a triaged set of goods that permit agency and then applies them generally through public policy.

With respect to defeasibility: Either account may be justifiable, but possibly not, depending upon outrider, boundary additions that one adds to understand the premises. One essay by Dale Jacquette takes this position against my argument for the moral status of basic goods.[16] Jacquette suggests that my argument and Kant's argument for the first form of the categorical imperative both require additional information on the nature of agents in order to gain epistemic and moral justification—he cites this as a rather innocuous form of defeasibility.[17] In Kant's case, Jacquette believed that his characterization of the agent's understanding of the needs of others (as in the second form of the first categorical imperative) would give Kant enough space to make his argument for the first form to be defensible. In my case, it was the inclusion of the personal worldview imperative[18] that was said to provide the extra conceptual context that allowed the conclusion to be supported. But what about Gewirth? What might count for the boundary conditions that would allow for the acceptance of his argument for the PGC? Certainly, Gewirth says that the PPA must have minimum skills in deductive and inductive logic. By this, he meant that one could apply logic to daily life: 1. My pay was cut from 1,000 units to 750 units, 2. rent should be no more than 30 per cent of one's monthly income, therefore, 3. I need to move from my apartment that costs 300 units to one that costs 225 units. Or, 4. many of my friends at work who didn't get the flu shot ended up getting the flu, 5. I don't want to get the flu, therefore, 6. I will increase my chances for health by getting the flu shot.

These are rather minimal conditions. Even when we factor in his last book, *Self-Fulfillment,* some detractors of the defeasibility ilk may say it is not enough.[19] This is a controversial subject that has been raised recently in response to James Griffin's book *On Human Rights.*[20] The jist of many of these objections revolves around the opaqueness of the terms 'freedom' and 'well-being'. If they are insufficiently specified in some intersubjective sense, then there may indeed a problem.[21]

Another way Gewirth or those working on the deontological agency strategy of justification (including myself) might emphasize to greater success is an analysis of the law of non-contradiction. This is especially relevant to the indirect version of the PGC justification (set out above). The power of this approach involves one reading of the law of non-contradiction— especially that proposed by Aristotle. Therefore, it is of some keen interest to briefly examine Aristotle's approach as a way to support the indirect version of Gewirth's PGC.

ARISTOTLE AND THE PRINCIPLE OF NON-CONTRADICTION[22]

In *Metaphysics*, Aristotle presents the principle of non-contradiction by setting up and defeating seven possible objectors. While it is beyond the scope of this chapter to carefully examine each, a few general points may be made that are instructive to this chapter.[23]

Aristotle begins at (1005b 18–1007a 21) by describing what it means to set out an enunciation. This involves metaphysics and epistemology. One begins with beliefs, but how are they substantiated? There have to be criteria, or else everything is gibberish. 'Ox!ltpv' might make sense as a password for one of your internet accounts, but otherwise, it is nonsensical. The essence of Aristotle's initial observation is that though sceptics may not want to admit to closure on some particular proposition, this is not the same as saying that both sides are 'true'. Rather, they are saying that 'x *could* possess F' and that 'x *might not* possess F'. Such statements are modal operators that harken back to his discussion of a sea battle in the future (*On Interpretation* 9). This lack of closure is not problematic to the law of non-contradiction, but just sets out why the sceptics are only about lack of closure (indecision).[24] This initial observation ends by affirming that the sceptic cannot support his position (because to support any proposition requires the acceptance of the law of non-contradiction).

The other objections refer to the process of predication by which some primary substance may or may not possess the given property *present in* the primary substance (according to the *Categories*) essentially or accidentally. If accidental, then the apparent wiggle room is illusionary since accidental properties cannot be a part of a definition (*A. Po.* I.4) because properties in a definition are per se connections (*kath' auto*). Thus, the apparent wiggle room disappears.

Aristotle thinks that these various 'contradiction-seeking models' only make sense if we accept Heraclitus's and Protagoras's notions or radical ontological relativity, which leads to epistemological relativity. Of course, to that approach, there is no reply. Such a situation would defy intersubjective

54 Boylan

reports about *what is*. This is a primitive posit. Few would support this sort of radical relativity. But those who do cannot defend the position (because otherwise, they would end up in a self-referential contradiction themselves—saying something really *is*). Those who don't can only throw up their hands.[25]

The cogency to Gewirth is this: In the indirect form of the argument, there is clearly a supposed interlocutor and a possible objector. If we accept the force of Aristotle's argument, then no one could reasonably contend that he or she would deny for him or herself the goods of freedom and well-being in an imaginary conversation. Further, if this interaction is repeated countless times (e.g., 7 billion times), then no single actual instance of an agent making a claim could deny that they possess freedom and well-being. We cannot cogently *imagine* someone denying the principle of non-contradiction to another individual. To detractors, the reply is: Dictate such a conversation so that we might evaluate it. Obviously, no one could.

This gets around any manoeuvers of Universal Generalization. It is no longer necessary. All that is needed is an indirect argument (aka *reductio ad absurdum*) in which the rules are: Bring me any particular person who denies that he or she possesses the right to freedom and well-being and I can show how they are involved in a contradiction via Aristotle's analysis. Thus, the boundary condition 'on pain of contradiction' becomes a central player.

If this is true, then the direct argument becomes secondary to the indirect argument in the overall presentation. This was not Gewirth's intent when writing *Reason and Morality*, but the good news is the PGC is saved. It is impossible to defeat it under these terms.[26]

SOLVING THE PROBLEM WITH AGENCY JUSTIFICATION

A broader implication of this chapter is that those who wish to create a necessary foundation to morality need to do so via agency justification (grounding human nature in the ability to act, or to contemplate and will action).[27]

Kant offers insight into the way to solve the difficulties with agency justification and the way that the principle of non-contradiction might work. If we look at the formulation of the first form of the categorical imperative, it sets out several conditions:[28] 1. Find the generic description of the possible prohibition in question; 2. imagine that the maxim in question was universalized to cover a possible society; 3. examine whether there is a contradiction involved in executing 2.; 4. if there is a contradiction, then the maxim is absolutely prohibited (because it is incoherent, viz., violates the principle of non-contradiction); if it does not entail a contradiction, then it is a permission—one may do it or not according to prudential reasons.[29]

What makes this an effective strategy is that it moves directly to a generic description and remains in that realm until the outcome is achieved and then can be applied back to the individual (via logical subsumption). Abstract principles (such as the principle of non-contradiction) work best in the generic realm. They do not do so well when applied to the particular since the particular is often set out in ambiguous or equivocal terms. This is also what Aristotle set out in his argument against detractors to the law of non-contradiction. Some (like those quibbling about particular predication and about non-closure scepticism) want to remain in the domain of the individual and not make any general commitments. One does not have this luxury in the realm of the general. This is why *the general* is the language of science. Though individuals may vary, for the most part, the laws of biology cover the various individuals in a comprehensive way. But clearly, using the model of biological laws is problematic for our exercise. It will not be adequate to say that *murder* (the killing of an innocent at will), *for the most part* is wrong. *Au contraire*, it must be wrong all the time. What we need is a model other than biology.

Now we must be clear, that the aim of Kant, Gewirth, and Boylan is not to cover people for the most part. Thus, unlike Aristotle's biology,[30] what these agency authors aspire to is something rather different: it is a law-like imperative that operates rather like a law of physics (in which a single counterexample disproves the whole project). On the upside, this gives the argument tremendous power. On the downside, there is a great burden of proof.

Where everything comes together is where you can apply the law of non-contradiction. In the three authors discussed, I would set out the moment as follows:

Gewirth (indirect argument)[31] utilizes the principle of non-contradiction to set out premise #s 13, 13, 16, and 19 (in the aforementioned reconstruction). Kant utilizes this in the first and second forms of the categorical imperative (at the moment of examining possible logical contradictions in generalization for prohibitions, and at the moment of examining possible material contradiction in willing someone not coming to his aid if he were at risk, *ceteris paribus*). And I utilize the principle of non-contradiction in my argument for the moral status of basic goods in premise #a 8, 10, and 11. Here the force (like Gewirth and Kant's first form) is purely logical. Without the principle of non-contradiction, these arguments fail. With the acceptance of the law of non-contradiction, there is a claim that goes to our fundamental human nature: that we are rational beings.[32] To deny it is to deny that we are human.

CONCLUSION

So how do you want to justify a moral theory? The anti-realists most often turn to general agreement, contractarianism.[33] For those who are committed to there being no absolute truths in metaphysics or epistemology, this is the prudent strategy. In the Anglo-American philosophical world at present, it is this writer's view that this is the majority view. Ethics becomes

56 Boylan

a subcategory of sociology and anthropology. Some practitioners of philosophy of language have been responsible for this. Others seek for more certainty in the realm of human action. This chapter has set out three of these: Alan Gewirth, Immanuel Kant, and Michael Boylan as following this alternate route. How can they claim such certainty in a world that seems to many to be constantly changing? The answer is nuanced, but it begins with the recognition of the law of non-contradiction and its impact on agency theories of ethics.

NOTES

1. My primary target here is J. Rawls, *A Theory of Justice* (Cambridge, MA: Harvard University Press, 1971) and his notion of the original position that creates unreal boundary conditions to generate his desired result. I call this the thought experiment fallacy—see Michael Boylan, *The Good, the True, and the Beautiful* (London: Bloomsbury, 2008), pp. 211–12.
2. My vocabulary here is meant to reflect Aristotle's emphasis in *APo.* I.3–4, 72b 5–74a 4.
3. M. Boylan, *A Just Society* (Oxford and Lanham, MD: Rowman and Littlefield, 2004), Chapter 1.
4. M. Boylan, *Basic Ethics,* first edition (Upper Saddle River, NJ: Prentice Hall, 2000), IV.3 (see the connections to Gewirth set out here).
5. M. Boylan, *Natural Human Rights: A Theory* (New York and Cambridge: Cambridge University Press, 2014), Chapter 1.
6. For a quick, general recitation of the potential problems of postmodernism within this context see: T. Eagleton, *The Illusion of Post-Modernism* (Oxford: Blackwell, 1996).
7. For an example of this see Boylan, *Natural Human Rights: A Theory,* Chapters 2 and 3.
8. A. Gewirth, *Reason and Morality* (Chicago: University of Chicago Press, 1978), p. 135.
9. This might seem like a version of the golden rule. However, Gewirth would demur—Gewirth *Reason and Morality,* pp. 169–71, 272–3. This is because this sort of evenhandedness is a necessary condition for a single principle theory, but it is not sufficient. Contrary examples abound. Following Augustine, one might say, 'Because I want to sleep with your wife, you may sleep with my wife'. The reciprocal attitude is important in ethics, but it presupposes that one has the right attitude in the first place.
10. This is my reconstruction from 'Introduction', in M. Boylan (ed), *Gewirth: Critical Essays on Action, Rationality, and Community* (Lanham, MD and Oxford, 1999), p. 3.
11. See my depiction of Richard Brandt, who makes the same move: M. Boylan, *Natural Human Rights: A Theory,* pp. 129–30.
12. The most complete surveys of the early claims of either defeasibility or invalidity are taken on by D. Beyleveld, *The Dialectical Necessity of Morality: A Defense of Alan Gewirth's Argument to the Principle of Generic Consistency* (Chicago: University of Chicago Press, 1992).
13. For a toggle between Aristotle and modern science in this respect, see M. Boylan, *The Origins of Ancient Greek Science: Blood—A Philosophical Study* (London: Routledge, 2015), Chapter 4.

'On Pain of Contradiction' 57

14. See M. Boylan, *Morality and Global Justice: Justifications and Applications* (Boulder, CO: Westview, 2011), pp. 95–6.
15. See Boylan, *A Just Society*, pp. 53–4; Boylan, *Morality and Global Justice*, pp. 42–3; Boylan, *Natural Human Rights: A Theory*, pp. 184–7.
16. The argument for the Moral Status of Basic Goods—Boylan, *A Just Society*, Chapter 3:

   1. All people, by nature, desire to be good—Fundamental Assertion
   2. In order to become good, one must be able to act—Fact
   3. All people, by nature, desire to act—1, 2
   4. People value what is natural to them—Assertion
   5. What people value they wish to protect—Assertion
   6. All people wish to protect their ability to act—3–5
   7. Fundamental interpersonal 'oughts' are expressed via our highest value systems: morality, aesthetics, and religion—Assertion
   8. All people must agree, upon pain of logical contradiction, that what is natural and desirable to them individually is natural and desirable to everyone collectively and individually—Assertion
   9. Everyone must seek personal protection for her own ability to act via morality, aesthetics, and religion—6, 7
   10. Everyone, upon pain of logical contradiction, must admit that all other humans will seek personal protection of his or her ability to act via morality, aesthetics, and religion—8, 9
   11. All people must agree, upon pain of logical contradiction, that since the attribution of the basic goods of agency are predicated generally, that it is inconsistent to assert idiosyncratic preference—Fact
   12. Goods that are claimed through generic predication apply equally to each agent and everyone has a stake in their protection—10, 11
   13. *Rights and duties are correlative—Assertion*
   14. Everyone has at least a moral right to the basic goods of agency and others in the society have a duty to provide those goods to all—12, 13.

17. D. Jacquette, 'Justification in Ethics', in J.-S. Gordon (ed) *Morality and Justice: Reading Boylan's A Just Society* (Lanham, MD and New York: Lexington Books, 2009), pp. 54–69.
18. Boylan, *A Just Society*, Chapter 2: '*All people must develop a single comprehensive and internally coherent worldview that is good and that we strive to act out in our daily lives*'.
19. A. Gewirth, *Self-Fulfillment* (Princeton: Princeton University Press, 1998), esp. Chapter 4.
20. James Griffin, *On Human Rights* (Oxford: Oxford University Press, 2008), see Part II. I discuss some of these controversies over freedom and well-being in Boylan, *Natural Human Rights: A Theory*, Chapter 5.
21. This quandary about specificity has driven this author to set out possible goods of agency in a table of embeddedness in which each possible good of agency is set out according to its proximity to agency (which I call 'embeddedness'). See Boylan, *A Just Society*, Chapter 3 and Boylan, *Natural Human Rights: A Theory*, Chapter 6.
22. Aristotle, *Metaphysics* IV.3–IV.6: 1005b18–1009a5/The Principle of Non-Contradiction

   1. The most certain of all principles states that it is impossible for the same attribute to both belong and non-belong to the same thing in the same relation—A/1005b 18–20

58   *Boylan*

2. There could be no definition without it being necessarily so that there is a definitive law of stable attribution of a property to its substance—F/1005b 22–4

3. [Definitions are necessary for argument and argument is necessary for obtaining knowledge]—A

4. [Obtaining knowledge is what we primarily do as humans—'All men by nature desire to know']—A

5. It is impossible (*adunaton*) for someone to [authentically] grasp (*hupolambanein*) that something is **and** is not (*einai kai me einai*)—1–4/1005b 25

6. Heraclitus argues that what a man says does not necessarily represent what he believes—F/1005b 26

7. Those who hold contrary (inconsistent) beliefs, by nature, must hold one of them true and the other false—5,6/1105b 27–32

8. Some natural philosophers [sceptics] hold that something may both be and not be and demand a proof for any who think otherwise [those who support the law of non-contradiction]—F/1006a 1–10

9. The proponents of #8 when queried can, themselves, cite nothing more certain than the law of non-contradiction—A/1006a 5–11

10. [To be able to set out anything of significance to oneself and to another one must set out a starting point or else be liable to begging the question]—A

11. [Demonstration requires a starting point]—F (From *A. Po.*, I.1)

12. The proponents of contradiction must begin by setting out what they think is significant or not to himself and to another—10–11/1006a 20–4

13. [To set out a firm starting point is to agree to the law of non-contradiction]—A

14. The proponents of contradiction cannot argue their case—9–13/1006a 25–8

15. The principle of non-contradiction ('to be' and 'not to be' have different and mutually exclusive meanings)—A/1006a 29–34

16. The proponents of a law of contradiction (#8) cannot accept the burden of proof that they themselves put forward in premise #8–5, 9, 14, 15/1006a 15–18

17. Some who are against the principle of non-contradiction say that there are various ways to be a man, which, for example, has several definitions—F/1006a 34

18. There is a difference between arguments about attributes (accidents on the Categories of Predication) and substances—A/1006b 1–10

19. What is at issue is questions of being and not multiple attributions of accidents—A/1006b 15–30

20. Multiple claims about accident predication do not put the law of non-contradiction into jeopardy since 'being man or being not-man' is logically different than 'being white' and 'being not-white'— 17–19/1007a 1–5

21. *Opponents to this principle when stating their case must be asked whether they are or are not answering our argument: if they say 'yes', then they have contradicted themselves; if they say 'no', then they have no rebuttal—*F (1007a 10–21)

22. Those who take the position of premise #21 often take the position that there is no difference between substance and essence because they believe everything to be an accident (so that there is no essentialism: substance and essence (*ousia* and *to ti hen einai*)—A (1007a 21–3)—Objection #1

23. The Objection #1 folk base their case on everything being an accident (*sumbebekenai*) so that there is no such thing as there being 'essentially man' or 'essentially animal'—F (1007a 23–6)

24. If there is any signification of anything, as such, then what is signified is *that* and not something else—F (1007a 27–8)

'On Pain of Contradiction' 59

25. Accidents always imply predication of a property to a subject, so that if there is no substance, then there can be no predication and no accidents: but this is impossible—F (1007a 33–1007b 7)
26. [Objection #1 fails]— 21–5
27. If all contradictory predications are true, then all will be one—A (1007b 19–23)—Objection #2
28. If everything is equally possible, then the same thing can be a trireme, and a wall, and a man (as Protagoras is committed to asserting)—A (1007b 23–5)
29. Premise #28 creates a second-order self-referential loop: If a man is a trireme, then it is just as true that he isn't a trireme, then it is just as true that he is a trireme, *et al.*—F (1007b 25–7)
30. [Self-referential loops are absurd and should always be rejected]—F
31. [Objection #2 is refuted]— 27–30
32. If it is true of X that he is both man and not-man, then it is equally true that he is *not* either man or not-man—F (1108a 3–6)—Objection #3
33. One can take premise #32 to be true, then one could take that compound of two propositions and count it as one proposition and then deny the compound with another of the same character with opposite truth value, *et al.*—F (1108a 6–8)
34. [Premise #33 creates an infinite sequence]—F
35. [Infinite sequences are absurd and should always be rejected]—F
36. [Objection #3 is refuted]— 32–5
37. Some will contend that they do not universally deny predication, but do so only situationally (this applies to both accidents and substances)—F (1008a 9–11)—Objection #4
38. Premise #37 states either: (a) the negation will be true wherever the affirmation is true, and the affirmation will be true wherever the negation is true, or (b) the negation will be true wherever the assertion is true, but the assertion will not always be true where the negation is true—A (1008a 12–16)
39. [Premise #38-a has been dealt with above (Objections #2 and #3), so that #38-b is the heart of Objection #4]—A
40. Premise #38-b implies that the negation is knowable even when the assertion is not—F (1008a 20–1)
41. When the negation is knowable, then what is denied is truly asserted separately vis-à-vis predication, e.g., that a thing is not-white or that it is white, but if the 'thing' is in question, then there is nothing knowable [the understanding of non-truth becomes part of a universal statement]—F (1008a 20–5)
42. If there is no substance, then the person making the claim is also nothing and that everything is both true and false—including the proposition 'that everything is both true and false' [another form of the self-referential paradox]—F (1008a 30–4)
43. [Objection #4 is refuted]— 38–42
44. If the assertion is true and the negation is false, then when the negation is true it will be impossible to assert or deny the proposition's truth value—A (1008b 1–3)—Objection #5
45. Seen in temporal terms, one cannot at the exact same time assert a proposition to be both true and false—A (1008b 2)
46. Perhaps premise #45 begs the question—A (1008b 3)
47. [Objection #5 is rejected]— 44–6
48. (a) Some would say a thing is so or is not so; (b) some would say that both are right—F (1008b 4–5)—Objection #6
49. The first view in premise #48 is asserting that nothing has any definite nature and therefore is meaningless [and to be rejected]—A (1008b 6)

60 *Boylan*

50. The second view, which is a little stronger (because reality has a definite nature), says that at one time this proposition (that reality has a definite nature) will be true and not be true—A (1008b 8–9)
51. According to #48-b, all men are equally right and wrong, so that he refrains from judgment—F (1008b 9–11)
52. [It is in the nature of man to come to epistemological closure and in so doing to make judgments about perceived events]—or else they cannot practically exist in the world (such as which fork to take on the way to Megara)—A (1008b 12–31)
53. [We must be attentive to what is necessary to live in the world, i.e., making choices and unqualified judgments]—A
54. [Objection #6 is rejected in both of its forms]— 48–53
55. Inherent in the nature of things is variation by the less [and the more]; thus, this may tell against exact essentialism [which the law of non-contradiction seems to require]—A (1008b 31–3)—Objection #7
56. [The 'more and less' are a part of nature] so that it is the case that there are variations in being right, e.g. 4 is not 5, but it is closer to 5 than it is to 1,000—F (1008b 33–1009a 1)
57. That which is closer to the truth is more true than that which is farther away, and this conforms to nature—56 (1009a 1–3)
58. [One could not engage in speculation about 'closer to the truth' unless there was a truth that was determinate]—F
59. [Objection #7 is refuted]— 55–7

60. [The law of non-contradiction is upheld against all objections]— 5, 14, 16, 20, 26, 31, 36, 43, 47, 54, 59

23. There is a rich discussion of this topic in the relatively recent literature and I am engaged in an essay to fit into this tradition. For the reader wishing to get the high points of the controversies, I would suggest: J.P. Anton, 'On Aristotle's Principle of Contradiction: Its Ontological Foundations and Platonic Antecedents', *Philosophia: Yearbook of the Research Center for Greek Philosophy at the Academy of Athens* (1972), pp. 266–80; A. Code, 'Aristotle's Investigation of a Basic Logical Principle: Which Science Investigates the Principle of Non-Contradiction?', *Canadian Journal of Philosophy*, 16:3 (1986), pp. 341–57; Marc S. Cohen, Aristotle on the Principle of Non-Contradiction', *Canadian Journal of Philosophy*, 16:3 (1986), pp. 359–70; T.D. Praetere, 'The Demonstration by Refutation of the Principle of Non-Contradiction in Aristotle's Metaphysics, Book IV', *Logique et Analyse*, 36:144 (1993), pp. 343–58; M. Furth, 'A Note on Aristotle's Principle of Non-Contradiction', *Canadian Journal of Philosophy*, 16:3 (1986), pp. 371–81; J.-L. Hudry, 'Aristotle on Non-Contradiction: Philosophers vs. Non-Philosophers', *Journal of Ancient Philosophy*, 7:2 (2013), pp. 51–74; Pierre Joray, 'The Principle of Contradiction and Ecthesis in Aristotle's Syllogistic', *History & Philosophy of Logic*, 35:3 (2014), pp. 219–36; Jan Lukasiewicz, 'On the Principle of Contradiction in Aristotle', *Review of Metaphysics*, 24:3 (1971), pp. 485–509; V. Raspa, 'Lukasiewicz on the Principle of Contradiction', *Journal of Philosophical Research*, 24 (1999), pp. 57–112; and M.V. Wedin, 'Aristotle on the Firmness of the Principle of Non-Contradiction', *Phronesis: A Journal of Ancient Philosophy*, 49:3 (2004), pp. 225–65.
24. For a discussion of non-closure among the sceptics, see M. Boylan, *The Origins of Ancient Greek Science: Blood—A Philosophical Study* (London: Routledge, 2015), Chapter 4.
25. I am in the process of writing a more complete essay that focuses upon Aristotle's seven arguments and how they have been understood.

'On Pain of Contradiction'   61

26. Of course, it is important to realize just *what* we have saved: it is that no one can deny for himself or to others that he possesses freedom and well-being and so does everyone else so that a reciprocal relation of recognition and observance comes about.

27. See my discussion of various approaches in Boylan, *Natural Human Rights: A Theory,* Chapter 6.

28. I discuss this in Boylan, *Basic Ethics*, first edition, IV.3 (note the connection here to Gewirth).

29. Of course, the obligations are taken up under the second form of the categorical imperative, through imperfect duties that involve imagining oneself in the disadvantaged position and being able to will that someone who could help them without significant risk to himself do so without violating the law of nature that dictates survival.

30. For a discussion of this issue in terms of the rules of the *Posterior Analytics* v. the biological works, see M. Boylan, *Method and Practice in Aristotle's Biology* (Lanham, MD and New York: UPA/Rowman and Littlefield, 1983) and *The Origins of Ancient Greek Science: Blood—A Philosophical Study,* Chapter 3.

31. In the direct argument it is between the stages: 1 to 2, and 2 to 3.

32. It should be mentioned that in my personal worldview imperative, I also bring in a second facet of human nature, the affective good will. My personal worldview imperative states: *All people must develop a single comprehensive and internally coherent worldview that is good and that we strive to act out in our daily lives* (Boylan, 2014, p. 166). In order to satisfy the first of these four requirements, completeness, I have argued that the agent must develop both a rational and emotional good will. The emotional good will starts with empathy (a rational understanding of how others view the world). It then proceeds to sympathy (the level connection of two emotional beings). From there a care response occurs, which is active helping. This entire process I characterize as philosophical love.

33. For further discussion on this, see my chapter on the ontology of human rights, Boylan, *Natural Human Rights: A Theory,* Chapter 7, cf. Boylan, *Basic Ethics,* second edition (Upper Saddle River, NJ: Prentice Hall, 2009), Chapters 1 and 3.

WORKS CITED

Anton, J. P., 'On Aristotle's Principle of Contradiction: Its Ontological Foundations and Platonic Antecedents', *Philosophia: Yearbook of the Research Center for Greek Philosophy at the Academy of Athens, vol. 2* (Athens: Academy of Athens, 1972), pp. 266–80.

Beyleveld, D., *The Dialectical Necessity of Morality: A Defense of Alan Gewirth's Argument to the Principle of Generic Consistency* (Chicago: University of Chicago Press, 1992).

Boylan, M., *Method and Practice in Aristotle's Biology* (Lanham, MD: UPA/Rowman and Littlefield, 1983).

———, *Basic Ethics*, 1st edition (Upper Saddle River, NJ: Prentice Hall, 2000).

———, *A Just Society* (New York and Oxford: Rowman and Littlefield, 2004).

———, *The Good, The True, and The Beautiful* (London: Bloomsbury, 2008).

———, *Basic Ethics*, 2nd edition (Upper Saddle River, NJ: Prentice Hall, 2009).

———, *Morality and Global Justice: Justifications and Applications* (Boulder, CO: Westview, 2011).

———, *Natural Human Rights: A Theory* (New York and Cambridge: Cambridge University Press, 2014).

62   Boylan

———, *The Origins of Ancient Greek Science: Blood—A Philosophical Study* (London: Routledge, 2015).

Boylan, M., ed. *Gewirth: Critical Essays on Action, Rationality, and Community* (New York and Oxford: Rowman and Littlefield, 1999).

Code, A., 'Aristotle's Investigation of a Basic Logical Principle: Which Science Investigates the Principle of Non-Contradiction?', *Canadian Journal of Philosophy*, 16:3 (1986), pp. 341–57.

Cohen, M. S., 'Aristotle on the Principle of Non-Contradiction', *Canadian Journal of Philosophy*, 16:3 (1986), pp. 359–70.

Eagleton, T., *The Illusion of Post-Modernism* (Oxford: Blackwell, 1996).

Furth, M., 'A Note on Aristotle's Principle of Non-Contradiction', *Canadian Journal of Philosophy*, 16:3 (1986), pp. 371–81.

Gewirth, A., *Reason and Morality* (Chicago: University of Chicago Press, 1978).

———, *Self-Fulfillment* (Princeton: Princeton University Press, 1998).

Griffin, J., *On Human Rights* (Oxford: Oxford University Press, 2008).

Hudry, J.-L., 'Aristotle on Non-Contradiction: Philosophers vs. Non-Philosophers', *Journal of Ancient Philosophy*, 7:2 (2013), pp. 51–74.

Jacquette, D., 'Justification in Ethics', in J.-S. Gordon (ed.), *Morality and Justice: Reading Boylan's a Just Society* (Lanham, MD and New York: Lexington Books, 2009), pp. 54–69.

Joray, P., 'The Principle of Contradiction and Ecthesis in Aristotle's Syllogistic', *History & Philosophy of Logic*, 35:3 (2014), pp. 219–36.

Lukasiewicz, J., 'On the Principle of Contradiction in Aristotle', *Review of Metaphysics*, 24:3 (1971), pp. 485–509.

Praetere, T. D., 'The Demonstration by Refutation of the Principle of Non-Contradiction in Aristotle's Metaphysics, Book IV', *Logique et Analyse*, 36:144 (1993), pp. 343–58.

Raspa, V., 'Lukasiewicz on the Principle of Contradiction', *Journal of Philosophical Research*, 24 (1999), pp. 57–112.

Rawls, J., *A Theory of Justice* (Cambridge, MA: Harvard University Press, 1971).

Wedin, M. V., 'Aristotle on the Firmness of the Principle of Non-Contradiction', *Phronesis: A Journal of Ancient Philosophy*, 49:3 (2004), pp. 225–65.

4 Dialectical Necessity and the 'Is-Ought' Problem

Stuart Toddington

INTRODUCTION

The centrepiece of Gewirth's Ethical Rationalism is the argument for the Principle of Generic Consistency (PGC), and Gewirthian scholars (and perhaps even those with a mere passing acquaintance) are familiar with its three-stage structure as presented in Gewirth's *Reason and Morality*. Gewirth says:

> First, every agent implicitly makes evaluative judgments about the goodness of his purposes and hence about the necessary goodness of the freedom and well-being that are necessary conditions of his acting to achieve his purposes. Second, because of this necessary goodness, every agent implicitly makes a deontic judgment in which he claims that he has rights to freedom and well-being. Third, every agent must claim these rights for the sufficient reason that he is a prospective agent who has purposes he wants to fulfill, so that he logically must accept the generalization that all prospective purposive agents have rights to freedom and well-being.[1]

This argument has had a long gestation. Its central ideas were developed in numerous publications prior to the appearance of the account with which we are now familiar. One such is the 1973 article, 'The "Is-Ought" Problem Resolved',[2] in which Gewirth claimed to have resolved a problem that empiricists have long held to be logically intractable. Since Hume, it has been widely accepted that bridging the inferential gap between factually descriptive and morally prescriptive statements is impossible. But not only did Gewirth produce a compelling contribution to the solution of the problem, he did a better job than any writer hitherto in setting out its parameters and presenting it in its most challenging form. This is no small achievement. For, rare as it is to find consensus in matters of moral philosophy, it is still surprising that the simple suggestion that one cannot derive an 'ought' from an 'is' turns out to demand so much accomplished epistemological effort in its explication. The reason for this is that the problem requires considerable interpretation if it is to be rendered in its strongest form, and, if clarification

64 Toddington

and reformulation in this regard are not to be seen as evasions, then a defensible epistemological interface between empiricist and positivist tenets on the one hand, and, broadly rationalist approaches to the relationship between the conceptual and empirical on the other, must be established. This foundational clash is unavoidable. It is only by way of a radical analysis of the issues that we can ensure that the blanket ban on 'is-ought' derivations—or the lifting of it—is not merely a product of stipulation.

The 'is-ought' problem known as *Hume's Law* exposes the incongruities of the relations of implication held to obtain between contingent empirical propositions and moral imperatives. Hume's original formulation in *The Treatise* focuses upon the connections (or as Hume says, 'copulations') that frequently appear to be invoked when an interlocutor purports to move inferentially from contingent descriptions of the world, to claims about how things ought to be. Essentially, the solution to the 'is-ought' problem must take the form of a grounded *theory* of the process by which 'this new relation can be a deduction from others, which are entirely different from it'.[3] I want to show how Gewirth sets out to *clarify* the 'is-ought' problem by first securing the shackles that prevent a logical escape from it more securely than any presentation of it hitherto. By engaging directly with what is regarded as Hume's inviolable *law* of empiricist logic, this clarification allows us to see what is conceptually essential about the problem and, through its suggested solution, exposes the constraints of empiricist and positivist conceptions of moral theory that Hume's Law seeks to enshrine. Secondly, with some background analysis of why a positivistic confidence in the intractability of 'is-ought' derivations persists, I want to suggest that, in the context of the conception of rational agency, the orthodox logic of Gewirth's dialectically necessary method can create a normative inferential pathway leading from the empirical conditions of action to the necessary categorical commitments immanent in the axiological and instrumental dimensions of prudence. In other words, the synthesis that emerges from Stage 1 and Stage 2 of Gewirth's argument for the PGC *is*, in effect, the explanation that Hume, in this famous passage, demanded we produce for his inspection.

1. WHAT IS AN 'OUGHT'?

Hume's 'Law' declaring the impossibility of deriving 'ought' from 'is' is one of the great totems of Scientific Positivism. It is, via the bifurcation of reason into inductive and deductive modes, the source of the 'fact-value distinction' and lies behind the Verificationism, Emotivism, and Moral Scepticism of the Vienna Circle that effectively characterized moral judgement as the antithesis of scientific thinking. But in the original passage from Hume, we see not a blunt injunction to desist from the attempt to justify moral claims

Dialectical Necessity and the Is-Ought Problem 65

on empirical premises, but a genuine invitation to reflect upon how or why, if such an argument were to succeed, '. . . this new ['ought'] relation can be a deduction from others . . . entirely different from it'. Hume says:

> In every system of morality, which I have hitherto met with, I have always remark'd, that the author proceeds for some time in the ordinary way of reasoning, and establishes the being of a God, or makes observations concerning human affairs; when of a sudden I am surpriz'd to find, that instead of the usual copulations of propositions, *is*, and *is not*, I meet with no proposition that is not connected with an *ought*, or an *ought not*. This change is imperceptible; but is however, of the last consequence. For as this *ought*, or *ought not*, expresses some new relation or affirmation, 'tis necessary that it shou'd be observ'd and explain'd; and at the same time that a reason shou'd be given, for what seems altogether inconceivable, how this new relation can be a deduction from others, which are entirely different from it.[4]

Taking up this invitation, Gewirth begins by clearing up the different senses in which we use the word 'moral'. These differences provide the five vital characteristics of moral claims (in relation to the empirical conditions antecedent to them) with which a comprehensive articulation of the 'is-ought' problem is concerned. The first is that the 'ought' in question is seen to be 'moral' in the sense that it contains the assertion that one ought to take positive account of the interests of other persons—especially in regard to forms of well-being; these being 'indicated in the antecedent "is"-statements that provides the reasons for the actions urged in the "ought"-judgements'.[5] Secondly, the 'oughts' in question are intended to be action-guiding or prescriptive in the sense that they 'guide or influence actions . . . set forth as required by the facts [*ises*] presented in the antecedents'. These empirical antecedents 'serve not to qualify or restrict the "oughts" but rather to indicate the facts or reasons which make them mandatory'.[6] Thirdly, the 'oughts' are egalitarian in that they require that 'at least basic well-being be distributed equally'.[7] Fourthly, the 'oughts' purported to be derived from the antecedent *ises* should be determinate. By this, Gewirth means that whatever is prescribed contains 'definite contents such that the opposite contents cannot be obtained by the same mode of derivation in question'. The fifth characteristic is that the 'oughts' or moral norms held to be derivable from the empirical antecedents that constitute the 'is' of the argument are to be seen to be 'categorical, not merely hypothetical'. More precisely,

> the requirements set forth therein are normatively overriding and ineluctable or necessary, in that their bindingness cannot be removed by, and hence is not contingent on or determined by, variable, escapable features either of the persons addressed or of their social relations.[8]

66 Toddington

So, on the basis of this analysis, and what we can refer to henceforth as *Clarification (1)*, the 'is-ought' problem should be stated as follows: '[H]ow can "ought" judgements having these five characteristics be logically derived from, or be justified on the basis of, premises which state empirical facts?'[9] But this formulation suggests, says Gewirth,[10] a sixth condition, that of 'non-circularity', that is, 'the premises from which the "ought"-conclusions [in a successful solution of the problem] are derived must not themselves be moral or prescriptive'.[11] Appended to *Clarification (1)*, this can be referred to as *Clarification (2)*.

The issue of *circularity* is fundamental. In terms of, and to what degree, arguments might be considered 'vicious' or 'virtuous' in this regard, rests the distinction between Empiricism (and pragmatism) and rationalism. Gewirth returns to it in the passages where he discusses the 'external' and 'internal' positions on the possibility of overcoming the derivation of 'ought from is' (and also reviews seven of what he considers to be unsuccessful attempts to overcome it).[12] The 'internal' position is broadly optimistic, but Gewirth's main concerns lie with problems arising from what he calls the 'external' insistence on the unbridgeable gap between '*is*' statements and 'ought' conclusions. And it is to these 'external' objections that I now turn.

There are three that require examination: The first is the view that there is an unbridgeable gap between, on the one hand, empirical description, and on the other, 'oughts' which 'take a stand for or against something by advocating or guiding action'. The alarming descriptive-*cum*-action-guiding example that Gewirth notes as a plausible (but inadequate) retort, 'There is a cobra curled up right behind you',[13] fails to overcome the objection (as Gewirth points out), because the empirical statement in itself assumes that the person to whom it is addressed has 'a want or desire to which the fact presented . . . bears some means-end or other causal relation'.[14] The second 'external' objection expresses the non-cognitivist position that assumes that moral judgements 'unlike empirical statements, have no truth-value and hence cannot follow logically from statements having truth-value'.[15] This account of the assumed logical and semantic chasm between 'fact' and 'value' is a feature of Emotivism, physicalist correspondence theories, and the stringent demands of Verificationism (and falsificationism). There has been no shortage of responses to these varieties of moral non-cognitivism, but Gewirth believes that while many of the replies to the truth-value concerns are sound, they 'do not go far enough to satisfy the conditions of the real "Is-Ought" Problem'.[16] In short, while suggesting that, ontologically moral judgements have correspondence, we are not sure what they must correspond *to*, and if we are to suggest that, epistemologically, moral judgements are, at least in principle, subject to confirmation or disconfirmation, then it has not as yet been shown '*how* categorical moral "ought"-judgments . . . are to be confirmed or disconfirmed.'[17] But the *third* 'external' objection should be of particular interest to those who might consider themselves to be Ethical rationalists, because it is, or should be, a rationalist objection in itself. It is simply that an 'ought' cannot be derived exclusively and directly from an 'is', because whatever appears in the

Dialectical Necessity and the Is-Ought Problem 67

conclusion of an argument must be present in the premises—and the problem is simply that there are no 'oughts' in the premises. Gewirth says:

> This argument is easily refutable by a consideration of non-syllogistic modes of inference. But, as I shall go on to show, this refutation does little to resolve the real "Is-Ought" problem, for the derivations it authorises do not satisfy the condition of determinacy.[18]

Talk of 'non-syllogistic' or alternative logic in any form spells sudden death for any credibility in the face of a challenge to Hume's Law, and in any event, Gewirth insists that the reasoning involved in arriving at the conclusion of the argument for the PGC is to be understood 'in a strict sense as comprising only the canons of deductive and inductive logic, including among the latter its bases in particular sense perceptions'.[19]

What we find respectively in Gewirth's listing of the relevant 'external' objections is simply this: (External *i*) hypothetical or conditional imperatives (as opposed to the categorical ones which we seek to derive) pose no threat to the jurisdiction of Hume's Law—they are simply examples of instrumental prudence in relation to a *given* objective. *If* you do not want to be bitten by the cobra, *then* you ought to move away. (External *ii*) without nailing one's colours to the masts of Emotivism or Physicalism, one must come up with a convincing account of what gives a categorical moral imperativea truth-value, and this means giving a reasonable account of conditions of correspondence or the conditions and criteria of confirmation or disconfirmation. (External *iii*) it appears inexplicable that a premise that is semantically devoid of any normative-moral content could produce a normative-moral conclusion. Thus, rather than rising heroically to what is an impossible challenge, rationalists could, and should, accede to this point without demur. In fact, it is the consideration of this formidable obstacle in (External *iii*) that will eventually lead us to the purest distillation of the problem.

To see this, we should recall some influential thinking on the matter. It is Kant, of course, who points out that Reason suggests that any *particular* moral imperative presupposes a more general one, and that a justificatory regress becomes immediately apparent. In other words, the validity of any particular moral norm implying some corresponding duty to act does not merely presuppose a more general normative ground; it points to the existence of a *supreme* moral principle.[20] And it is not only moral objectivists like Kant who see this inevitability: The most austere of Legal Positivists, Hans Kelsen, makes this inference leading to the notion of the Basic Norm or *Grundnorm* that supports the *Pure Theory of Law*. Whether we are talking about moral norms or legal norms, the hierarchical logic of validity and inference is the same. Kelsen says:

> The legal order is not a system of coordinated norms of equal level, but a hierarchy of different levels of legal norms. Its unity is brought about

68   Toddington

by the connection that results from the fact that the validity of a norm, created according to another norm, rests on that other norm, whose creation in turn, is determined by a third one. This is a regression that ultimately ends up in the presupposed basic norm.[21]

When, in *Clarification (2)*, Gewirth first appends the sixth condition (of non-circularity) to the five original characteristics he insists must be present in a legitimate solution, he says that this means that 'the premises from which the "ought'-conclusions are derived must not themselves be moral or prescriptive'.[22] But the objection in (External *iii*) suggests that this sixth condition cannot be met. This apparent impasse prompts Gewirth to reflect further on the issue of circularity: He says that the kind of 'ought' judgements we must come up with if we are to be successful in our quest cannot be assumed to be self-evident, and thus must be derived in some way from other statements. These other, justifying statements necessarily must be either moral or non-moral. If the *former*, 'there recurs the question of how *they* are to be justified', and if we are to have recourse to the latter, and thus *empirical* statements, 'then there is the difficulty that the "ought-judgments" are not derivable from those statements either inductively or deductively, unless we *define* ought in empirical terms'.[23] The upshot of this is that if the 'is-ought' problem is to be reformulated as more than a positivistic contrivance, we might as well cut to the chase and in the light of *Clarification (2)* ask, not merely, *how does one go about justifying moral imperatives?* But rather, because we know that any particular moral norm presupposes a more general one, *how do we go about justifying a supreme moral principle?*

2. WHAT IS AN 'IS'?

Gewirth's argument for the PGC looks inwardly and reflectively upon the presuppositions and implications of the way practical reason relates to action, but it is not a purely metaphysical set of speculations. On the contrary, the judgements of practical reason that Gewirth maintains are *dialectically necessary from the standpoint of the agent* are mundanely rooted in the context of our everyday experience of action in the world and in the conditions that must be met if the prospect of acting for any purposes whatsoever is to be regarded as viable. In 'The "Is-Ought" Problem Resolved', Gewirth says that to state that some person performs an action, or for an agent to describe himself as acting purposively by saying, (1) 'I do X for purpose E', is to make empirical statements.[24] For the sake of argument at this point, let us assume that this is the case. Gewirth also wants to say that someone who makes the alleged empirical judgement about themselves in (1) must now necessarily accept— at least from their point of view—that, (2), 'X and E are good'.[25] Gewirth holds that (2) expresses a value judgement. Again, let us provisionally accept this characterization of (2). Gewirth gets from (1) to (2) on the basis of two

Dialectical Necessity and the Is-Ought Problem 69

compelling assumptions: the first being the simple rationale behind the idea of the dialectically necessary method, namely the attribution to the agent of the 'acceptance of beliefs on the basis of their being entailed by other propositions he [or she] accept',[26] and secondly, that in purposive action that is unforced or *voluntary*, the purpose 'E' aimed at in (1) above

> is regarded by the agent as worth aiming at or pursuing; for if he did not so regard it he would not unforcedly choose to move from quiescence or non-action to action with a view to achieving the goal. This conception of worth constitutes a valuing on the part of the agent.[27]

So, because Gewirth thinks that (1) is an empirical statement and that (2) is a value judgement, he believes that 'to this extent from the standpoint of the agent the "fact-value" gap, even if not the "is-ought" gap, is already bridged in action'.[28]

We are familiar with the next move:

> The agent's positive evaluative judgment extends not only to its particular action and purpose but also to the generic features which characterise all his actions. Since action is a means to attaining something he regards as good, even if this is only the performance of the action itself, he regards as good the voluntariness or freedom which is an essential feature of his action, for without this he would not be able to act for any purposes at all. He also regards as good those basic aspects of his well-being which are the necessary conditions both of the existence and of the success of all his actions, and which hence are not relative to his particular purposes . . .[29]

If the characterization of action that Gewirth presents to us is accepted as arising from a combination of sense and reasoning that might be regarded as *inductive*, then we can see where this project is heading in respect of overcoming the 'is-ought' problem. For, if I employ means to ends unforcedly chosen—and which function as reasons for my actions—then it seems I must value those ends, and either value the means to achieving them, or give up the ends. Of the various means I must deem necessary for specific and particular purposes, I must acknowledge the hard empirical fact that the biological, cerebral, psychological, and cognitive facts about my constitution as an agent in relation to the natural and social worlds determine the minimal conditions under which it is *possible* for me to act *per se*. We could refer to this diversely constituted *minima* as the 'generic features of action' or 'generic conditions of action'. Whatever we call it, it seems that *reasonable* agents have to come to terms with the *fact* that the generic aspects of their freedom and well-being are necessary means to whatever particular purposes they might have, and in this sense, *reasonable* agents must regard their freedom and well-being as vitally important.

70 *Toddington*

Now, there are strenuous objections to almost every inference and every conceptualization that appears in Gewirth's Argument for the PGC, and there is a particular set of objections that relate directly to Gewirth's claim to have solved the 'is-ought' problem. In respect of the latter, there have been some important exchanges in collections devoted to the analysis and critique of Gewirth's ethical theory, and, in particular, to Gewirth's claims that the foundational premise in his argument for the PGC is of an *empirical* nature. Two such contributions (from Gary Seay[30] and from A. W. Hudson[31]) appear to converge in relevant respects. These are important contributions to the literature, but I treat of them only briefly here for several reasons. One is that that, in moving towards the concluding section of this discussion, I would not wish to defend the claim that the conception of agency that appears in Stage 1 of Gewirth's Argument for the PGC is an 'empirical' statement. It is certainly not the kind of contingent empirical observation relating to 'some event' or some 'conjunction of events' that Hume had in mind when he invented the problem. Another is that Beyleveld (and, in respect of Hudson, Gewirth) considered these issues many years ago. I merely summarize their responses here in preliminary support of what below I will suggest might be seen as a broader 'Gewirthian Perspective'. Seay says:

> I am inclined to agree with his [Gewirth's] conclusion that the Principle of Generic Consistency does provide an ethical first principle that is categorically binding on all persons in so far as they are agents; yet I am not convinced that he has succeeded in providing a logical derivation of value judgments from factual statements.[32]

Why does Seay come to this conclusion? After a pristine exposition of the argument, he says,

> In effect, it [the argument to the PGC] derives an "ought" from another "ought". This is clear in the very first step of the argument as Gewirth proposes it, where he attempts to show that a judgment of value is logically entailed by a descriptive statement of fact. The proof operates, I believe, chiefly through a confusion of the assertoric and dialectical methods: hence, I hold that Gewirth's proof fails.[33]

He goes on:

> For, from the point of view of the agent, it is his specific intention that brings the action into being; yet the commitment to a purpose is already present in the intention; hence the element of value must be perceived by the agent as added to his object by him at the very beginning, in deciding to undertake the action. What Gewirth's dialectical argument discloses is not a derivation of value from fact, but a derivation of value from an antecedent value.[34]

Dialectical Necessity and the Is-Ought Problem   71

Hudson has a similar take on the initial steps of the argument and rejects outright Gewirth's claim that being an agent or engaging in action can be described in 'pure, unadulterated statements of fact'. The 'is' that is alleged to appear in the statement, 'I do X for purpose E', says Hudson, is both descriptive of the agent's action *and prescriptive* for the agent: It has 'both constative and prescriptive illocutionary force'.[35] Beyleveld's response to Seay (which, I suggest, simultaneously counters Hudson's objection) is that, 'The dialectically-necessary method does not begin with actions, but with *statements* to which a PPA is committed *by virtue of voluntary purposive agency*'.[36]

Beyleveld says:

> Within the point of view of the PPA, [I do X for purpose E → E is good] is a *logically* required inference; and "I do X for purpose E" refers to the fact of my agency, even though, within my point of view as a PPA, this fact is imbued with evaluative significance. . . . [Seay] . . . Is right if he means that the fact that I do X for purpose E does not justify that E *is* good assertorically. But he is wrong if he thinks that the fact that I make this statement does not commit *me* to *holding that it is the case that E is good* (though this judgment need not be a judgment of definitive goodness).[37]

This is impeccable analysis, but these brilliant responses are forced into increasingly more conceptual, ideal-typical, and stringently dialectical modes the more they are required to counter what empiricists and positivists would consider to be the crux of the 'is-ought' problem. What Beyleveld is saying to Seay and Hudson is perhaps what Gewirth had wanted to say from the moment he set down his pen after writing the 1973 article. That is, while still maintaining that he believes that the statement in question is a factual one, and after all the sweat and toil, Gewirth declares in his 1984 response to Hudson,

> My main concern is not with the "is-ought" problem; it is, rather, to show that every agent logically must accept certain moral "ought"-judgments. Hence, if being an agent, or engaging in action, is not something that can be stated as a "pure, unadulterated statement of fact," this does not affect my general thesis. What it would show instead is that the *factual world* of human action is "loaded with values" for every agent; and this is something I would gladly accept so long as the facts and values in question are held to be ineluctable for every agent. [38]

Let us, then, reflect upon this weariness in respect of the demands of fidelity to the purely empirical. For, despite the technical wrangling over the empirical-prescriptive nature of the initial premise in Gewirth's Argument for the PGC, there is a genuine and compelling sense in which one *could* say that Gewirth has overcome the problem set down for us by Hume. But in what follows, my

72 Toddington

point will be that an obsession with the empiricist and positivist understanding of the Humean problem can legitimately be set aside if we adopt a more ecumenical view of the essential epistemological task.

Ironically, it seems that Gewirth's engagement with Hume in the 'The Is-Ought Problem Resolved', and in his replies to those who felt that he had failed in that regard, effectively suggest that we might disregard it, and instead, set about explaining the methodology of concept formation appropriate to the justification of a supreme moral imperative. But if this approach is adopted, it cannot remain a local dispute: It requires us to revisit historically entrenched and conceptually radical divisions in our epistemological outlook. It would be gratifying to think that this was a novel direction in which Gewirthian scholarship could be extended; however, as with most of the *particular* objections, either Gewirth himself [39] or Beyleveld have preempted this most general and vital one. On page 116 of his unparalleled defence of Gewirth, Beyleveld notes the following objection from Gregory Lycan, headed: 'If PPAs are logically required to conform to the PGC, then the PGC is analytic, and hence purely linguistic'.[40] This is in fact a substitution instance of the central theorem of the Logical positivist *Credo* that affirms that all *a priori* truth is *merely* tautologous. This is a dogma licentiously derived from Hume's famous 'Fork' that splits reasoning into two seemingly irreconcilable pathways.

3. FACTS AND VALUES, IS AND OUGHT

The issue, of course, is about the distinction between fact and value, and the 'is-ought' problem rendered as Hume's Law is a provocative assertion of the positivistic hegemony that crushes, by Humean fiat, the prospect of moral and social *critique* in the sphere of scientific discourse. This is an intellectual tyranny of such imperious influence that it belies its fragile foundations. Hume tells us that reason deals with a twofold division: 'relations of ideas' and the 'relations between matters of fact and existence'. '[F]acts of existence' are what we are able to observe to be *contingently* the case by use of our physical senses, whereas 'relations of ideas' or conceptual relations, present themselves to our understanding in terms of *necessity* or contradiction. This classification of reasoning is sensible and plausible, and on the face of it, there is no reason why we should challenge it. However, if we are asked to accept that *only* propositions concerning 'matters of fact and existence' convey any *meaningful and genuinely informative* (synthetic) knowledge, whereas the realm of the *a priori*—however complex its appearance—reduces simply to empty tautology, then we must question why and how this is supposed to follow from 'Hume's Fork' *per se*. But we should not complain about the suggestion that an external world of natural objects observable to our senses might be described in terms of *contingent* factual propositions backed by *inductive* reasoning.

Dialectical Necessity and the Is-Ought Problem 73

Hume's account of inductive reasoning is prefigured almost entirely in Bacon,[41] but what we should understand by 'inductive' reasoning in contemporary discourse arises from Hume's diligent focus: The appropriate form of reasoning to be applied to the world of observable and tangible objects arises not from *a priori* reflection, but from our experience. Hume says:

> All reasonings concerning matter of fact seem to be founded on the relation of *Cause and Effect*. By means of that relation alone we can go beyond the evidence of our memory and senses.[42]

But when Hume says that our understanding of cause and effect arises from our 'experience', he is careful to confine the scope of that judgement to the simple observation of sensible bodies and *conjunctions of events* involving sensible bodies. His argument in the *Enquiries* points to a mysterious gap between our sensory observations of the *sensible qualities* of objects, on the one hand, and the *secret powers* that we all too readily assume they contain.[43] Hume's critique of the crucial distinction, epistemologically speaking, between on the one hand, the proposition that '*I have found that such an object has always been attended with such an effect*', and, on the other, '*I foresee, that other objects, which are, in appearance, similar, will be attended with similar effects*' and his refusal to accept it as a *sequence* of sound inference is what we understand by the Problem of Induction. Hume says, cautiously:

> I shall allow, if you please, that the one proposition may justly be inferred from the other: I know, in fact, that it always is inferred. But if you insist that the inference is made by a chain of reasoning, I desire you to produce that reasoning. The connexion between these propositions is not intuitive.[44]

But why does Hume say that one proposition might *justly* be inferred from the other?

> There is some other principle which determines [us] to form such a conclusion. This principle is Custom or Habit. For wherever the repetition of any particular act or operation produces a propensity to renew the same act or operation, without being impelled by any reasoning or process of the understanding, we always say, that this propensity is the effect of *Custom*. By employing that word, we pretend not to have given the ultimate reason of such a propensity. We only point out a principle of human nature, which is universally acknowledged, and which is well known by its effects. [45]

This is perhaps the most unsatisfactory epistemological argument in the history of philosophy. It is so unsatisfactory that it provoked Immanuel Kant

74 Toddington

to construct the transcendental analysis in the *Prolegomena* as an alternative account of the principle in question. But either way, both authors seem to agree that in dealing with matters of fact, *human nature* (broadly speaking) forms a customary propensity in us to rely on deeper, indispensable assumptions underpinning the confidence in our experiences that point to an all-pervasive future persistence of causal relations obtaining between sensible objects. We can agree to refer to these judgements about object relations as 'empirical observations' or as 'empirical facts', and attribute knowledge of them to *inductive* reasoning which, when properly directed, furnishes us with what is undoubtedly useful, factual information about the world.

It seems equally obvious that this approach to acquiring knowledge of sensible objects in the world is entirely different from the processes of ratiocination we employ when we explore, as Hume would say, 'relations of ideas'. Hume has a quick definition of what might be subsumed under this label, namely, 'Every affirmation which is either intuitively or demonstratively certain'. The famous theorem of Pythagoras is cited, as is a simple illustration of arithmetical multiplication and division. Propositions of this kind, says Hume, 'are discoverable by the mere operation of thought, without dependence on what is anywhere existent in the universe'.[46] But one reason why we should not place complete confidence in Hume's analysis of the nature and scope of the *a priori* in general, or of the logic of moral concept formation in particular, is that we are given contradictory guidance in this regard. In the *Enquiries* of 1748, moral reasoning is not only juxtaposed to 'matters of fact and existence', in that we are to accept that, '[a]ll reasonings may be divided into two kinds, namely, demonstrative reasoning, or that concerning relations of ideas, and moral reasoning, or that concerning matter of fact and existence',[47] but we are also told that there is merely a difference in *degree* between mathematical and moral concepts. In the *Philosophy of Morals of 1751*, however, Hume announces, 'Men are now cured of their passion for hypotheses and systems . . . and will hearken to no arguments but those which are derived from experience'.[48] Men will, of course, still endeavour to 'find those universal principles, from which all censure or approbation is ultimately derived',[49] but 'this is a question of fact, not of abstract science'.[50] We have, then, the 'fork', but are now unsure upon which prong to skewer moral concepts.

But accepting the broad division of the faculties, we could ask whether the kind of demonstration appropriate to the justification of affirmations concerning relations of ideas is in some important sense homogeneous, or might there be significantly different types of 'demonstration'—perhaps correlative to different types of necessity. For example, is the 'demonstrative reasoning' definitive of the class of *a priori* concerns appropriate to the set of 'relations of ideas' that constitute the discipline of geometry, identical to the 'demonstrative reasoning' that might be required by the set of 'relations of ideas' that constitutes moral reasoning? We can, for example, deduce, *a priori*, (i) the sum or quotient of any given numerical set of relations, we can

Dialectical Necessity and the Is-Ought Problem   75

fathom (ii) the size of an unknown third angle given the two other angles in a triangle and so on—and we can even compute (iii) the rate of acceleration of an object by means of differential calculus, enabling us to construct a graph of this motion that would allow us to determine the location of the object at any given time. Less interestingly, knowing (iv) that Fido is a dog, and being aware that dogs are canine quadrupeds, we can infer, *a priori* that Fido is a canine quadruped. And less interestingly still, our ability to understand relations between ideas allows us to infer (v) that a dog is a dog. This list of *a priori* propositions shows us at a glance that reasonings about 'relations of ideas' are not flatly homogeneous. Some, like the inferences in (i)—(iii), seem important and interesting and—as Hume affirms—take us from what is known to what was unknown;[51] whereas others, like (iv) and especially (v) are what we usually understand by 'tautology'. But what, then, of, say, (vi) 'John is an agent'? Does this imply (vii), 'John values his purposes'? Or perhaps, (viii) 'If John is an agent, then John, dialectically speaking, must value his purposes'. One can only assume that the necessity of (viii) depends upon what we mean by 'agent'. As Hume says, 'Truth or falsehood consists in an agreement or disagreement either to the *real* relations of ideas, or to *real* existence and matter of fact'.[52] But are these kinds of propositions *meaningful*? Do they admit of truth and falsity? Are they useful and informative? Are they 'purely' empirical? Only someone with a vested interest in not only defending a purely experiential epistemology, but in undermining the scientific importance of the idea of conceptual necessity in theory construction would ask these strange questions, because it seems clear, following the most radical and most influential empiricist since Hume, that all these propositions point to a mixture of *analytic* and *synthetic* elements as a precondition of their intelligibility and that to deny this is an execrable *dogma*.[53]

'Hume's *Fork*' does not imply Hume's *Law*, such that we must accept that we can never derive 'an ought from an is', or that there is an unbridgeable gap between 'fact and value'. Rather, it raises some complex questions for those who want to make capital out of the uncontentious claim that reason, when called upon, can operate in an empirical and 'inductive' mode when dealing with the contingencies of natural phenomena *and* it can operate in a conceptual and deductive mode when dealing with the logical necessities that obtain between ideas, or between the meanings we glean from, or perhaps assign to, concepts. Two questions thus suggest themselves. The first is whether there is any obvious reason why we should be fastidious about conferring the status of facticity *exclusively* upon claims arising from 'inductive' or 'empirical' judgements about *contingent* states of affairs. It seems reasonable to say that 'it is a fact that the square of three is equal to 9', or that 'the angles of a triangle add up to 180°', in just the same way that one might say 'it is a fact that . . .' or 'it is the case that . . .' or '. . . there is coal in Yorkshire'. If these locutions are to be taken as indicating merely that the proposition in question is held to be *true*, then it would seem irrelevant in this regard to ask *what* was held to be true—even though it would be interesting to ask, 'Under which Theory

76 Toddington

of Truth is this statement to be filed?' Gewirth would say straightforwardly that the truth of the conditional proposition in (viii) above, was true by virtue of it correspondence 'to the concept of a rational agent'.[54] But if the epithet of 'factual' is to be attached only to statements relating to contingent states of affairs held to be true by virtue of inductive reasoning and evidence, so be it. But this is pure stipulation, for nothing of any epistemological import turns upon it. The incantation of the 'fact-value distinction' on this basis would not scatter very many metaphysical daemons if it was interpreted as merely expressing the view that 'there are rationally justifiable propositions concerning contingent causal relations between sensible objects, as distinct from rationally justifiable propositions concerning 'relations of ideas'. The 'fact-value' distinction does, of course, frequently express a deeper prejudice, namely that *only* propositions describing contingent states of affairs supported by inductive reasoning and empirical evidence have truth-values, and thus they alone are to be regarded as amenable to scientific reasoning. This dogma cannot be challenged within the context of the positivistic notion of facticity that constitutes the 'is-ought' discourse. Rather, the foundational stages of the argument for the PGC arise from a concept of agency which melds the implicitly value-laden concept of *voluntary* purposive action with the brute, empirical exigencies of the generic requirements *for* action. A conceptually ideal understanding of what is constitutive of rational agency is thus *indispensable* to our claims to empirical knowledge of individual and social action.[55] This does not make the premises of the argument for the PGC empirically *contingent*, but it does show that it is possible to derive a non-circular justification of a supreme moral principle.

NOTES

1. A. Gewirth, *Reason and Morality* (Chicago: The University of Chicago Press, 1978), p. 48.
2. A. Gewirth, 'The "Is-Ought" Problem Resolved', *Proceedings and Addresses of the American Philosophical Association*, 1:47 (1973–1974), pp. 34–61.
3. D. Hume, *A Treatise of Human Nature*, L. A. Selby-Bigge and P. H. Nidditch (eds) (Oxford: Clarendon Press, 1978), Book III i, p. 469.
4. Ibid.
5. Gewirth, 'The "Is-Ought" Problem Resolved', p. 35.
6. Ibid.
7. Ibid.
8. Ibid., p. 36.
9. Ibid.
10. Ibid.
11. Ibid.
12. Ibid., p. 40.
13. Ibid., p. 38.
14. Ibid., p. 38.
15. Ibid., p. 39.

Dialectical Necessity and the Is-Ought Problem   77

16. Ibid., 39–40.
17. Ibid., p. 40; emphasis added.
18. Ibid.
19. Gewirth, *Reason and Morality*, p. 22.
20. I. Kant, *The Metaphysics of Morals*, Mary Gregor (ed and trans) (Cambridge: Cambridge University Press, 1996), p. 4 [6:207].
21. H. Kelsen, *Pure Theory of Law*, Max Knight (ed) (Berkely and Los Angeles: University of California Press, 1967), p. 221.
22. Gewirth, 'The "Is-Ought" Problem Resolved', p. 36.
23. Ibid., p. 37; emphasis added.
24. Ibid., p. 50.
25. Ibid., p. 51.
26. Ibid., p. 50.
27. Ibid., p. 51.
28. Ibid., p. 51.
29. Ibid., pp. 51–2.
30. G. Seay, 'Fact and Value Revisited: Why Gewirth Is Not a Cognitivist', *Journal of Value Enquiry*, 17:2 (1983), pp. 133–41.
31. A. W. Hudson, 'The Is-Ought Problem Resolved?', in E. Regis Jr. (ed) *Gewirth's Ethical Rationalism: Critical Essays with a Reply by Alan Gewirth* (Chicago: Chicago University Press, 1984), pp. 108–27.
32. Seay, 'Fact and Value Revisited: Why Gewirth Is Not a Cognitivist', p. 134.
33. Ibid., p. 138.
34. Ibid., p. 140.
35. Hudson, 'The Is-Ought Problem Resolved?', pp. 119–22.
36. D. Beyleveld, *The Dialectical Necessity of Morality* (Chicago: The University of Chicago Press, 1991), p. 134.
37. Ibid.
38. A. Gewirth, 'Replies to My Critics', in E. Regis Jr. (ed), *Gewirth's Ethical Rationalism: Critical Essays with a Reply by Alan Gewirth* (Chicago: The University of Chicago Press, 1984), pp. 192–255, on pp. 223–4.
39. Ibid., pp. 171–7.
40. Beyleveld, *The Dialectical Necessity of Morality*, p. 116.
41. I refer to Sir Francis Bacon's *Novum Organum* (1620).
42. D. Hume, *Enquiries Concerning Human Understanding and Concerning the Principles of Morals* [1777], L. A. Selby-Bigge and P. H. Nidditch (eds) (Oxford: Clarendon Press, 1975), p. 26.
43. Ibid., p. 33.
44. Ibid., p. 34.
45. Ibid., pp. 42–3.
46. Ibid., p. 25.
47. Ibid., pp. 42–35.
48. Hume, *Enquiries Concerning Human Understanding and Concerning the Principles of Morals*, pp. 174–5.
49. Ibid., p. 174.
50. Ibid.
51. Hume, *Enquiries Concerning Human Understanding and Concerning the Principles of Morals*, pp. 289–0.
52. Hume, *A Treatise of Human Nature*, Book III i, p. 458.
53. W. V. O. Quine, 'Two Dogmas of Empiricism', *Philosophical Review*, 60:1 (1951), pp. 20–43.
54. See: Gewirth, 'The "Is-Ought" Problem Resolved', p. 60.
55. See: Gewirth, *Reason and Morality*, pp. 171–7.

78   Toddington

WORKS CITED

Bacon, Sir F., *Novum Organum* (1620).

Beyleveld, D., *The Dialectical Necessity of Morality* (Chicago: The University of Chicago Press, 1991).

Gewirth, A., 'The "Is-Ought" Problem Resolved', *Proceedings and Addresses of the American Philosophical Association*, 1:47 (1973–1974), pp. 34–61.

———, A., *Reason and Morality* (Chicago: The University of Chicago Press, 1978).

———, A., 'Replies to My Critics', in E. Regis Jr. (ed.), *Gewirth's Ethical Rationalism: Critical Essays with a Reply by Alan Gewirth* (Chicago: The University of Chicago Press, 1984), pp. 192–255.

Hudson, A. W., 'The Is-Ought Problem Resolved?', in E. Regis Jr. (ed.), *Gewirth's Ethical Rationalism: Critical Essays with a Reply by Alan Gewirth* (Chicago: The University of Chicago Press, 1984), pp. 108–127.

Hume, D., *Enquiries Concerning Human Understanding and Concerning the Principles of Morals* [1777], eds. L. A. Selby-Bigge and P. H. Nidditch (Oxford: Clarendon Press, 1975).

Hume, D., *A Treatise of Human Nature*, eds. L. A. Selby-Bigge and P. H. Nidditch (Oxford: Clarendon Press, 1978).

Kant, I., *The Metaphysics of Morals*, ed. Mary Gregor (Cambridge: Cambridge University Press, 1996).

Kelsen, H., *Pure Theory of Law*, ed. Max Knight (Berkely and Los Angeles: University of California Press, 1967).

Quine, W. V. O., 'Two Dogmas of Empiricism', *Philosophical Review*, 60:1 (1951), pp. 20–43.

Seay, G., 'Fact and Value Revisited: Why Gewirth is Not a Cognitivist', *Journal of Value Enquiry*, 17:2 (1983), pp. 133–41.

Part II
Gewirthian Contributions

5 A Dialectically Necessary Approach to the Sociological Understanding of Power and Real Interests[1]

Stephen A. Brown

Understandably, because Alan Gewirth[2] is a philosopher who situates his work in moral philosophy, and between the political stances of liberalism and communitarianism, much of the secondary commentaries on his work are philosophical or legal in nature. However, it is my contention in this chapter to argue that the import of Gewirth's work is central to the discipline of sociology. Whereas Stuart Toddington[3] demonstrates the indispensability of Gewirthian reasoning to concept formation in the social sciences, this chapter will argue that it is also essential to the understanding of the fundamental sociological concept of power.

Steven Lukes,[4] with some similarities to Ralf Dahrendorf,[5] articulates a theory of real, objective interests in his 'third dimension' of power. His argument is that a theory of real, objective interests is necessary as a means by which to identify how and why policy preferences or 'wants' can be shaped and manipulated by the powerful into something contrary to those real interests.

Ultimately, Lukes backs away from the radical and powerful implications of these insights and fudges the issue, arguing that to follow through on these insights would be ethnocentric. What Lukes is guilty of here is something common to both positivistic and Weberian epistemologies, namely the proposition that value judgements are incapable of being subject to rational justification, and thus are outside the remit of social scientific concept formation or investigation. Whereas it is beyond the remit of this chapter to offer a substantive justification of Gewirth's method, or his conclusions, the chapter will argue that Gewirth can offer an effective moral justification and underpinning of Lukes's notion of real interests. That acknowledgement of being a Prospective Purposive Agent (PPA) and the correlative implications of this as detailed in the Principle of Generic Consistency (PGC) can and does provide clear and authoritative guidelines of what an agent's real interests are, and under what conditions they can be pursued. In so doing, ethical reasoning is shown to be indispensible to social science concept formation.

A familiar argument is that human rights are only acknowledged or perceived in certain socio-historical epochs, and that to try to ascribe these rights to certain peoples is like asking a Stone Age man to write you a cheque. In

82 Brown

this chapter, I will demonstrate why Gewirth's is not a socio-historical contingent theory, or guilty of the charges of ethnocentricism. Once this has been established, I shall begin to look at the extent to which it is possible that, rather than a social-historical context creating a basis for rights-claims, the exercise of power inhibits or diverts a PPA from maximizing its freedom and well-being, and conforming to the PGC.

One misconception about Gewirth's philosophy, according to Toddington,[6] surrounds his use of epistemological individualism, which has encouraged those who wish to criticize the present organization of society to link Gewirth with those determined to propound libertarian propaganda. Those concerned with the unwholesome consequences of this argue that a philosophy beginning with an analysis of the isolated individual is both egocentric and rules out the possibility of a critique of bourgeois individualism, on the grounds that only I matter, therefore I need not worry about the consequences of my actions on others. Toddington argues that this is not so. He, like Deryck Beyleveld,[7] notes that Gewirth's theory is not egocentric, and neither is it imputing individual rather than communitarian motives to anyone. This is because Gewirth does not believe that these rights are the products of any form of social organization; rather, his argument is concerned with the justification of those rights. He is not even arguing that his theory is the most relevant to societies or cultures which attach supreme importance to individuals or that PPAs treat their purposes as in competition with others. Gewirth's theory is perfectly consistent in societies where individuals equate their purposes with the common good, or even where individuals subordinate their identity to that of a community.

So, as Toddington notes, those who argue for a collective and cooperative way of life have nothing to fear from an individualist rationality. However, these arguments about the social context of rights-claims have been pursued further, and Beyleveld spends a great deal of time examining them. Adamantia Pollis[8] argues that Gewirth's theory is both ethnocentric and ahistorical. It ignores Eastern philosophical traditions, where objectivity and individualism are often meaningless. In the West, the autonomous individual only came into being in modern political philosophy during a recent historical epoch. Elsewhere, Gewirth's agent is conceptually and empirically non-existent. Also, Gewirth's theory is not underpinned by an ontology, and it stems from the positivist tradition by arguing for objectively important needs. That rationality governs action precludes those possessing minimal rationality, as well as emotions and irrationality.

In terms of the charge of being ahistorical, Gewirth points out that even certain socio-historical epochs do not have a word for rights; the concept of rights can be found in all cultures, for instance, in property rights or criminal assault.[9] Furthermore, as both Gewirth[10] and Beyleveld[11] note, Gewirth's theory is not ahistorical, but transhistorical in the sense that he derives the PGC not from any cultural norms, but from the necessary universal features of agency, which transcend historically specific social institutions, practices, and conceptions of the self. The necessary conditions of successful agency apply to all humans in all times.

Gewirth is not claiming that these universal rights have always, in all circumstances, been recognized. He only argues that they rationally ought to be recognized as belonging to all PPAs by all PPAs. Gewirth is not engaged in a social anthropology of rights-claims, but a moral epistemology of them. When Pollis argues that autonomous individuals do not exist in certain societies, she means that PPAs exist who do not have their freedoms recognized. Beyleveld notes that Gewirth operates with a normative and prescriptive, rather than a recognitional concept of having a right, and Pollis's objection here is irrelevant, because this normative conception is universally valid. Furthermore, Gewirth does not argue for an objective theory of needs, but rather, there are needs that all PPAs must value for themselves.

Beyleveld notes that contra Pollis, Gewirth's theory does have a fundamental conception of ontology. Pollis believes that Gewirth tries to derive universalistic conclusions from the extant diversity of human rights conceptualizations.[12] This ignores the dialectically necessary nature of the claim to the generic features of agency, which are necessarily claimed by all PPAs and thus constitute an ontological basis to the theory.[13]

Gewirth does not deny the legitimacy of feelings or emotions, but rather, he provides a specification of what constitutes rational emotions. Put another way, Gewirth's concept of rationality involves what can be dialectically derived inductively and deductively from being a PPA, and as such, it undergirds all forms of reason.[14] As such, it undergirds reason. Immoral action is behaviour that contradicts being a PPA (and therefore the PGC) and as such, by definition, is irrational.

However, it is Bernard Williams[15] who highlights the familiar point that Gewirth's argument presupposes that people are equal in terms of power and abilities, when they are not like that. By ignoring difference, such as class, racial, and sexual differences, we are left with a mere idea of a person, what he refers to as conjured phantoms.

Williams is arguing that it seems strange to ask what a PPA would do as a PPA and nothing more. PPAs differ as to power and position, and a more powerful PPA may view its interests differently than a less powerful one. We must also acknowledge Beyleveld's point that that Gewirth's criterion of rationality is not based on prudence, but logical consistency. Also, Gewirth equips a PPA with more than rationality; he gives a PPA purposes and justificatory frameworks that are applicable to any social context.

It is of course true to point out that Gewirth's PPA is an ideal-type in the Weberian sense, but I would not argue this to be a weakness, but a strength. In order to focus on the universality of agency, I cannot conceive of any other methodology that would be as effective. Gewirth[16] himself argues that those differences referred to by Engels are irrelevant to the distribution of generic rights. His theory does not deny these differences, but a theory based on differences must be able to abstract from them, and be able to subject them to

84   Brown

moral evaluation. Because Gewirth's rights are universal and generic, they must be viewed in abstract from those phenomena that are usually of interest to sociologists. However, this does not mean that being a PPA is not of interest to real people, because the generic features of action that any PPA must claim rights to are necessary conditions for any form of social action, which are typically of interest to theorists such as Marx, Max Weber, Émile Durkheim, and Habermas, who pay more attention to the 'real world'.

Virginia Held[17] raises a number of similar points. She doubts the legitimacy of an egalitarian, universalistic morality on the basis that we plainly do not live in an egalitarian world. She argues, like Williams, that PPAs are not PPAs and no more, but have contingent, individual skills and attributes that may be better served under an unequal society.[18] Her example is of the rich in eighties America, whom she argues were acting rationally in voting for Reagan in that he pledged to protect their advantageous position.[19] Thus, Rawls's original position is of little use here, because it ignores 'real people', but Held criticizes Gewirth for the arbitrariness of his categories, and fails to accept that we should concentrate on the generic features of action, rather than, for instance, on an individual's wealth.[20] The rich claim things quite different to others, for instance, to utilize their greater resources, or to act competitively, as would an individual with great sporting prowess. Held concludes by arguing that if Gewirth's theory is one for real people in real societies (which is the contention of this chapter), then it is unacceptable, sociologically and philosophically, to argue that we all claim rights to the same things.

Beyleveld[21] comments at length upon this objection. Gewirth's rights-claims do not extend to unnecessary features of action, such as a Ferrari, but only to those things necessary for purposive behaviour; otherwise, a PPA contradicts itself as a PPA. Therefore, if a PPAs purposes are to be a great swimmer, then it seems fair for a PPA to claim a right to stop others obstructing this, as PPA would to all its purposes, as long as a PPA's desires do not interfere with the freedom and well-being of some Other Prospective Purposive Agent (PPAO).

Beyleveld[22] makes the point that Gewirth notes that PPAs might claim rights to their particular purposes, but they must (and must only) claim rights to the generic features of action. PPAs do not all claim rights to the same things, and they need not claim rights to their ocurrent purposes. But they must claim rights to the generic features of action, in order for their ocurrent purposes to become possible and practical.

Held tries to argue that PPAs universalize their rights on the basis of their particular occurrent purposes, while of course, Gewirth's universalization is based upon the generically necessary features of action. Beyleveld[23] consents that Held may well be aware of all this, but her argument is not based upon a misrepresentation of Gewirth's, but is a study of how actual PPAs actually reason. Beyleveld argues that PPAs may have a Subjective Viewpoint on Practical Reasonableness (SPR). Their purposes may be to be a deontic egoist, or any other irrational pursuit. Beyleveld's point is that a deontic egoist can deny that it is a deontic egoist, but it cannot deny that it is a being with purposes. Accepting that a PPA is a PPA contradicts that it is a deontic egoist. To deny that a PPA is a PPA is to deny that PPA is a being with the necessary features of action to be a deontic egoist. Put another way, both characteristics cannot be held without contradiction, and a PPA's denial of being a PPA cannot be held without contradiction.

Unless a PPA claims and possesses freedom and well-being, a PPA cannot pursue or achieve any purposes; therefore, a PPA must value them or deny that a PPA has any purposes, which thus denies that PPA could be a deontic egoist. A PPA may have all manner of SPRs. But if any of these SPRs conflict with a PPA's freedom and well-being, then a PPA denies that it is a PPA, and consequently, that it holds an SPR for its purposes.

From this, Beyleveld denies that being a PPA is purely abstract, or of no interest to 'real people':

> Thus, Gewirth's argument to the PGC is not an argument from "abstract" or "ideal" PPAs (those who lack varying contingent features, or lack knowledge of which such features they possess). It is an argument from the necessary features that "actual" PPAs possess, regardless of their contingent differences, and the contingent purposes for which they act. Thus, the argument is directed at, and binding for, "actual" PPAs.[24]

Gewirth and Beyleveld have said enough to show that a) sociology, which is concerned with historically specific forms of social organization, has nothing to fear from a Gewirthian conception of agency that is universal, and b) a Gewirthian transhistorical notion of agency (and the deductions made from it) can exist within radically different historical and socio-economic forms of social organization. We have also seen that Gewirth's theory is not incompatible with theorists who wish to proclaim a communitarian way of life. So we have now reached a point where we can address what I wish to be my principle argument. Despite the fact that Held's and Williams's objections to Gewirth were unsuccessful, for Gewirth's theory to be of use to sociology, which I can believe it can be, we need to be able to explain why 'actual' PPAs do act immorally and irrationally towards a PPAO. In short, why do certain groups/institutions/individuals inhibit the freedom and well-being of other groups/individuals, often in a systematized and structured fashion?

For Gewirth's theory to have the importance in critical social theory and a critical sociology that it deserves, we need to integrate into it a critical account of the most sophisticated way in which power is exercised. This is not to say that Gewirthianism is somehow incomplete as a philosophy, for I hope that enough people have said enough to refute this. Gewirth has succeeded in accomplishing what he set out to do, to show that PPAs act irrationally if they do not acknowledge themselves as PPAs, which entails

86 Brown

acting in accord with the PGC. I am merely arguing that to apply Gewirthianism to sociology, to explain actually occurring behaviour and the brutality of social life, we have to be able to call upon theorists of power who have a different agenda than Gewirth. If this is successful, then I believe we will have succeeded in a morally charged social theory which can accurately describe, from the point of view of PPA, those social conditions which cause PPA to behave in the way that it does, and also objectively, be able to ascertain where, if anywhere, immoral, irrational action occurs, and what is its (equally immoral) cause. Consequently, its usage for social policy ought to be immense. For the rest of this chapter, I wish to outline the particular conception of power I feel to be most suited to sociology.

Lukes's theory of power fits most comfortably with Gewirth's distinction between rational and irrational action. Lukes analyses and criticises two different dimensions of power, arguing that his own three-dimensional view is superior to the others.

Lukes attributes the one-dimensional conception of power to the American pluralists, notably Robert A. Dahl,[25] Nelson W. Polsby,[26] and Raymond E. Wolfinger.[27] Lukes[28] argues that the label of pluralist is somewhat misleading because it assumes that this conclusion was built into their initial assumptions. Lukes argues that this was not so. Their methodology was routed in empiricism and behaviourism, that power is to be judged by the observation of its activity. Power is no more than A getting B to do what B may otherwise not do. We record this by observing A's commands or influence over B. The pluralists, according to Lukes, can hardly be blamed for this tag, because pluralism is exactly what they found in their analysis of the American political system. If power had been exercised in a non-pluralist fashion, e.g., slavery, or a mechanical consensus, then this is what they would have observed and recorded. Lukes concludes from this that the one-dimensional view is more sophisticated than its critics have allowed for.

Their methodology arose from a critique of the Marxist conception of power. The pluralists understood Marxism as being inherently ideological, in that its critique of the power of capitalism was derived from an advocacy of the communal ownership of the productive forces, which would eliminate alienation, and form a society in accord with the species-being of humanity.

The pluralist analysis confirmed that power is not confined to a small powerful elite, ruling class, or oligarchy, but is distributed amongst the population as a whole through the vote. The individual uses this nomination as a vote of confidence to whichever political party or individual it feels best represents its desires. This system gains its legitimacy and name by the existence of a sufficient number of political parties, each of which have distinct political agendas, and between them, cover the whole spectrum of political persuasions and debate, from 'left' to 'right', so that the individual has a 'true' choice, and not merely a vote between two identical parties who commit themselves to the same policies.

A Dialectically Necessary Approach to Power   87

Of course, the party that achieves the power to implement its policies is the one with the largest number of votes. However, all these parties are subject to lobbying from all manner of pressure groups with their own agendas that wish the parties to adopt their recommended measures. These pressure groups could represent environmental, trade union, business, human rights, and health issues. In this pluralist society, it is the task of the media, (and some sociologists) to inform the population, in a fair way, of the policies and strategies of the various parties.

Power, in this dimension, manifests itself in situations of conflict over specific issues. The group with power, in any society, is that which concretely controls and exercises the decision-making process in the face of opposition to these measures. In a pluralist society, this opposition comes from political parties of a differing persuasion, and/or from pressure groups. In extreme cases, a political party whose concrete decisions are massively unpopular and fly in the face of public opinion may well be voted out of control of the decision-making process.

Lukes notes, in preparation for his own conception of power, that the notion of interests here, is confined to, and synonymous with, an individual's expressed wants or policy preferences. Lukes[29] is concerned in his discussion of the two-dimensional conception of power with the work of Bachrach and Baratz,[30] whose basic idea is that power is not just A's authority over B, but also A's power to limit the consideration of issues which are to face the decision-making process to those issues which are least likely to adversely affect A. Bachrach and Baratz[31] are referring here to the mobilization of bias, or the extent to which issues, through the media, can be organized in to and out of the public agenda. An example of this would be the power of MPs who could manipulate the media by discussing issues that avoid consideration of other issues which may possibly affect that MP's power base. What we have here is a situation of non-decision-making where problematic issues are concerned.

This typology of power, according to Lukes, includes issues such as coercion, influence, and manipulation.[32] However, Lukes does not believe that the differences between the one and two-dimensional views of power are that great. Whereas the two-dimensional view does offer a qualified critique of the behaviourism included in the one-dimensional view, by concentrating on the way in which issues are excluded from discussion, Bachrach and Baratz argue that the process of making non-decisions are observable decisions; therefore, they two are similarly behaviourist. In addition, like the one-dimensional view, the second dimension of power conceives of the individual's interests as subjective, expressed policy preferences. Its strengths lie in its concentration on potential issues and covert conflict. Its weaknesses become apparent in Lukes's discussion of his own three-dimensional view.[33]

We can see three principal strengths in Lukes's third-dimension of power: its concern with latent conflict, its critique of behaviourism, and, most importantly for us, its notion of real, objective interests, that an individual's

88 Brown

real interests may be independent from, and something different to, the individual's expressed policy preferences, and therefore may not be themselves observable. Put another way, what the individual wants to do and what the individual ought to do may be two different things. Those advocating either the one- or two-dimensional view of power argue that because they cannot be determined empirically, the notion of real interests should not be included in the sociological concept of power, and should be abandoned for the consideration of philosophers. What I hope to show is that they are mistaken, and that real interests are of concern to both sociologists and philosophers.

Lukes's critique of the second dimension of power hinges on its commitment to behaviourism[34] that, like the pluralist methodology which it seeks to criticize, it too is only concerned with empirically justifiable behaviour, which encompasses both decisions, and the decision not to make a decision. Lukes argues that this is a misleading picture of the way in which power is exercised in society. Groups, individuals, and institutions are often able to mobilize bias in a result that may not have been the original choice, which means that power is not as directly a conscious action as Bachrach and Baratz maintain. Power is sustained not just by chosen acts, but by behaviour that is socially conditioned and culturally patterned. Lukes attributes this failure to the use by the earlier theorists of power of methodological individualism. Here, we should note that Lukes's notion of methodological individualism is different from that of Gewirth's. Lukes's notion refers to the empirically justifiable act of individuals or groups realizing their wills or goals, whereas Gewirth's refers to the logical conditions for successful, rational action, which any PPA must accept.

Lukes also argues that overt conflict is not necessary to the study of power.[35] Put another way, the exercise of power that involves conflict may be its most unsuccessful manifestation. Power may indeed involve A getting B to do what B does not want to do, but A's task may be somewhat easier, and less likely to lead to B's mutiny if A can shape or condition B's desires, so that B wants what A wants B to want. Lukes argues that this can take a mundane form through control of information in the media or even in the work place. However, the most interesting way of studying this is through socialization.

Lukes[36] now brings his notion of real interests back into his argument. So far, we have seen that the earlier theorists of power have equated an individual's interests with its wants, exhibited through expressed policy preferences. However, what Lukes is interested in is the extent to which real power is exercised by A wanting something, which another individual or group wants A to want, but may in fact be against A's interests. An example of this could be a union of miners, who vote for the usage of certain materials in the mine that may have toxic effects. They agree to the materials on the ground that it will cut costs and lead to fewer redundancies. What Lukes would argue here is that the miners have voted for something against their interests, even though they wanted it. Here, Lukes equates a person's interests with

A Dialectically Necessary Approach to Power 89

what they would want if they were uncoerced and rational. In the rest of this chapter, we shall try to form this into something much less vague.

So Lukes's critique of the earlier dimensions of power is that empirically, if no expression of grievances can be observed, the social scientist must assume that no one's interests are being harmed, because if they were, they would have been expressed. Lukes disagrees:

> [I]s it not the supreme and most insidious exercise of power to prevent people, to whatever degree, from having grievances by shaping their perceptions, cognitions and preferences in such a way that they accept their role in the existing order of things, either because they can see or imagine no alternative to it, or because they see it as natural and unchangeable, or because they value it as divinely ordained and beneficial? To assume that the absence of grievance equals genuine consensus is simply to rule out the possibility of false or manipulated consensus by definitional fiat.[37]

The third dimension of power offers the most sophisticated way of the three, of conceptualizing how potential issues are denied entry to the decision-making process in a situation of latent conflict. The potential for conflict may in fact never occur. The latent conflict 'consists in a contradiction between the interests of those exercising power and the real interests of those they exclude'.[38] Lukes assumes that there would be a conflict if the powerless were aware of their interests.

To conclude this discussion, we need to find common ground between Lukes and Gewirth in order for Gewirthianism to be applicable to sociology. This common ground is the concept of real interests, which we discussed in connection with Lukes. However, we need not become overcomplicated in order to see this notion as implicit within Gewirth's theory. Gewirth argues that it is rational for a PPA to acknowledge itself as a PPA, and to live by the PGC if it wishes to avoid the warranted sanctioning of its freedom and well-being. It is no great leap of the academic imagination to see that what is objectively rational for a PPA is the same as saying that it is in a PPA's real interests to act rationally. It is in a PPA's interests to subscribe to the PGC. A PPA acts against its interests if it endangers its freedom and well-being, insofar as a PPA's freedom and well-being are necessary for a PPA to act. To act against its interests as a PPA is for a PPA to act irrationally.

So the way to synthesize rational (Gewirth) with irrational (Lukes) action is to argue this: Gewirth's importance to the study of power is achieved when we acknowledge that a PPA could be susceptible to suggestions from whatever source may, unwittingly or otherwise, lead a PPA to hold SPRs that endanger the freedom and well-being of a PPAO. This is to act irrationally as a PPA, and is also against a PPA's interests, as it is to invite the legitimate censuring of the PPA's freedom and well-being.

Another way of viewing this is to replace Lukes's notion of real interests with Herbert Marcuse's[39] concept of false needs. Ian Craib[40] writes that a

90   Brown

false need, like Lukes's concept of a want opposed to one's interests, is created by the culture industry as an unsatisfactory way of only partially, (if at all) dealing with a real problem. The result of this is that an agent's powers only become partially developed or 'one-dimensional':

> A "true" need is a need that can be defined as deriving from or expressing the creative and rational powers that make me a human being; it is a need which, if satisfied, will enable me to extend control over my life in conjunction with others, and to deepen and enrich my relationships with others.[41]

Here, we can see even more clearly that a true need, or what is in our real interests, is to realize that 'I am a PPA'. Craib's comments about our creative and rational powers, and control over our lives is impossible without, and inseparable from, making a rights-claim to freedom and well-being, even though we may not necessarily use our freedom and well-being in a creative, or relationship-enriching way.

Craib[42] gives a couple of examples of this. The first is within feminism, and the way in which its goals have been sidetracked. Feminism is a campaign by a group of people who have been excluded from large areas of social life. Its goals are social equality, freedom, and to forge deeper and more meaningful social relationships which are not based on property. These true needs are transformed by popular culture into false needs. The demand for equality is transformed into the demand for women to subject themselves to the same alienating, competitive, career-orientated conditions as men, surrendering the fight for more 'human' intimate satisfactions and qualities, or in Marxist terms, a life in accord with the species-being of humanity, for more shallow, exploitative relationships, where the model of the career woman is as plastic as the modern man.

Craib's[43] second example centres on the current concern with health and fitness. Because of the wealth of information concerned with the relation between ill health and social conditions, we could argue that our true needs in this case would be satisfied only by a collective effort to fight poverty and pollution. But again, popular culture, advertising, etc., has perverted this into an issue that only the individual can do anything about, hence the preoccupation with jogging, healthy eating, and personal fitness. Self-righteousness over smoking and drinking replaces the individual's true need to clear the environment. In addition, the personal quest for health is questionable. Jogging in the inner city probably results in the individual breathing in more lead. As Craib says, no amount of wholemeal bread will give the miner the same life expectancy as a university professor.

In both of these cases, we can see how a PPA's real interests or needs, which will enhance its freedom and well-being, are transformed into false needs or wants that fail to improve or even reduce its freedom and well-being. Our true need for freedom of choice is transformed into a choice of

A Dialectically Necessary Approach to Power 91

a plurality of washing powders, our need for freedom of speech becomes an excuse for a few individuals to publish ignorant, empty newspapers, and the need to stop a nuclear war becomes the desire to stop smoking.

From this, we can see two differing kinds of interests or needs that can be different from our wants. In Gewirthian terms, a PPA's interests are best served by the rational maximization of freedom and well-being, whatever the social context. Therefore, a PPA's interests, to be a PPA and live by the PGC, are *a priori* to the situation presented. The other kind of interests or needs may be unrelated to Gewirth only if the PPA's freedom and well-being are not harmed when they are violated. These interests, however serious, are contingent and historically specific. For example, it is against a PPA's interests to buy a loaf of bread from a shop, when the same bread in the same condition can be bought cheaper elsewhere, but we would not say that the PPA's freedom and well-being were harmed in this situation. Neither would we say that this had any bearing on the generic rights of other PPAs. However, in the example of a motorway being built in a PPA's back garden, both types of interest could be harmed. The PPA's contingent interests would be harmed in that its environment would lose its previous tranquillity and peacefulness. Also, the PPA's generic interests have been harmed, because the PPA may now suffer from lead poisoning from the car fumes. The additional noise may cause sleeplessness and nervous stress. In many ways, the PPA's freedom and well-being have been harmed. In this case, the PPA must do all it can to end this state of affairs, and indeed, censure its behaviour to make sure it does not allow anyone else to infringe on its generic rights. This action would have consequences for the PPAO.

An important amendment to Lukes from the point of view of Gewirth would be that real interests are objective in the dialectic sense, i.e., they must be so from the necessary point of view of every PPA.

To conclude his argument, Lukes[44] discusses a number of difficulties that he sees within his theory. The irony in his principal difficulty is that it leads him to the unwarranted belief that the application of his theory may be impossible, a problem that Gewirth's theory can rectify:

> Can we always assume that the victims of injustice and inequality would, but for the exercise of power, strive for justice and equality? What about the cultural relativity of values? Is not such an assumption a form of ethnocentricism?[45]

Here, Lukes argues that unlike the scenario of miners' lives being endangered, or a situation of people being poisoned, in other, less emotive situations where agents' interests are being harmed, they may not necessarily prefer an alternative. To start with, enough has been said to allay fears of ethnocentricism in Gewirth's theory. As to Lukes's first question, in light of Gewirth, we cannot say that those who fare badly in society necessarily would, once aware of their condition, fight for justice and equality. Such a

92 Brown

hypothesis has plagued Marxists since Marx.[46] All we can say, following Gewirth's analysis, is that they necessarily must seek these things if they are to attain freedom and well-being and fulfill themselves as PPAs, whatever other, contrary values may persist. Here, therefore, is one answer to the age-old problem of the supposed dichotomy of the right-wing liberals between freedom and equality.

Where Gewirth really supplies Lukes's deficiencies is over the definition of real interests. Lukes's definition of what an agent would do if it were aware of the results of all possible actions and free of ideological restraint sounds good, but is vague and flabby, and remains open to the charge of the basic irrationality of the human species. Lukes also fails to comment on how those who are mentally defective are to be conceptually defined or dealt with as agents. Gewirth says enough to leave his argument untainted by such problems, except where writers attribute these problems to Gewirth without having read or been aware of what he wrote on these issues.

Gewirth's sociology, then, would have to rely on what a PPA ought to do, given this exercise of power, or any other social context, rather than try to predict what a PPA will necessarily do. The principle problem within this theory is the difficulty in applying it. However, this need not be insurmountable. The problem is that many may find it unconvincing to argue that every case of irrational action (given Gewirth's definition of irrational action) is caused by the exercise of power, whether that be the power of an individual or group, or the result of the structurally determined 'behaviour' of a societal institution. Again, part of the answer is contained in the notion of 'ought' rather than 'will'. However, the reason for a specific PPA's deviant or irrational behaviour may not be the presence of an anti-PGC influence, but rather the lack of any influence at all. Instead of trying to find out why some commit deviant acts, some sociologists, e.g., Steven Box,[47] have tried to see why others do not. In short, control theory argues that certain people or groups are more likely to commit crime than others are because they have less to lose. They do not have the same investment in society, or as much to achieve from it. This is not to forget what we noted earlier, that philosophically, the PPA's complete absence from a social context, i.e. with no PPAO, does not mean that the PPA does not ascribe to the obligations being a PPA entails; merely that sociologically, the PPA's alienation (and I use this term in its loosest sense) from the PPAO for whatever reason may be enough to convince the PPA against committing itself to the PGC. The legitimacy of this could be investigated by examining many sociological accounts of the influence of alienation in society.

One objection to the argument constructed here is that a variant of it has already played itself out within an early, classical period of sociological thought. Weber's work on rationality contains a number of different ideal-types of rationality, with the most familiar being practical rationality. For the purpose of this argument however, two other kinds are substantive and formal rationality.[48] Substantive rationality refers to the extent to which human action is determined by values and ethical considerations such as

A Dialectically Necessary Approach to Power   93

justice and equality, and this is contrasted with formal rationality, where the calculation of quantitative, numerical, and expenditure criteria come into play. I am not suggesting that Lukes's conception of the manipulation of an agent's wants to something against his or her real interests is the same as Weber's notion of formal rationality, but nevertheless, the problem discussed in this chapter has connotations and resemblances with the contrast Weber articulates. Furthermore, Weber's articulation of ultimate values within substantive rationality would, if Gewirth is to be taken seriously, necessarily include a commitment to the PGC. Jürgen Habermas's work on the tension between the system and lifeworld is a more contemporary articulation of the same problem Weber was grappling with.[49]

These problems are not insurmountable if worked through in the context of this theory. It would be strengthened also by looking at the issues Lukes raises about how to identify both the exercise and the result of the exercise of power. This may be achieved only by applying the theory and working through any difficulties that way. I am convinced that tackling these problems and placing Gewirth's theory of the PPA at the centre of this social theory is infinitely more productive than abandoning the theory, and, in all probability, abandoning the attempt to solve these important problems.

NOTES

1. My thanks to Stuart Toddington, Glen Newey, Neil Stammers, and Andrew Chitty for their comments on earlier versions of this chapter. As always, errors and contentious arguments are my responsibility only.
2. A. Gewirth, *Reason and Morality* (Chicago: University of Chicago Press, 1978).
3. S. Toddington, *Rationality, Social Action and Moral Judgement* (Edinburgh: Edinburgh University Press, 1978).
4. S. Lukes, *Power: A Radical View*, second edition (Basingstoke: Palgrave Macmillan, 2004).
5. R. Dahrendorf, *Class and Class Conflict in Industrial Society* (Stanford, CA: Stanford University Press, 1959).
6. Toddington, *Rationality, Social Action and Moral Judgment*, pp. 148–9.
7. D. Beyleveld, *The Dialectical Necessity of Morality* (Chicago: University of Chicago Press, 1991), p. 448.
8. A. Pollis, 'Review of Human Rights by Alan Gewirth', *Graduate Faculty Philosophy Journal (New School for Social Research)*, 10:1 (1984), pp. 183–6.
9. A. Gewirth, *The Community of Rights* (Chicago: University of Chicago Press, 1996), pp. 66–8; Gewirth, *Reason and Morality*, pp. 98–102.
10. A. Gewirth, *Self-Fulfillment* (Princeton: Princeton University Press, 1998), pp. 200–4.
11. Beyleveld, *The Dialectical Necessity of Morality*, pp. 156–9.
12. Pollis, 'Review of Human Rights by Alan Gewirth', p. 185.
13. Beyleveld, *The Dialectical Necessity of Morality*, p. 159.
14. Gewirth, *Reason and Morality*, pp. xii, 44; Beyleveld, *The Dialectical Necessity of Morality*, pp. 158–9.
15. B. Williams, *Ethics and the Limits of Philosophy* (Harvard, MA: Harvard University Press, 1985), pp. 62–3.

16. Gewirth, *Reason and Morality*, pp. 127–8.
17. V. Held, 'Reason and Economic Justice', in K. Kipnis and D.T. Meyers (eds), *Economic Justice: Private Rights and Public Responsibilities* (Totowa, NJ: Rowman and Allanheld, 1985), pp. 33–41.
18. Held, 'Reason and Economic Justice', pp. 35–6.
19. Ibid., p. 37.
20. Ibid., p. 38.
21. Beyleveld, *The Dialectical Necessity of Morality*, pp. 310–6.
22. Ibid., p. 312.
23. Ibid., p. 313.
24. Ibid., p. 316.
25. R.A. Dahl, *Who Governs? Democracy and Power in an American City* (New Haven: Yale University Press, 1961).
26. N.W. Polsby, *Community Power and Political Theory* (New Haven: Yale University Press, 1963).
27. R.E. Wolfinger, 'Nondecisions and the Study of Local Politics', *American Political Science Review*, 65 (1971), pp. 1063–80.
28. Lukes, *Power*, pp. 16–9.
29. Ibid., pp. 20–5.
30. P. Bachrach and M.S. Baratz, 'The Two Faces of Power', *American Political Science Review*, 56 (1962), pp. 947–52; P. Bachrach and M.S. Baratz, 'Decisions and Nondecisions: An Analytical Framework', *American Political Science Review*, 57 (1963), pp. 641–51; and P. Bachrach and M.S. Baratz, *Power and Poverty: Theory and Practice* (New York: Oxford University Press, 1970).
31. Bachrach and Baratz, *Power and Poverty*, pp. 43–4.
32. Lukes, *Power*, pp. 21–2.
33. Ibid., pp. 25–9.
34. Ibid., p. 25.
35. Ibid., p. 27.
36. Ibid., pp. 28–9.
37. Ibid., p. 28.
38. Ibid., pp. 28–9.
39. H. Marcuse, *One-Dimensional Man* (1964) (London: Routledge, 1991), pp. 4–8.
40. I. Craib, *Modern Social Theory*, second edition (Hemel Hempstead: Harvester Wheatsheaf, 1992), pp. 217–8.
41. Ibid., p. 217.
42. Ibid., pp. 217–8.
43. Ibid., p. 218.
44. Lukes, *Power*, pp. 49–58.
45. Ibid., p. 49.
46. H. van der Linden, *Kantian Ethics and Socialism* (Indianapolis, IN: Hackett Publishing Company, 1988), p. 251, attempts to solve the problem as to why workers ought to opt for communist values by linking together Marxism with Kantian ethics. Without doing so, Marx can only provide the necessary conditions for socialism, not the sufficient ones. My argument would be that Gewirth could do the work of Kant here.
47. S. Box, *Deviance, Reality and Society* (New York: Holt, Rinehart and Winston, 1971).
48. K. Morrison, *Marx, Weber, Durkheim: Formations of Modern Social Thought*, second edition (Basingstoke: Palgrave Macmillan, 2006), pp. 437–46.
49. S. Applerouth and L. Desfor Edles, *Sociological Theory in the Contemporary Era*, second edition (London: Sage Publications, 2011), pp. 484–95.

WORKS CITED

Applerouth, S. and Desfor Edles, L., *Sociological Theory in the Contemporary Era*, 2nd edition (London: Sage Publications, 2011).

Bachrach, P. and Baratz, M. S., 'The Two Faces of Power', *American Political Science Review*, 56 (1962), pp. 947–52.

——, 'Decisions and Nondecisions: An Analytical Framework', *American Political Science Review*, 57 (1963), pp. 641–51.

——, *Power and Poverty: Theory and Practice* (New York: Oxford University Press, 1970).

Beyleveld, D., *The Dialectical Necessity of Morality* (Chicago: University of Chicago Press, 1991).

Box, S., *Deviance, Reality and Society* (New York: Holt, Rinehart and Winston, 1971).

Craib, I., *Modern Social Theory*, 2nd edition (Hemel Hempstead: Harvester Wheatsheaf, 1992).

Dahl, R. A., *Who Governs? Democracy and Power in an American City* (New Haven: Yale University Press, 1961).

Dahrendorf, R., *Class and Class Conflict in Industrial Society* (California: Stanford University Press, 1959).

Gewirth, A., *Reason and Morality* (Chicago: University of Chicago Press, 1978).

——, *The Community of Rights* (Chicago: University of Chicago Press, 1996).

——, *Self-Fulfillment* (Princeton: Princeton University Press, 1998).

Held, V., 'Reason and Economic Justice', in K. Kipnis and D. T. Meyers (eds.), *Economic Justice: Private Rights and Public Responsibilities* (Totowa, NJ: Rowman and Allanheld, 1985).

van der Linden, H., *Kantian Ethics and Socialism* (Indianapolis, IN: Hackett Publishing Company, 1988).

Lukes, S., *Power: A Radical View*, 2nd edition (Basingstoke: Palgrave Macmillan, 2004).

Marcuse, H., *One-Dimensional Man* (1964) (London: Routledge, 1991).

Morrison, K., *Marx, Weber, Durkheim: Formations of Modern Social Thought*, 2nd edition (Basingstoke: Palgrave Macmillan, 2006).

Pollis, A., 'Review of Human Rights by Alan Gewirth', *Graduate Faculty Philosophy Journal (New School for Social Research)*, 10:1 (1984), pp. 183–6.

Polsby, N. W., *Community Power and Political Theory* (New Haven: Yale University Press, 1963).

Toddington, S., *Rationality, Social Action and Moral Judgement* (Edinburgh: Edinburgh University Press, 1978).

Williams, B., *Ethics and the Limits of Philosophy* (Cambridge, MA: Harvard University Press, 1985).

Wolfinger, R. E., 'Nondecisions and the Study of Local Politics', *American Political Science Review*, 65 (1971), pp. 1063–80.

6   Gewirth's Moral Philosophy and the Foundation of Catholic Social Thought

Christoph Hübenthal

There is no real necessity to value religious people and communities positively. From a secular point of view, it normally suffices to tolerate them within reason. However, secular contemporaries pursuing a moral project, the objectives of which lie beyond their personal sphere, are usually looking for allies to contribute to their enterprise. The more comprehensive a project appears to be, the more they must wish that every possible agent, be it an individual or collective, participates in the attempt to achieve the project's objectives. If therefore—to put it bluntly—non-religious people pursue the *moral shaping of the entire human lifeworld*, they will necessarily seek support from all potential agents, including religious agents. So, tentatively, if we take for granted that every agent is ethically obligated to pursue the moral shaping of the entire human lifeworld, it follows that, from a secular perspective, religious people and communities should not only be tolerated, but rather be regarded as possible cooperation partners, at least in ethical matters. This applies all the more because religious agents usually have strong moral convictions and motivations.[1]

Of course, this is not to say that every religious morality has to be endorsed just like that. The last decades have sufficiently shown how inhuman religiously informed moralities can be, and evidence of this has not only been provided on a theoretical level but, much worse, also on a practical level. There is certainly no warranty that secular and religious actors can always cooperate successfully when it comes to shaping human life conditions in accord with moral standards. The reason for this incompatibility is quite obvious. Whereas secular proponents of an ethical project are supposed to justify their moral goals by arguments generally accessible to everyone, religious actors usually employ sources as, for instance, private revelations, Holy Scriptures, or authoritative doctrines that are normative only for those who share their religious beliefs. As in many other cases, therefore, it is the often quoted discordance between *universalist* and *particularist* moralities that impedes a fruitful cooperation between secular and religious people.

On closer inspection, however, even from the viewpoint of a universalist secular ethics, not all religious moralities appear to be particularist. At least one remarkable exception can be found in the social teaching of the Catholic

Church, usually called *Catholic Social Thought* (CST).[2] This ethical doctrine explicitly claims to be comprehensible not only to Catholics, Christians, or other people of religious affiliation, but to every human being of good will. The rationale for this is that CST is based on *natural law*. Natural law, for its part, appears to be a cognitivist and non-relativist ethical approach seeking to bring to the surface the normative implications of nature in general and of human nature in particular. Likewise, it objects to any form of legal positivism, that is, to the opinion that laws are valid simply by virtue of their being a result of a positive act of the legislator. Instead, natural law holds that every judicial norm eventually has to be justified through recourse to human or non-human nature.[3] Even at first glance, it should be clear that any religious morality based on natural law might be a possible ally for secular actors pursuing the moral improvement of the entire human lifeworld. So the question arises of whether CST could in fact be such an ally.

In this chapter, I will try to develop a cautiously positive answer. In its current version, however, CST cannot meet the requirements it should meet from a secular point of view. The reasons for this are, on the one hand, that CST employs a kind of natural law theory which is not as universalist as it claims to be, but still draws on *hidden religious presuppositions*, and, on the other hand, that CST's natural law theory also suffers from a serious *meta-ethical inconsistency* in that it builds on a dubious moral realism. Both problems, however, can be resolved by substituting Alan Gewirth's moral philosophy for natural law theory. Such a replacement, as I will argue, allows for a consistent reconstruction of CST's basic principles as well as a coherent reformulation of its essential content. Moreover, substitution of the natural law theory by Gewirth's moral philosophy does not inevitably reduce CST to a secular ethics. On the contrary, the genuinely theological purpose of CST can presumably be pursued better on the basis of a completely rational ethical system than on the basis of clandestine religious morality. To defend these theses, I will first briefly sketch CST and lay bare its foundational and meta-ethical problems. In the second section, Gewirth's moral philosophy—particularly his social ethics as unfolded in *The Community of Rights*[4]—will be presented as a cogent basis for CST. In the last section, I will try to show how CST can still remain a religious ethics, though one that proves to be a credible ally for everyone who seeks to morally shape all conditions of human life.

STRENGTHS AND WEAKNESSES OF CATHOLIC SOCIAL THOUGHT

Charitable activities have been part of the core business of the Church from the outset, but it was not before the end of the nineteenth century that theologians and the magisterium provided a systematic reflection on such activities. By that time, the Church first began to realize that the causes of

98 *Hübenthal*

poverty lie not only in the vicissitudes of human fate, but primarily in cultural, political, and economic *structures*. Ironically, this insight was partly indebted to socialist and communist theoreticians who decades earlier had discovered that the misery of the working class was strongly related to the functioning of the capitalist economy. Of course, the Church was anything but willing to share communist ideas. Due to the socialist challenge, however, it nevertheless felt compelled to think through the systemic conditions in which human privation, poverty and suffering evolve. In this way, the Church realized that it could not limit its social engagement to occasional forms of charity, but also needed a reliable theory to understand the structural causes of human hardship and to combat these structures efficiently. The first ecclesial document bearing witness to these new insights was Pope Leo's XIII encyclical letter *Rerum Novarum*, published in 1891. Generally, this document is considered to be the birth certificate of CST.

Almost by nature, the further development of CST was influenced by a multitude of internal and external factors. Different theological, philosophical, and sociological accounts had varying impacts on the shaping of the Church's social teaching, while at the same time, the historical, cultural, and political situations addressed by CST underwent considerable changes. Furthermore, the magisterium gradually recognized the enormous multiformity of the contexts and issues to which the social doctrine was to be applied.[5] Against the backdrop of increasing complexity, Pope John Paul II instructed the Pontifical Council for Justice and Peace to compile an orderly account of the Church's social teachings. The council's efforts eventually resulted in the publication of the *Compendium of the Social Doctrine of the Church* in 2004,[6] which—according to its authors—'intends to present in a complete and systematic manner . . . the Church's social teaching'.[7] Indeed, the *Compendium* can be seen as an impressive attempt to present the entire substance of CST in an integral and unified way. Among other things, this is shown by the fact that the *Compendium* introduces the four central principles that are said to constitute the basis of CST and to warrant its coherence. 'These are the principles of: *the dignity of the human person*, . . . which is the foundation of all the other principles and content of the Church's social doctrine; *the common good*; *subsidiarity*; and *solidarity*'.[8]

These few remarks by themselves nurture the assumption that CST might be a promising ally for secular ethical endeavours seeking to morally improve the entire human lifeworld. After all, the *Compendium* unmistakably contends that the principle of *human dignity*—in combination with its three corollaries—serves as the foundation of CST, which, for its part, claims to be a complete and systematic ethical edifice. Building a religious ethical approach on human dignity and, moreover, seeking to unfold it in a consistent and coherent manner is certainly not the worst way possible to initiate a discussion between such an approach and secular enterprises pursuing similar purposes.[9] The decisive question, then, is whether the *Compendium* succeeds in fulfilling these self-imposed tasks. Unfortunately, it is

Gewirth and Catholic Social Thought 99

doubtful that it does and, strangely enough, the doubt primarily pertains to the *natural law theory*, which is usually regarded as a guarantor of general accessibility as well as the internal consistency of an ethical system.[10] Indeed, the *Compendium* decidedly uses this theory because of its 'universal character, which precedes and unites all rights and duties'.[11] But, as can be argued, the natural law theory actually fails to meet these expectations due to both a foundational and a meta-ethical shortcoming.

To begin with, the *foundational* problem becomes apparent when one examines a series of assertions concerning the rationality and universal accessibility of the natural law. Throughout the entire document, the *Compendium* contends that the natural law can be conceived comprehensively only in the light of faith and revelation. In a historical retrospective, for instance, it is said that Pope Leo XIII examined the labour question exhaustively in *Rerum Novarum* and provided a proper evaluation of it by applying 'doctrinal principles founded on Revelation and on natural law and morality'.[12] In a section on human freedom, the *Compendium* stresses that the precepts of natural law 'are not clearly and immediately perceived by everyone ... [but] only with the help of Grace and Revelation. The natural law offers a foundation prepared by God for the revealed law and Grace, in full harmony with the work of the Spirit'.[13] And in another passage, it is even alleged 'that the power to decide good and evil does not belong to man but to God alone'.[14] These and countless other passages sufficiently indicate that, according to the magisterium, an all-encompassing understanding and interpretation of the natural law is not possible without grace-filled inspiration and theological knowledge about its divine origin. Almost as stereotypes, we see expressions such as 'knowledge illuminated by faith', 'reason illuminated by revelation', and 'knowledge enlightened by faith', which altogether relate to the prerequisites for a proper hermeneutics of the natural law.[15] Against this background, it is certainly not unwarranted to conclude that CST in general and the *Compendium* in particular presuppose a *theonomous foundation* of the natural law so that non-believers are eventually impotent to get a grip on its full meaning and content.

In spite of this clear plea for theonomy, however, the magisterium still holds that the natural law is universally valid. The *Compendium* reads, for instance: 'To man, "as he is involved in a complex network of relationships within modern societies", the Church addresses her social doctrine'.[16] Obviously, this does not only pertain to believers, but basically to every human being. In another passage, the *Compendium* explicitly claims applicability to the 'responsibilities regarding the building, organization and functioning of society, that is to say, political, economic and administrative obligations—obligations of a secular nature'.[17] And in still another context, it is said that the Christocentric character of CST 'does not weaken or exclude the role of reason and hence does not deprive the Church's social doctrine of rationality or, therefore, of universal applicability'.[18] We may conclude from all of this that the magisterium decisively stresses a theonomous foundation of the

100 Hübenthal

natural law and its social doctrine, but nevertheless is still of the opinion that the normative entailments of the natural law apply to every human being and to all social structures. Even a close reading of the entire *Compendium*, though, does not provide a satisfying answer to the question of how these two claims fit together meaningfully, that is, how a normative framework can be comprehensible only to a minority of the moral subjects and at the same time be compulsory for all.

One might think that this problem could be easily resolved by furnishing the natural law with a non-theonomous foundation. After all, from the beginning of the modern age, theoreticians have sought to conceptualize the natural law 'etsi Deus non daretur', that is, as if God did not exist. If these attempts had been successful, the intelligibility of the natural law would indeed no longer depend on the adoption of a religious faith, but would basically be accessible to all. In fact, however, this is not a viable option, since the natural law theory, as employed by CST, is not only theonomously justified, but also suffers from a serious *meta-ethical deficiency*. The *Compendium*, as can be shown, decidedly presupposes a divine inscription of normativity in the reality of creation, and in doing so, takes up a problematic form of *moral realism*. In a relevant passage, the document explicitly speaks of 'the laws of nature that God inscribed in the created universe, so that humanity may live in it and care for it in accordance with God's will'.[19] Apparently, the problem here is not only the theonomous foundation of the natural law, but also the assumption that the empirical reality as such bears normative implications.

The concrete implications become visible when we look at a passage in which the *Compendium* firmly rejects the opinion that gender identity is merely a cultural construct and emphasizes instead the existence of a male and female sexual identity. The complementarity of these identities, so it is argued, finds its ultimate expression in the institution of marriage, and the *Compendium* then concludes: 'According to this perspective, it is obligatory that positive law be conformed to the natural law, according to which sexual identity is indispensable, because it is the objective condition for forming a couple in marriage'.[20] Obviously, here it is said that a presumed biological fact, namely the complementarity of the male and female sexual identity, contains a normative fact which then ought to find expression in legal norms protecting and fostering the institution of heterosexual marriage. Another example of the inscription of normativity in the empirical reality can be found in a passage where the *Compendium* derives the natural right to work from the simple empirical fact that work is necessary for maintaining a family.[21] In a speech held before the German parliament in 2011, Pope Benedict XVI emphatically complained about modern positivist reason which, according to him, draws a sharp line between 'is' and 'ought' and thus proves to be incapable of discerning the natural law as the normativity of the whole natural reality.[22]

Meta-ethically speaking, CST's natural law theory thus draws on a *moral realism* that presupposes the inscription of moral facts into the empirical

Gewirth and Catholic Social Thought 101

world and so, in a sense, enforces the re-enchantment of nature. Against the backdrop of the meta-ethical debates of the twentieth century, however, this proves to be a highly dubious undertaking. The underlying theoretical problem can be spelled out in a nutshell as follows: Either there is a *logical relation* between empirical facts and the assumed moral facts, in which case it would be possible to determine the moral value of empirical facts by simply describing them,[23] and natural science and ethics would coincide, though beyond the scope of CST, no natural scientist or ethicist would ever endorse such a coincidence, or there is *no logical relation* between empirical and moral facts, in which case two entities sharing all significant descriptive features may still differ in their moral values. This is fairly implausible, to say the least.[24] A third option would be to *negate* once again *a logical relation* between empirical and moral facts, but nevertheless to hold that, in the face of empirical facts, it is possible to recognize moral facts intuitively. This, however, raises severe ontological and epistemological questions, for now one has to ask what sorts of things moral facts actually are and how they can be recognized reliably. It is hard to see how these questions can be answered in a satisfactory way.[25]

In short, we may conclude that the natural law theory of CST suffers from two shortcomings, in that it draws on a *theonomous foundation* and a problematic *meta-ethical conception of moral realism*.[26] In spite of our first impression, therefore, CST in its current version cannot be seen as a serious discussion partner for a secular ethics seeking to morally improve the entire human lifeworld. At the end of the day, CST cannot fulfill its high ambitions to build up a unified and coherent ethical edifice that—based on the principle of human dignity and its corollaries—is generally comprehensible to everyone. Nonetheless, even from a secular point of view, it is still a worthwhile project to reshape CST in such a way that it fulfils its ambitions, for—as has been pointed out in the introductory remarks—secular ethicists must be interested in competent religious partners.

GEWIRTH'S JUSTIFICATION AND CONCEPTUALIZATION OF THE SUPPORTIVE STATE

Generally speaking, one could say that the application range of CST resembles a particular application range of Gewirth's moral philosophy, which he himself calls the 'supportive state'.[27] So if it can be shown that Gewirth provides a logical account of the supportive state that avoids the foundational and meta-ethical problems just mentioned and, moreover, succeeds in systematically reconstructing the basic principles and content of CST, then his moral philosophy can indeed be taken as a cogent foundation of the Church's social teaching.

The idea of the supportive state belongs to the indirect applications of the Principle of Generic Consistency (PGC), that is, the supreme moral principle,

102 Hübenthal

which Gewirth convincingly justified in *Reason and Morality*.[28] Throughout his work, Gewirth did not get tired of emphasizing that the PGC primarily serves as the foundational basis of human rights. In his last book, *Self-Fulfillment*, he then explicated an idea that implicitly had always lain at the bottom of the method he utilized to justify the PGC, that is, the 'dialectically necessary method'. In short, the idea is that every agent, on pain of self-contradiction, must necessarily attribute dignity to himself or herself. Only due to this attribution, he or she is also logically committed to claim rights, and since this rights-claim is grounded in the very fact that the agent is an agent, he or she necessarily has to attribute rights to every other agent, too. To clarify the complex relation between dignity and human rights, Gewirth notes that 'although the existence of human rights follows dialectically from the worth or dignity that every agent must attribute to himself, the content of that dignity is in turn morally modified by the universal and equal human rights in which the argument eventuates'.[29] The necessary attribution of dignity is thus the starting point for the derivation of the PGC and human rights, which, for their part, further specify what dignity means and consists of. *Human dignity*, in other words, forms the basis of Gewirth's entire ethical edifice, which in itself is bound to serve this dignity by means of human rights.

It is exactly against this background that the supportive state is to be considered. The supportive state, as has been said, belongs to the indirect applications of the PGC. Just as direct applications, indirect applications seek to protect and to promote human dignity and human rights. Unlike direct ones, however, they do not primarily pertain to individual actions, but to social rules and societal institutions.[30] More precisely, the supportive state belongs to the dynamic indirect applications of the PGC, which means that its main purpose is not to maintain a static, already existing equality with regard to human rights, but the gradual overcoming of inequalities.[31] In the first chapters of *Reason and Morality*, Gewirth had already pointed out that the content of human rights is defined by the necessary conditions of human agency or the generic features of action, that is, by 'freedom and well-being'. Well-being, in turn, is further specified in terms of certain goods, namely 'basic goods', 'non-substractive goods', and 'additive goods'.[32] Against this backdrop, the main goal of the supportive state can be determined as the promotion of an equal distribution of freedom and well-being among all members of a given society.

One of Gewirth's central aims in *The Community of Rights* is to show that the establishment of a supportive state has a *community*-building effect. For once it becomes clear that—due to the universal validity of the PGC—all members of a society are at the same time rights holders and duty bearers, they find themselves in an overall network of mutual relations which obligates the better off to support the weaker and the weaker to actively cooperate in order to improve their own situation.

> Because this principle of human rights entails the requirement of mutual respect (and of mutual aid when needed and practicable), it is a principle

of *social solidarity*, as against exclusive preoccupation with personal interest. This solidarity requires institutions whereby hitherto deprived groups can be brought nearer to equality. By the effective recognition of the mutuality entailed by human rights, the society becomes a *community*.[33]

The supportive state represents thus not merely a technical arrangement to promote the equal distribution of freedom and well-being, but also bears affective and conative components. Gewirth does not even shy away from calling the supportive state an 'institutionalization of love'.[34] In another context, he explains that positive duties towards the worse off do not only pertain 'to actions and institutions but also to attitudes and motivations'.[35] So each member of the society is supposed to acquire particular virtues, which serve as an intrinsic motivation to contribute to the institutional setting of the supportive state. From all this, we may conclude that the indirect application of the PGC, which in itself is derived from a necessary and universal attribution of *dignity*, systematically generates the idea of a communitarian supportive state which is unified by the virtue of *social solidarity*.

By the same token, it can be demonstrated that CST's corollary principles of *subsidiarity* and *common good* also form essential features of the supportive state and thus follow from the PGC. Though Gewirth does not mention the subsidiary principle literally, his overall construction of the supportive state still shows a better understanding of this principle than the commentaries of many a specialist. While such experts often interpret the principle one-sidedly by only emphasizing the state's, or the higher body's, obligation not to interfere with matters that the individual, or the lower body, can regulate on his or her own, Gewirth unambiguously makes clear that, in fact, the supportive state is the addressee of a twofold obligation: Firstly, it *must not* interfere with individual matters which individuals, or lower bodies, can manage themselves; and secondly, it *has to* provide support in matters which individuals, or lower bodies, cannot manage themselves.[36] The aim of the second obligation, however, is not to continue a relation of dependency, but rather, to promote a particular kind of autonomy that Gewirth calls 'productive agency'. In the specific sense that Gewirth attributes to this notion, productive agency means the ability to generate products or to provide services that have a practical value and can therefore be sold on markets.[37] So the more an agent acquires productive agency with the help of the supportive state's institutions, the less he or she will depend on these institutions and the more he or she will be able to make a positive contribution to the supportive state. It follows that the state's two obligations as defined by the subsidiarity principle find their counterpart in the individual's obligation to acquire productive agency to the extent feasible.[38] Generally, these considerations indicate that Gewirth clearly recognizes the actual meaning of the subsidiarity principle by highlighting the supportive state's long-term goal, namely, to abolish the immoral conditions to which it owes its existence as far as possible.[39]

104   *Hübenthal*

Gewirth exhibits a comparable clarity in his delineation of the *common good*. In *Reason and Morality*, he stated that 'the PGC's requirement with regard to well-being may also be put as the principle of the Common Good: every transaction must be for the good of the recipient as well as of the agent'.[40] In *The Community of Rights*, he further distinguishes between a distributive and a collective meaning of the common good. While the distributive meaning unambiguously stresses that commonality implies that all single members of the society have equal human rights, the collective meaning pertains to a good that the community possesses as a whole. This, however, could mean that not every member of the community participates in the good.[41] The community, so one could further argue, would then be treated as an entity on its own, the good of which can be pursued separately from the good of the single members. Eventually, this could lead to a conflict between the common good and the good of the members as epitomized by their human rights. Hence, the collective meaning of the common good is inconsistent with the PCG, so that only the distributive interpretation is acceptable.[42]

These considerations, as has been indicated, were intended to show that Gewirth's moral philosophy can indeed be taken as a cogent foundation of CST. This moral philosophy and CST both have *human dignity* as their point of departure, and Gewirth uses this point of departure and the dialectically necessary method to derive the PGC, which serves as the human rights principle. Among other things, the PGC asks for an indirect dynamic application in order to fight inequalities with respect to human rights, and so seeks to promote equality. The instrument to achieve this purpose is the supportive state. The supportive state, however, appears not only to be an arrangement of technical institutions, but eventually proves to be a community held together by virtue of *solidarity*. Furthermore, the supportive state is committed to the principle of *subsidiarity*, since, on the one hand, it gives every member of the community the help necessary for them to acquire productive agency as much as possible. At the same time, the recipients of this help are obligated to cooperate actively in the acquirement and improvement of their productive agency. On the other hand, the supportive state aims at societal conditions under which such help is no longer needed. In this way, it can comply more and more with the first obligation of the subsidiarity principle, the obligation of non-interference. Finally, it can be argued that the aim of the supportive state consists of the full actualization of the *common good*, provided that this principle is given a distributive meaning, not a collective one.

Of course, much more could be said about the striking substantial similarities between CST and Gewirth's moral philosophy.[43] But even these few remarks will have made clear that Gewirth provides a *rationally justified basis* for an ethical edifice that he and CST largely have in common. Above all, however, Gewirth provides a basis that avoids the foundational and meta-ethical shortcomings that CST is suffering from. In the context of his

Gewirth and Catholic Social Thought 105

moral philosophy, human reason is not reliant on a revelatory illumination to comprehend the entirety of morality, but can suffice with the 'canons of deductive and inductive logic'.[44] So his moral philosophy can do without a *theonomous foundation*. Likewise, he abstains from the dubious *moral realism* which assumes a (divine) inscription of normativity into the empirical reality. After all, Gewirth's greatest achievement can be seen in the discovery of the evaluative structure of human agency. The PGC, as has been said, results from the logical necessity by which agents have to attribute worth, dignity, and rights to themselves as well as to every other agent or prospective agent. Therefore, once it has been recognized that human agency implies unavoidable valuations, there is no need to presuppose values inscribed in nature anymore.

IS THE CHRISTIAN IDENTITY THREATENED?

No matter how plausible it now may seem to substitute the Gewirthian approach for the natural law basis of CST, such a replacement might still cause discomfort to religious people, and perhaps even to non-religious people (the reason for this will be explained shortly). After all, the theonomous foundation and the assumption of a divine inscription of normativity into nature have ensured that CST can be easily identified as a religious ethics. If these traits are dropped, CST threatens to become a purely secular ethics, and Catholicism loses one of its most distinctive characteristics. So the question arises of whether replacing the natural law theory with Gewirth's account actually jeopardizes the *Christian identity* of CST. It can be argued that this is decisively not the case.

To begin with, the fact that the PGC determines the primary content of human rights as well as the direct and indirect modes of its application does by no means imply that, in moral or political matters, everything is fixed from the outset. On the contrary, with regard to the well-being component of human rights, Gewirth himself points to a 'historical variability'.[45] Moreover, he asserts that many of the social rules are not determined beforehand, but result from deliberative and democratic processes.[46] Within an ethical framework built on the PGC, there is thus sufficient space for a historical adaptation and specification of moral and political norms. It must also be noted at this point that such adjustments can immensely benefit from a religious reading of ethical conceptions like justice, peace, liberation, or redemption. Since a religious interpretation of such notions often bears on ideas of infinity and absoluteness, the moral and political deficiencies of our conditioned and finite world become more visible when contrasted with these ultimate conceptions. This is exactly the reason why a non-religious thinker like Jürgen Habermas contends that public debates within a post-secular society still depend on the semantic potentials of religious traditions.[47] And in the same way, Gewirth notes, 'In certain circumstances, religion also has

106   *Hübenthal*

been a powerful force for justice because of its doctrine of the equal worth of all humans as children of God'.[48] It follows that there is certainly no need for a religious ethical tradition such as CST to give up its Christian identity when basing itself upon a purely rational foundation. It still can contribute to the adaptation and specification of moral and political norms by building on its inherited images, symbols, and narratives, which shed a light of absoluteness on our finite social reality and so might eventually reveal the actual extent of our moral liability.

A second argument supporting the assertion that CST does not have to give up its Christian identity when it replaces its natural law foundation with a foundation in the PGC is a little bit more complicated. To get the point, one should first notice that the social teaching of the Church does not only aim at societal and global conditions within which human dignity is recognized, solidarity and subsidiarity are practiced, and the common good is pursued, but first and foremost, '[t]he teaching and spreading of her social doctrine are part of the Church's evangelizing mission'.[49] So CST is not an end in itself, but has to be seen in the broader context of evangelization. From a secular perspective, one could thus argue that the Church has a hidden agenda when it seeks to realize its ethical programme, since it actually strives for social conditions by means of which its religious ideology can successfully be communicated. In this way, the whole of the social doctrine is merely an *instrument* to achieve decisively religious purposes. But is this accusation right? As long as the Church upholds the natural law theory, it can hardly point out why such a critique would be wrong. For in this case, as has been shown, the entire social teaching would depend on assumptions which no one outside the Church can reasonably share. CST could then rightly be suspected of being tailored only in accordance with the religious purposes it has to serve. If Gewirth's approach is substituted for natural law theory, however, the picture changes. For in that case, the ethical programme would be justified as an *end in itself*, and not only because it is an instrument to achieve religious aims. Though the societal implementation of the ethical programme may still be regarded as a means to promote communication conditions suitable for the purpose of evangelization, a society that guarantees human rights, practices solidarity as well as subsidiarity, and realizes the common good is nevertheless a society that must be pursued on its own.

By adopting Gewirth's moral philosophy, the Church can thus objectively justify the means to its major end, that is, evangelization. But there is more to it. In fact, it can be shown that even this end is objectively justified to some extent. In *Self-Fulfillment*, Gewirth convincingly points out that the question of the *meaning of life* cannot be ignored if one wants to live a fulfilled life, that is, if one wants to satisfy one's deepest aspirations and develop one's best capacities. The delineation of a comprehensive meaning can thus be seen as a significant aspect of a fulfilled human life. After having discussed some possible interpretations of such a meaning, Gewirth himself provides a rather formal definition. 'The meaning of life', he says, 'consists

Gewirth and Catholic Social Thought 107

in the values that the agent who lives the life regards as most worth pursuing'.[50] Then he further qualifies these values by noting that they have to be organized in accord with a coherent overall plan, they must be regarded as attainable, and they must meet certain evaluative, primarily moral, standards. As these qualifications already indicate, the quest for comprehensive meaning is fairly demanding and requires a number of personal and societal conditions to be met. Agents must, for instance, possess the basic and non-substractive goods to live at least a decent life, they must have enjoyed a good education and they must already have developed their best capacities before they can authentically decide what the meaning of life is for them. As long as these conditions are not fully met, any decision on the meaning of life is in danger of being a heteronomous or even manipulated decision. It is exactly for this reason that Gewirth strongly emphasizes that the preconditions for self-fulfillment and for the ability to take an authentic decision on one's meaning of life belong to the objects of human rights. At the same time, however, he also stresses 'that self-fulfillment, while being facilitated by the appropriate context of human rights, must be an achievement of the autonomous individual'.[51]

To what extent can these considerations be viewed as a justification of the Church's primary purpose, namely to conduct its evangelizing mission? The answer is: If every human being is entitled to have the preconditions that enable him or her to make an autonomous decision on the meaning of life, these preconditions include *information* about traditional and current ways of *articulating the meaning of life*. If, furthermore, evangelization means nothing but to provide such information and thereby to invite people to freely affirm the Christian interpretation, this purpose is absolutely justified by the core of Gewirth's moral philosophy. The adoption of this philosophy as the basis of CST is thus by no means a threat to the Christian identity of the Church's social doctrine but, on the contrary, can serve as a rational justification of both CST as a means and evangelization as its end.

NOTES

1. See J. Habermas, 'Religion in the Public Sphere', *European Journal of Philosophy*, 14:1 (2006), pp. 1–25.
2. See, for example, J.M. Thompson, *Introducing Catholic Social Thought* (Maryknoll, NY: Orbis Books, 2010).
3. See E. Schockenhoff, *Natural Law and Human Dignity: Universal Ethics in an Historical World* (Washington, DC: The Catholic University of America Press, 2003), pp. 10–2.
4. A. Gewirth, *The Community of Rights* (Chicago, IL: Chicago University Press, 1996).
5. See K.R. Himes *et al.* (eds), *Modern Catholic Social Teaching: Commentaries and Interpretation* (Washington, DC: Georgetown University Press, 2005).
6. Pontifical Council for Justice and Peace, *Compendium of the Social Doctrine of the Church* (Città del Vaticano: Libreria Edrice Vaticana, 2004) (hereinafter *Compendium* with paragraph numbers).

108 *Hübenthal*

7. *Compendium*, n. 8.
8. *Compendium*, n. 160.
9. For the centrality of human dignity, see M. Düwell *et al.* (eds), *The Cambridge Handbook of Human Dignity: Interdisciplinary Perspectives* (Cambridge: Cambridge University Press, 2014).
10. See, for example, J. Finnis, *Natural Law and Natural Rights* (Oxford: Clarendon, 1980).
11. *Compendium*, n. 140.
12. *Compendium*, n. 89.
13. *Compendium*, n. 141.
14. *Compendium*, n. 136.
15. See particularly, *Compendium*, nn. 72–8.
16. *Compendium*, n. 61 (the passage in double quotation marks is taken from: John Paul II, *Centesimus Annus*, n. 54).
17. *Compendium*, n. 83; see also n. 397.
18. *Compendium*, n. 75.
19. *Compendium*, n. 37.
20. *Compendium*, n. 224.
21. See *Compendium*, n. 294.
22. The speech can be found in G. Essen (ed), *Verfassung ohne Grund? Die Rede des Papstes im Bundestag* (Freiburg: Herder, 2012), pp. 17–26.
23. Against this kind of ethical naturalism, G. E. Moore already posed his famous *open-question argument*; see G. E. Moore, *Principia Ethica*, revised edition (Cambridge: Cambridge University Press, 1993), p. 67.
24. For the problem of supervenience, see S. Blackburn, *Essays in Quasi-Realism* (New York: Oxford University Press, 1993), pp. 111–29.
25. See J. L. Mackie, *Inventing Right and Wrong* (Harmondsworth: Penguin, 1977), pp. 38–42, where Mackie develops the 'argument from queerness'. Some years ago, J. McDowell tried to answer these questions by conceptualizing moral facts as 'secondary qualities' that are recognizable after an educational process. We can leave open here whether this is a plausible solution. However, it is still true that he did not have an answer to the problem of supervenience. See J. McDowell, *Mind, Value, and Reality* (Cambridge, MA: Harvard University Press, 1998), pp. 131–51.
26. At this point, one might ask whether there are other forms of natural law theory which do not exhibit the deficiencies mentioned. Of course, this cannot be discussed here exhaustively. It can be argued, however, that each natural law theory either suffers from similar problems or is based on valuations which are said to be natural inclinations but, on closer inspection, turn out to be non-necessary assessments.
27. Here, the reservation must be made that CST covers a broader field in that it also applies, for instance, to developmental ethics (see Paul VI, *Populorum Progressio*; Benedict XVI, *Caritas in Veritate*) or to environmental ethics (see Francis, *Laudato Si'*). It can reasonably be argued, however, that due to its universal scope, Gewirth's moral philosophy also allows for an extension to other ethical realms. This is partly shown in Gewirth's book *Human Rights: Essays on Justification and Applications* (Chicago, IL: University of Chicago Press, 1982).
28. A. Gewirth, *Reason and Morality* (Chicago, IL: Chicago University Press, 1978). As the first section of the present volume extensively deals with the PGC and its justification, it is not necessary to go into that here. Yet, it could be added that the justification of the PGC might be seen as an application of a *discursive concept of reason to the notion of agency*. Seeing it in this way, one can counter the *transcendentally pragmatic* objection that Gewirth's derivation

Gewirth and Catholic Social Thought 109

of the PGC is purely *monological*. For this point, see my *Grundlegung der christlichen Sozialethik: Versuch eines freiheitsanalytisch-handlungsreflexiven Ansatzes* (Münster: Aschendorff, 2006), pp. 249–66.

29. A. Gewirth, *Self-Fulfillment* (Princeton, NJ: Princeton University Press, 1998), p. 170.
30. See Gewirth, *Reason and Morality*, p. 272; see also Gewirth, *Human Rights*, p. 61.
31. See Gewirth, *Reason and Morality*, p. 312.
32. Ibid., pp. 53–8.
33. Gewirth, *The Community of Rights*, p. 6 (my emphases).
34. Ibid., p. xv.
35. Ibid., p. 42.
36. This corresponds perfectly with the first mention of the subsidiary principle. See Pius XI, *Quadragesimo Anno*, n. 79.
37. See Gewirth, *The Community of Rights*, pp. 132–3.
38. See Gewirth, *The Community of Rights*, pp. 231–5, where Gewirth argues that there is not only a right, but also a duty to work.
39. See Gewirth, *The Community of Rights*, p. 127.
40. Gewirth, *Reason and Morality*, p. 211.
41. See Gewirth, *The Community of Rights*, pp. 94–5.
42. In the history of CST, there was a long controversy as to whether the common good is to be interpreted as a *service value* (which resembles the distributive meaning) or as a *value on its own* (which resembles the collective meaning). Fortunately, the distributive interpretation found its way into CST; see *Compendium*, n. 164.
43. It would be a worthwhile exercise to relate CST's 'preferential option for the poor' (see *Compendium*, nn. 182–4, 449) to Gewirth's 'deprivation focus' (see *The Community of Rights*, p. 110 passim), which serves as the starting point of the 'economic biography', which then leads from a state of absolute poverty to a full-fledged membership in the community of rights.
44. Gewirth, *Reason and Morality*, p. 22.
45. Gewirth, *The Community of Rights*, p. 14.
46. See Gewirth, *Reason and Morality*, pp. 304–11.
47. See J. Habermas, ' "The Political": The Rational Meaning of a Questionable Inheritance of Political Theology', in E. Mendieta and J. VanAntwerpen (eds), *The Power of Religion in the Public Sphere* (New York: Columbia University Press, 2011), pp. 14–33.
48. Gewirth, *Self-Fulfillment*, p. 176.
49. John Paul II, *Sollicitudo Rei Socialis*, n. 41 (quoted in *Compendium*, n. 7).
50. Gewirth, *Self-Fulfillment*, p. 186.
51. Ibid., p. 195.

WORKS CITED

Pope Benedict XVI, *Caritas in Veritate* (http://w2.vatican.va/content/benedict-xvi/en/encyclicals/documents/hf_ben-xvi_enc_20090629_caritas-in-veritate.html).
Blackburn, S., *Essays in Quasi-Realism* (New York: Oxford University Press, 1993).
Düwell, M., Braarvig, J., Brownsword, R., and Mieth, D. (eds), *The Cambridge Handbook of Human Dignity: Interdisciplinary Perspectives* (Cambridge: Cambridge University Press, 2014).
Essen, G. (ed.), *Verfassung ohne Grund? Die Rede des Papstes im Bundestag* (Freiburg: Herder, 2012).

110 *Hübenthal*

Finnis, J., *Natural Law and Natural Rights* (Oxford: Clarendon, 1980).

Pope Francis, *Laudato Si'* (http://w2.vatican.va/content/francesco/en/encyclicals/documents/papa-francesco_20150524_enciclica-laudato-si.html).

Gewirth, A., *Reason and Morality* (Chicago, IL: Chicago University Press, 1978).

———, *Human Rights: Essays on Justification and Applications* (Chicago, IL: University of Chicago Press, 1982).

———, *The Community of Rights* (Chicago, IL: Chicago University Press, 1996).

———, *Self-Fulfillment* (Princeton, NJ: Princeton University Press, 1998).

Habermas, J., 'Religion in the Public Sphere', *European Journal of Philosophy*, 14:1 (2006), pp. 1–25.

———, ' "The Political": The Rational Meaning of a Questionable Inheritance of Political Theology', in E. Mendieta and J. VanAntwerpen (eds.), *The Power of Religion in the Public Sphere* (New York: Columbia University Press, 2011), pp. 14–33.

Himes, K. R. and Cahill, L. S. (eds), *Modern Catholic Social Teaching: Commentaries and Interpretation* (Washington, DC: Georgetown University Press, 2005).

Hübenthal, C., *Grundlegung der christlichen Sozialethik: Versuch eines freiheitsanalytisch-handlungsreflexiven Ansatzes* (Münster: Aschendorff, 2006).

Pope John Paul II, *Centesimus Annus* (http://w2.vatican.va/content/john-paul-ii/en/encyclicals/documents/hf_jp-ii_enc_01051991_centesimus-annus.html).

Mackie, J. L. *Inventing Right and Wrong* (Harmondsworth: Penguin, 1977).

McDowell, J., *Mind, Value, and Reality* (Cambridge, MA: Harvard University Press, 1998).

Moore, G. E., *Principia Ethica*, rev. edition (Cambridge: Cambridge University Press, 1993).

Pope Paul VI, *Populorum Progressio* (http://w2.vatican.va/content/paul-vi/en/encyclicals/documents/hf_p-vi_enc_26031967_populorum.html).

Pope Pius XI, *Quadragesimo Anno* (http://w2.vatican.va/content/pius-xi/en/encyclicals/documents/hf_p-xi_enc_19310515_quadragesimo-anno.html).

Pontifical Council for Justice and Peace, *Compendium of the Social Doctrine of the Church* (Città del Vaticano: Libreria Edrice Vaticana, 2004).

Schockenhoff, E., *Natural Law and Human Dignity: Universal Ethics in an Historical World* (Washington, DC: The Catholic University of America Press, 2003).

Thompson, J. M., *Introducing Catholic Social Thought* (Maryknoll, NY: Orbis Books, 2010).

7 Confucianism and Gewirthian Human Rights in a Taiwanese Context

Shu-Mei Tang and Shang-Yung Yen

INTRODUCTION

In this chapter, it is argued that the Gewirthian theory of human rights, by being not only rationally justified but also by being similar in important respects to the teachings of Confucius, is especially suited to function as a foundation for human rights legislation in a Taiwanese context.

Human rights are an abstract concept. The premise of human rights should have valid moral criteria or principles that can justify the assertion that all humans, *humans qua humans*, have rights and hence also have correlative duties. In China, an original version of a human rights theory can be traced back to the Chou dynasty. Thus, even before the Confucian period, the Chinese had already considered the importance of humanity and the relationship between God and human beings. Confucianism, however, has had a profound influence on Chinese history. In fact, for more than two thousand years, the thoughts of Confucius have been dominant in both the political and legal spheres of Chinese culture. Now, there are similarities in content between the theory of Gewirth and the contributions of writers in the tradition of Confucian natural law. These similarities concern the view of human beings as agents, and the normative idea that an agent should treat other agents as he would have them treat himself. Given these similarities, Gewirth's theory is exceptionally well suited to safeguard human rights in Taiwan, as well as in any other country influenced by Confucian thought.

HUMAN RIGHTS IN TAIWAN

In today's Taiwan, at least 88 per cent of the population is of Chinese Han nationality;[1] therefore, traditional Chinese culture has been the dominant culture in Taiwan. Thus, the original version of a human rights theory in Taiwan can be traced back to the Chou dynasty of ancient China.[2] Even before the Confucian period,[3] the Chinese had already considered the importance of humanity and the relationship between God and human beings.[4] In fact, there is evidence to suggest that the philosophers of the time taught that the

112   *Tang and Yen*

purposes and rights of people should occupy a high place in the mind of the ruler.[5] The following periods, the so-called *Spring* and *Autumn*[6] and Warring States periods,[7] were probably the most unstable periods in Chinese history. Yet despite the social and political instability, it was a time when many different opinions about human thoughts were expressed and some concrete forms of philosophical thought on human rights were developed.[8] These ideas had a profound effect on the whole of Chinese history.

The People's Republic of China joined the United Nations in the 1971. Immediately thereafter, Taiwan was forced to withdraw from the United Nations. Since the late 1980s, the democratization process has slowly but thoroughly transformed the whole societal fabric of Taiwan, with the first direct presidential election being held in 1996. One party, the Kuomintang, had led the Taiwanese government for fifty years since 1949 until, for the first time in Taiwan's history, in 2000, power was handed over to the opposition party, the Democratic Progressive Party, in a peaceful and democratic manner. No doubt the development of democracy and human rights is still in its infancy in Taiwan. Taiwan is unfamiliar with international human rights standards. It is easy for the important issues of human dignity and human rights to be neglected by policy makers in Taiwan or restricted in a constricted concept of human dignity and human rights.

The current administrative systems of the Taiwanese government are unclear and ambiguous concerning the status of human rights. In order to safeguard these fundamental rights in Taiwan, it would be useful to pay attention to concepts of human rights that are both theoretically sound and practically realistic in a Taiwanese context. We believe that the Gewirthian Principle of Generic Consistency (PGC) could play a significant role here.

THE GEWIRTHIAN ARGUMENT FOR HUMAN RIGHTS

The premise is that human rights in Taiwan and everywhere should have valid moral criteria or principles which can justify the assertion that 'all humans, *qua* humans, have the rights and hence also the correlative duties'.[9] Rights and duties should be correlative and inseparable.[10] The field of moral criteria is full of controversy. Disagreements about moral principles concern its justificatory relationship to reason, religion, power, utility, and economic class or history.

> For not only do the divergences among philosophers reflect different views about the logical difficulties of justification in ethics; the conflicting principles they uphold, whether presented as rationally grounded or not, have drastically different implications about the right modes of individual conduct and social institutions. The problem of whether any of these principles can be rationally justified is hence of first importance for the guidance of human life.[11]

Confucianism and Gewirthian Human Rights 113

Now, Taiwanese morality has been deeply influenced by the idea of utilitarianism. The basic principle of utilitarianism is the Greatest Happiness Principle. This entails that the choice of action should be based on promoting the maximum happiness of as many people as possible, and to reduce harm to the minimum level. However, while maximizing happiness, this principle will sometimes sacrifice individual rights or the rights of small groups.[12] Unlike utilitarianism with its maximizing aim, regardless of the result for individuals, Gewirthian ethics focuses on rights that pertain to each and every individual agent.

The chief novelty of Gewirth's argument is the logical derivation of a substantial normative moral principle from the nature of human action.[13] The connection between human action and normative moral principles has long been recognized. For example, virtue ethics theories emphasize that a virtuous person's ideas of the virtues connect ethics to action.[14] The role of one's character and the virtues that one's character embodies determine an evaluating ethical behavior. In Kant's categorical imperative, the universal law states, '*Act only in accordance with that maxim through which you can at the same time will that it [should] become a universal law*'.[15] Gewirth's thesis is that every agent, by the fact of engaging in action, is logically committed to the acceptance of certain evaluative and deontic judgements and ultimately of a supreme moral principle, the PGC, which is addressed to every agent: *Act in accord with the generic rights of your recipients as well as of yourself.*[16]

The major argument that structured Gewirth's theory is called 'the dialectically necessary method',[17] deducing evaluative statements from the internal viewpoint of a prospective purposive agent (PPA). Every rational PPA must logically accept that he and all other PPAs have rights to freedom and well-being, the generic rights referred to by the PGC.

A PPA is an agent who acts voluntarily for a purpose he has freely chosen and who has the capacity to act on his choice, and every PPA wants to be successful in his actions. Hence, freedom (the agent's ability to control his behaviour in accordance with his unforced choice) and well-being (the agent's ability to act successfully to realize his purposes) will constitute necessary goods for all rational agents. As for well-being, it has three levels: 'basic', 'nonsubtractive', and 'additive'. While basic well-being refers to preconditions of agency, such as life, health, and mental equilibrium, nonsubtractive well-being refers to the good of being able to maintain an undiminished capacity for agency (not being stolen from or lied to, for instance) and additive well-being refers to the good of being able to expand one's capacity for agency (for instance, by having education and earning an income).[18] And since no rational agent can accept being deprived of freedom and well-being, every rational agent must also claim rights to these necessary goods of agency.

The PGC relies on the normative perspective of a rational agent considering the value of the needs of his agency and the necessary conditions of

114 *Tang and Yen*

successful agency. Universalizing his perception of freedom and well-being as necessary goods and as objects of rights-claims, every rational agent must accept that all agents have rights to freedom and well-being, which is the content of the PGC. The PGC proposes a convincing argument superior to the dominant utilitarianism as regards fair treatment of individuals and due respect for their rights.

THE CONFUCIAN THEORY OF ETHICS

Gewirth's ethical argument shows similarities to the ethics of Confucianism. As is well known, Confucianism has been the dominant philosophy throughout Chinese history. To a great extent, Confucian philosophy has had so much impact that it not only affects Chinese people's lives and society in every aspect, but has also become a representative symbol of Chinese culture. Now, for anyone who accepts the Confucian position, there is at least no reason why a Confucian would *not* be able to accept the PGC, since the contents of Confucian ethics are similar to the Gewirthian ethics and there is no conflict between these two theories. In order to show how and why the Gewirthian PGC might be accepted and applied in Taiwan, we will compare the Confucian theory of ethics to the PGC.

Confucius's thoughts were mainly collected in the *Confucian Analects*, which were the dialogues or discussions of Confucius with his disciples and others on various topics. His disciples digested the memoranda of Confucius's discourses and compressed it into twenty books. The central arguments in the *Confucian Analects* relate to the concepts of *Jen and Yuh*: While *Jen* denotes perfect virtue, *Yuh* denotes the life of action, including purposes, intentions, desires, wants. As the Chinese government of that period was corrupt, Confucius attempted, through the teaching of his disciples and through his travels throughout China, to persuade the government to restore virtue to the governmental system.[19]

Jen

Jen is the core essence in Confucian thought and was frequently mentioned by Confucius and his disciples.[20] In the Confucian sense, the whole concept of human merit should be enshrined in *Jen*, for it embodies the complete essence of perfect features. The traditional interpretation of *Jen* relies on features such as love,[21] goodness, benevolence, humanity, heartiness, and kindness.

The character for '*Jen*' is composed of the character for 'two' and the character for 'people', though it is worth noting that the Chinese character for 'two' can mean more than one, in other words, it can also mean three or three hundred. In addition, 'people' is the basic unit for the requirement of *Jen*. Thus, 'two people' here would mean more than one person and it

Confucianism and Gewirthian Human Rights 115

could be a family, a community, or a country, and this suggests that human merit should be established and should exist between people. In the usage of Confucius, *Jen* is the greatest and the summation of all virtues; it is the supreme principle of morality.

The main exponent of his theory, Mencius, followed the Confucian thought and elaborated *Jen* in detail,[22] showing that the essence and central dogma of morality is *Jen*. According to Mencius, the essence of a human being is *Jen* or kindness, and can be clearly distinguished from other opinions on life such as that the essence of a human being is evil[23] or neutral.[24] Mencius suggested that *Jen* is to love all human beings. This is an idea that is equivalent to saying that people should love and respect each other. This is the highest merit of human nature, so that *Jen* is the essence of human beings, in which he believes, and which already exists between people.

Yuh

The Book of Documents, which describes the duties of governmental officials, mentioned that 'the *Yuh* of people should be constantly borne in the mind of the ruler'.[25] The terms *Yuh* or *Yuann* had been represented in the *Analects* a number of times,[26] and could be interpreted as will, wish, want, intentions, choices, decisions, reasons, volition, purposes, aims, desires, ambition, aspiration, prospect, and expectation. For instance, Yen Yuen 'wishes' not to boast of his excellence, nor to make a display of his meritorious deeds. In the *Analects* 4:5, Confucius claims that riches and honours are what men 'desire'. If they cannot be obtained in the proper way, people should not hold such riches and honours.[27] Therefore, if I wished to achieve something for my own purpose, it would imply that I have some motives in doing so, so I am a purposive individual. The purpose I aim for is only for myself. Therefore, I have the capacity to act voluntarily to achieve these aims, which I have chosen.

The concepts of *Yuh* and *Yuann* imply the agent's autonomy, which includes the autonomy of thought, will, and action. The term *autonomy* is derived from the Greek, meaning being a law (nomos) unto oneself (autos), or setting one's law for oneself.[28] The autonomy of thought means the agent can evaluate his purposes with his own reason; the autonomy of will refers to the agent's free, unforced, voluntary reason for his action; the autonomy of action indicates the agent has the capacity to fulfill his purposes without infringed by others. However, the autonomy of thought, will, and action should be based on reason. An agent should have the autonomy of thought and will to evaluate and decide his wishes for himself and freely take action to reach his goals.

The desires for these purposes are both intentional and inclinational. The perceived value of some purpose provides individual agents with a desire to voluntarily carry out actions intended to bring about the purpose in question. *Yuh* and *Yuann*, in the Confucian sense, imply that the state of human

116 *Tang and Yen*

beings is that of a purposive state, individually motivated by goals determined by their individual perspectives. Therefore, if an agent wishes to act voluntarily for his purposes, his desires move him to the action; this would imply that he is a purposive agent. This concept of agency in Confucianism would be similar to the notion of PPAs as developed by Gewirth. In both cases, agents are supposed to act in pursuit of their desires, but also to be able to adjust these pursuits in accordance with reason.[29]

Tian

Tian refers to the 'mighty power' of nature that creates the universe and sets the rules for people to live in harmony. This 'mighty power', the Power of Nature, is different from the concept of 'God' in Judaism, Christianity, and Islam. Although these three religions have different definitions of 'God', the creation of the world all came from their 'God'. Confucius did not deny the existence of 'God', but he implied that such power derived from '*Tian*'.

There are some criticisms concerning Confucius suggesting that his teaching was mainly based on humanistic premises and therefore was anti-religious, for he has always been very reluctant to explore issues such as the immortality of the soul or the existence of God. His arguments indicate indeed that his philosophy centred on the issues of humanity and human relations. Confucius claimed that *Tian* is the origin of perfect virtues and that these virtues exist in all people. *Tian* has given intrinsic value to people by providing them with virtues as part of their nature. Confucius characterized people as: 'Man is born with virtue. If a man loses his virtue, and manages to live, his escape from death is the result of mere good fortune'.[30] 'If a superior man abandons virtue, how can he fulfil the requirements of that name?'[31] Hence, he held that these virtues intrinsically existed in humans as fundamental nature simply because these virtues were possessed at birth. These aspects of human fundamental nature cannot be denied if one has been recognized as a human being.

Confucius contended that all ethical criteria should be bound to *Tian* because *Tian* has provided basic rules for virtue. Hence, from the Confucian point of view, the application of *Jen* is expected to be in accordance with the rule of *Tian*, which could be defined as benevolence, love, righteousness, propriety, and wisdom.

THE RULE OF TIAN

This concept of virtue derived from *Tian*, which is naturally conferred in humans in Confucianism, has great similarity to the PGC of Gewirthian theory. It is the desire that makes an impetus for an agent to perform his action voluntarily. The desires of Chinese characters, *Yuh* and *Yuann*, in a Confucian sense, entail that a human being as a moral agent is usually

Confucianism and Gewirthian Human Rights   117

motivated by aims set from their individual perspectives. The concept in Confucianism that values humans as purposive agents is in line with the notion of PPAs, which was proposed by Gewirth.

Human autonomy is the core essence of Confucianism. As Hsun Tzu[32] said, 'man is born with *Yuh*'. That is, the nature of *Yuh* has endowed humans with the right to use their capacities of agency to pursue their choices. Yet it is not the ultimate value, which is harmony, in the Confucian sense. However, Confucius conceived that this goal is not attained easily, as he expressed in the *Analects*. The Master said, 'A gentleman seeks harmony, but not conformity. A vulgar man seeks conformity, but not harmony'.[33] In this way, a harmonious society can be achieved by accepting diversity from all the agents, which comes close to the Gewirthian idea that agents have individual purposes and goals of action, but still need to accept certain common values (rights). Further elaboration can be found in Mencius's discussion of human nature. Mencius suggests that the rulers should rule like sages, with commiseration, because all men have a mind that cannot bear to see the suffering of others, and this commiserating mind is *Jen*. 'My reason for saying that no man is devoid of a heart sensitive to the suffering of others is this. Suppose a man were, all of a sudden, to see a young child on the verge of falling into a well. He would certainly be moved by compassion, not because he wanted to get in the good graces of the parents, nor because he wishes to win praise of his fellow villagers of friends, nor yet because he disliked the cry of the child'.[34]

The core value in the Confucian *Analects* is 'what I do not wish men to do to me, I also wish not to do to them'.[35] The first occasion was recorded in the *Analects* 15:23. Confucius was asked by Tsze-Kung if there was one word which might serve as a rule of practice for all one's life. The Master said, 'Is not "reciprocity" such a word? What you do not want done to yourself, do not do to others'. Here, reciprocity is equivalent to consideration, and by consideration he meant to put oneself in the place of others. On another occasion, Chung-Kung asked Confucius about *Jen*. The Master said, '. . . not to do to others as you would not wish done to yourself'.[36] Mencius demonstrated what this principle would mean in everyday life: 'Treat with the reverence due to age the elders in your own family, so that the elders in the families of others shall be similarly treated; treat with the kindness due to youth the young in your own family, so that the young in the families of others shall be similarly treated'.[37] In the *Analects* 15:38, the Master said, 'There being instruction, there will be no distinction of classes'. Therefore, all agents' *Jen* and *Yuh* could be developed properly without considering any distinction of classes. Mencius emphasized that *Jen* is to love human beings and things. The 'no distinction of classes' implies the equal status of all beings and even extends to all things. There is no conflict here between Confucianism and the duties of Gewirthianism.

The agent and recipient equally possess the right of autonomy and reward, and the agent's desires and wishes ought to do no harm to his recipient *qua*

118 *Tang and Yen*

recipient. The desires and wishes should be in accordance with the rule of *Jen*. The same kind of argument appears in Gewirthian theory: 'Every agent must hold, from within his own prudential standpoint in purposive action, that he is entitled at least to non-interference with his freedom and well-being'.[38] Therefore, it is necessary to follow the rule of *Tian* as expounded by Confucius and apply it to the unforced chosen purpose. 'What I do not wish men to do to me, I also wish not to do to them'. Mencius further elucidated the principle of *Tian* as 'I wish to attain my purpose and I would also wish other people to reach their purposes'. Therefore, the agents who follow the rule of *Tian* can become superior people and by contrast, those who disobey the rules of *Tian* would be known as inferior humans. Tsze-Kung believed that he had to be constantly exercising the perfect virtue *Jen* and applied this principle as his life-rule. However, Confucius replied to him, 'You have not yet attained this'.[39] Thus, it is hard to attain the perfect condition; in fact, even Confucius did not dare to rank himself as a sage.[40] But it is possible for agents to become moral if an agent has followed the rule of *Tian* and constantly exercises the perfect virtue *Jen*.

Confucianists highlight the importance of establishing an individual's perfect virtue and then applying it to regulate their relations with other people. Although Confucius did not establish a logical argument to explain why all people are the same in status, nor explain completely why they should have respect for each other, through his authoritative teaching, a consistent structure of moral thought can be found. The law should be constructed along moral lines because, as Confucius discussed, the establishment of moral principles in everyday life is more important than setting laws to rule people.[41] Moreover, when constructing laws, human beings are the main factor that lawmakers need to consider; they and their moral right to live a free life are primary. Consequently, it is important that the establishment, development, modification, or abolishment of legal regulations should all depend upon the implications for human beings, and their relation to the overriding moral principle.

The lack of a well-constructed theory of Confucian thought has to do with the discursive and fragmentary shape of the *Analects*. We have illustrated the direction of Confucius's thoughts here. It can be seen that firstly, the mighty creator *Tian* creates human beings and endows them with *Yuh* as the characteristic of human beings. This implies that humans are purposive beings. They are free to pursue their aims. In addition, *Tian* endows humans with *Jen* (perfect virtue, benevolence, and love), meaning that the essence of human beings is the drive to pursue their purposes in accordance with moral rules. Both essences endowed by the creator, *Tian*, establish a basic equal status for all human beings. The purpose of action to be guided by *Jen* is similar to self-fulfillment as capacity-fulfillment in Gewirthian argument.[42] Self-fulfillment is defined by Gewirth in terms of 'carrying to fruition one's deepest desires or one's worthiest capacities'.[43] Now, self-fulfillment as capacity-fulfillment refers to the latter part of this definition, making the

Confucianism and Gewirthian Human Rights 119

best of oneself, which in turn involves acting in accordance with rational morality and being a 'Reasonable Self'.

All humans are equal and possess equal virtues in terms of *Jen* and *Yuh*. *Jen* is the rational element that can be used to justify and value a human's purposes (*Yuh*). In these terms, it can even be suggested that the essence of human beings, *Jen* and *Yuh*, is equivalent to an individual's dignity. Moreover, the agent cannot deny *Jen* and *Yuh* as they exist in all human beings. Human dignity is the essence of the human being and cannot be compromised. Following from the above theoretical principle, a reciprocal treatment has been established in practice. In order to be moral, however, it is necessary to follow the rule of *Tian*, as expounded by Confucius. Thus, those people who follow this principle can become superior people, and by contrast, those who disobey the rules of *Tian* would be known as inferior humans. It is possible for those superior people to become sages after constantly exercising the perfect virtue, *Jen*. In fact, as noted above, even Confucius did not dare to rank himself as a sage.

DIFFERENCES BETWEEN THE RULES OF *TIAN*, THE PGC, AND THE GOLDEN RULE

There are then similarities in terms of results between the work of Gewirth and those of writers in the past who have written in the tradition of natural law (e.g., between the notion of *Tian*, the PGC, and the Golden Rule (the principle of appetitive-reciprocal consistency)). The most important of these similarities is that an agent should treat his recipients according to the same rules that he would like them to apply to himself. It is now necessary to understand the differences between these theories.

As has been described above, the PGC was produced through Gewirth's dialectically necessary argument. Gewirth claims that every rational agent (PPA) voluntarily pursues his chosen purposes and makes evaluative judgements about the goodness of his purposes. Hence, because he wants to achieve his purposes, he must value the goodness of freedom and well-being, as these are the necessary conditions of all successful action. Every agent (PPA) implicitly claims that he has rights to possess the generic conditions for achieving his goals. Every agent, *qua* being a PPA, must claim that he possesses these rights because, and only because, they are necessary to his fulfilling his chosen purposes. Thus, given a principle of universalizability, he must accept that all other PPAs have equal rights to fulfill their purposes. The conclusion, therefore, of Gewirth's argument, is that all PPAs must accept the PGC if they are to be fully rational. If a PPA were to deny that he or she has the generic rights of freedom and well-being, then it will contradict their existence as PPAs.

The Golden Rule is the common moral denominator of all the world's major religions. In one of its most famous formulations it says, 'One should

120 *Tang and Yen*

not treat others in ways that one would *not* like to be treated'.[44] The rule can also be expressed in positive terms, as, for instance, in Matthew 7:12 of the New Testament,[45] 'Treat others as you want them to treat you. This is what the Law and the Prophets are all about'. The significant point here, though, is that the Golden Rule leaves it open to the agent to determine his actions in accord with his or her own principles. In other words, according to the Golden Rule, the content of the agent's wish or desire is indeterminate. Thus, for instance, it would be possible for a British agent to believe that it is right that the food of all other agents should be served with tomato sauce, because he wants his food to be served with tomato sauce. If this is the case, then it is very difficult to justify which claims to rights should be upheld and which claims to rights should be dismissed, because the basis of the Golden Rule is individual opinion. In the words of Gewirth: 'Different answers may yield extremely unpalatable results, as where a sadomasochist holds that he ought to inflict pain and suffering on other persons because he would want them to inflict pain and suffering on him'.[46]

Thus, the significant difference between the PGC and the Golden Rule is that the PGC focuses on what the agent must necessarily value as his generic rights on the basis of what goods are necessary in order to achieve his purposes. By contrast, the Golden Rule leaves the question of what the agent can and cannot legitimately claim to be his rightful purposes undetermined.

Confucius did not go as far as to establish an argument which explained why all people should possess the same status and hold each other in equal respect. Instead, he used his teaching to highlight the importance of *Jen* and to apply *Jen* in accordance with the rule of *Tian*. Although the rule of *Tian* seems similar to the Golden Rule, *Tian* endows the agent with *Yuh*, implying the agent's autonomy, where autonomy includes the autonomy of thought, will, and action. This ideal of autonomy upholds as of the highest importance the subjective action of individuals who are unforced and who can voluntarily value and aim for their own personal goals. Furthermore, one can interpret Confucius as believing that all human beings were fundamentally alike. If this is so, then the theory of *Tian* endows all agents with *Yuh* and *Yuann*. Thus, the similarity between the rule of *Tian* and the PGC seems greater than with the Golden Rule.

CONCLUSION

The concept of human rights is an abstract one. The premise is that human rights should have valid moral criteria or principles that can justify the assertion that all humans *qua* humans have rights and hence also correlative duties. Confucianism has had a profound influence on Chinese history. In fact, for more than two thousand years, the thoughts of Confucius have dominated in both the political and legal spheres of Chinese culture. Traditional Chinese culture has also been the dominant culture in Taiwan. Hence,

Confucianism and Gewirthian Human Rights   121

a human rights theory that is not only rationally justified but also at least consistent with Confucian thought would be well suited as a foundation for Taiwanese human rights legislation.

There are similarities in terms of content between the work of Gewirth and that of writers in the past who have written in the tradition of Confucian natural law. The most important of these similarities is that an agent should treat his counterparts according to the same rules that he would like them to apply to him.

From the Confucian point of view, the notions of *Yuh* indicate that purposiveness is a basic aspect of human nature. One could not take action without being motivated by the autonomy of thought. Likewise, the PGC implies that all rational agents can act purposively and that they should respect the rights of other agents to do so as well. Human rights are moral rights (in the simple descriptive sense that they are about what people ought to do), and the PGC provides a justification for them. It can also be argued that anyone who claims that they possess human rights must also accept the PGC or contradict their very status as agents altogether. The structure and rationales of Confucian thought provide a content that is equivalent to the PGC when it comes to defending human rights. The normative universality of the PGC can correspond to a practical universality, to the extent that the PGC can be universally accepted. The present argument has shown that the PGC is at least consistent with Confucian ethics, and there is hence no reason to assume that it could not be accepted in an East Asian context.

NOTES

1. A 2010–2011 survey demonstrated that 67.5 per cent of respondents self-identified as Minnans Han, 13.6 per cent as Hakkas Han, 7.1 per cent as Mainlander Han, and 1.8 per cent as aboriginals. The other 7.5 per cent of respondents self-identified as Taiwanese, and 1.9 per cent were unknown. This evidence demonstrates that people have intermixed, but also, importantly, that people identify with, and claim membership in, more than one group. Hakka Committee of Executive Administration Yuan, *Report on the National Population-Based Survey* 2010–2011 (Taipei: Hakka Committee of Executive Administration Yuan Press, 2011), p. 172.
2. The Chou dynasty was founded in 1111 BC and ended in 256 BC.
3. Confucius was born in the year 551 BC.
4. Some literature of this period mentioned the idea of people respecting God in order to have a prosperous and peaceful life. Furthermore, in *I Ching (The Book of Changes)*, the same kind of thought is found in connection with the teaching of poetry, history, religious rites, and music. Thus, at that time, Chinese people were already concerned with the spiritual aspects of human life. See S. Fang (ed), *I Ching (The Book of Changes)* (Taipei: Dai-Sing Publishing Co. Ltd, 1995).
5. *The Book of History in the Chou Dynasty*. This is a historical book describing an ancient government post in charge of secretarial duties. See X. Huang (ed), *The Book of History in the Chou Dynasty* (Hong Kong: Joint Publishing Co. Ltd, 1995).

122 Tang and Yen

6. This period started in 722 BC and ended in 481 BC.

7. This period started in 403 BC and ended in 221 BC.

8. Many different opinions about human thoughts were developed in that period. Thus, this period is known as the period of the 'hundred philosophers' (551 BC–233 BC). These philosophers include Confucius, Mo Tzu, Lao Tzu, Mencius, Chung Tzu, Hui Shih, Shang Yang, Kung-sun Lung, Hsun Tzu, Han Fei Tzu, and so on.

9. A. Gewirth, *Human Rights: Essays on Justification and Application* (Chicago: University of Chicago Press, 1982), p. 42.

10. A. D. Renteln, *International Human Rights: Universalism Versus Relativism* (Newbury Park: Sage Publications, 1990), p. 205; A. Clapham, *Human Rights: A Very Short Introduction* (New York: Oxford University Press, 2007), p. 5; and B. Orend, *Human Rights: Concept and Context* (Petersborough, ON: Broadview Press, 2002), p. 21.

11. A. Gewirth, *Reason and Morality* (Chicago: University of Chicago Press, 1978), p. ix.

12. J.J.C. Smart and Bernard Williams, *Utilitarianism: For and Against* (Cambridge University Press, 1973).

13. *Reason and Morality*, p. x.

14. In Western jurisprudence, most virtue ethics theories are derived from Aristotle, who declared that a virtuous person is someone who has ideal character traits.

15. Immanuel Kant, *The Moral Law. Kant's Groundwork of the Metaphysic of Morals*, A. W. Wood (ed and trans) (Yale University Press, 2002), p. 37.

16. *Reason and Morality*, p. 135.

17. Gewirth describes the dialectically necessary method as reflecting 'judgments all agents necessarily make on the basis of what is necessarily involved in action'. See ibid, p. 44.

18. Ibid., pp. 53–6.

19. *Confucian Analects* 13:20, One of Confucius' disciples, Tsze-Kung, inquired about the features of those people who were engaging in government in those days. Confucius replied to the inquiry in a morose way. 'Pooh! They are so many pecks and hampers, not worth being taken into account'. The reference of *Confucian Analects*, see J. Legge, *The Chinese Classics: With a Translation, Critical and Exegetical Notes, Prolegomena, and Copious Indexes*, Volume I: *Confucian Analects, the Great Learning, and the Doctrine of the Mean* (1861), revised second edition (1893) (Oxford: Clarendon Press, Reprinted by Taipei: SMC Publishing Inc, 1998).

20. The term *Jen* appeared in *Confucian Analects* more than forty times.

21. Fan Ch'e asked about benevolence. The Master said, 'It is to love all men'. He asked about knowledge. The Master said, 'It is to know all men'. See *Confucian Analects* 12: 22.

22. *The works of Mencius*. The reference to the works of Mencius, see J. Legge, Volume II: *The Works of Mencius* (1861), revised second edition (1895) (Oxford: Clarendon Press, reprinted by Taipei: SMC Publishing Inc, 1998).

23. The doctrines of the School of Hsun Tzu are a development of those of Confucius in the direction of naturalism and rationalism. According to Hsun Tzu, the essence of a human being is evil. See *The works of Hsun Tzu*, Chapter 23, Man's Nature is Evil, Hsün Tzu, *Hsün Tzu: Basic Writings*, B. Watson (trans) (New York: Columbia University Press, 1996).

24. According to Kao Tzu, the essence of a human being is flexible or natural. 'Man's nature is indifferent to good and evil, just as the water is indifferent to the east and west'. Under a good situation, humans will develop their kind nature;

Confucianism and Gewirthian Human Rights 123

under a poor situation, such as starvation, war, or flood, humans will develop their bad nature. See *The Works of Mencius*, Book 6, Part 1, Chapter 2.

25. *The Book of Documents*, Great Declaration I, 1.6, 'What the people desire, Heaven will be found to give effect to'. *The Book of Documents*, also known as *Classic of History* or *Shangshu*, is a collection of rhetorical prose attributed to figures of ancient China, and served as the foundation of Chinese political philosophy for over 2,000 years. See J. Legge, *The Chinese Classics: With a Translation, Critical and Exegetical Notes, Prolegomena, and Copious Indexes*, Volume III: *The Shoo King or the Book of Historical Documents* (London: Trubner. 1865; reprinted by Hong Kong: Hong Kong University Press, 1960).
26. *Confucian Analects* 5:11; 5:25; 6:28; 7:29; 12:2,10.
27. *Confucian Analects* 4:5.
28. R. Gillon, 'Autonomy and the Principle of Respect for Autonomy', *British Medical Journal*, 290 (1985), pp. 1806–8.
29. *Reason and Morality*, p. 22.
30. *Confucian Analects* 6:17.
31. *Confucian Analects* 4:5.
32. *The works of Hsun Tzu*, Chapter 19, Rites and Propriety.
33. *Confucian Analects* 13:23.
34. *The works of Mencius*, Book 2, Part 1, Chapter 6.
35. *Confucian Analects* 5:11.
36. *Confucian Analects* 12:2.
37. *The works of Mencius*, Book 1, Part 1, Chapter 7.
38. *Reason and Morality*, p. 73.
39. *Confucian Analects* 5:11.
40. *Confucian Analects* 7:33.
41. Confucius believed that '[i]f the people be led by laws, and uniformity sought to be given them by punishments, they will try to avoid the punishment, but have no sense of shame. If they be led by virtue, and uniformity sought to be given them by the rules of propriety, they will have the sense of shame, and moreover will become good'. *Confucian Analects* 2:3.
42. A. Gewirth, *Self-Fulfillment* (Chichester: Princeton University Press, 1998).
43. Ibid., p. 3.
44. For the definition of the Golden Rule, see A. Flew (ed), *A Dictionary of Philosophy* (London: Pan Books in association with The MacMillan Press, 1979), p. 134.
45. This version of the Bible has been produced by the British and Foreign Bible Society, 1997.
46. *Reason and Morality*, p. 169.

WORKS CITED

Clapham, A., *Human Rights: A Very Short Introduction* (New York: Oxford University Press, 2007).

Fang, S. (ed.), *I Ching* (*The Book of Changes*) (Taipei: Dai-Sing Publishing Co. Ltd, 1995).

Flew, A. (ed.), *A Dictionary of Philosophy* (London: Pan Books in association with The MacMillan Press, 1979).

Gewirth, A., *Reason and Morality* (Chicago: University of Chicago Press, 1978).

———, *Human Rights: Essays on Justification and Application* (Chicago: University of Chicago Press, 1982).

124   Tang and Yen

———, *Self-Fulfillment* (Chichester and Princeton: Princeton University Press, 1998).

Gillon, R., 'Autonomy and the Principle of Respect for Autonomy', *British Medical Journal*, 290:6484 (1985), pp. 1806–8.

Hakka Committee of Executive Administration Yuan, *Report on the National Population-Based Survey* 2010–2011 (Taipei: Hakka Committee of Executive Administration Yuan Press, 2011).

Hsün, Tzu, *Hsün Tzu: Basic Writings*, Translated by B. Watson (New York: Columbia University Press, 1996).

Huang, X. (ed.), *The Book of History in the Chou Dynasty* (Hong Kong: Joint Publishing Co. Ltd, 1995).

Kant, I., *The Moral Law. Kant's Groundwork of the Metaphysic of Morals*. Edited and Translated by A. W. Wood (New Haven and London: Yale University Press, 2002).

Legge, J., *The Chinese Classics: With a Translation, Critical and Exegetical Notes, Prolegomena, and Copious Indexes*, Volume I: *Confucian Analects, the Great Learning, and the Doctrine of the Mean* (1861), revised 2nd edition (1893) (Oxford: Clarendon Press; Reprinted by Taipei: SMC Publishing Inc, 1998).

———, *The Chinese Classics: With a Translation, Critical and Exegetical Notes, Prolegomena, and Copious Indexes*, Volume II: *The Works of Mencius* (1861), revised 2nd edition (1895) (Oxford: Clarendon Press; Reprinted by Taipei: SMC Publishing Inc, 1998).

———, *The Chinese Classics: With a Translation, Critical and Exegetical Notes, Prolegomena, and Copious Indexes*, Volume III: *The Shoo King or the Book of Historical Documents*. (London: Trubner, 1865; Reprinted by Hong Kong: Hong Kong University Press, 1960).

Orend, B., *Human Rights: Concept and Context* (Peterborough, Canada: Broadview Press, 2002), p. 21.

Renteln, A. D., *International Human Rights: Universalism Versus Relativism* (Newbury Park, CA: Sage Publications, 1990).

Smart, J. J. C. and Williams, B., *Utilitarianism: For and Against* (Cambridge: Cambridge University Press, 1973).

8 The Gewirthian Ideal of Self-Fulfillment
Enhancing the Moral Foundations of International Law

Robert A. Montaña

INTRODUCTION

The notion of international law—envisioned by Jeremy Bentham as the law of nations—is understood within the structures of public law and is concerned with the relationship between states or their components, which are considered as possessing independent and international statuses. Such a law ought to be treated as a distinct phenomenon because, unlike municipal laws and other such laws as considered by traditional philosophical systems, the legal framework of international law lacks an overarching authority capable of enforcing at all times its provisions with appropriate penalties. Born out of agreement in order to establish and maintain international peace and security, such a law would have to depend upon commonalities in economic, political, socio-cultural, and even humanitarian objectives by nations and states possessing various forms of agenda and interests. While the aspirations of the framers of the provisions of international law are ideal, its actual practice and applications are beset with conflicting elements.

Let us consider some examples. In November 2005, a Filipina was allegedly raped by Lance Corporal Daniel Smith, giving rise to a fierce custody battle between the Philippine courts and the American Embassy. Because the Visiting Forces Agreement between the United States and the Philippines was vague as regards the protocols governing erring servicemen, the US Embassy expressed its intent to retain custody of Smith until after the end of all judicial proceedings, including appeals. The Philippine Supreme Court, on the other hand, had already ordered the transfer of Smith to a Philippine facility. Without a clear timeframe, however, the defenders of Smith were able to secure an acquittal from the Philippine Court of Appeals, ending the impasse.

Another case happened in April 2012, in which another Filipina accused Erick Bairnals Shcks, a Panamanian diplomat, of rape. He was able to leave, however, after he was cleared by Justice Secretary Leila De Lima who cited immunity privileges granted by the 1961 Vienna Convention on Diplomatic Relations.

In another case, the Philippine Supreme Court junked the petition of environmental activists for a *Writ of Kalikasan* in relation to the grounding of

126 *Montaña*

the US Navy's USS Guardian in Tubbataha Reef on January 2013. Despite the environmental damage this negligence has caused, the Supreme Court ruled that the Principle of State Immunity—applicable both to the Philippines and to the United States—had established jurisdictional limits to its powers.

These instances expose a fundamental contradiction between the egalitarian-universalist formulations of international law and the actual application of private international law. The Philippine experience discloses flaws as protectionism overrides egalitarian protocols in a seemingly blurred global power structure. In the absence of a moral ground that can establish rational consistency, international law is likely to fall into its positivist interpretation, according to which such would be governed by mere agreements, conventions, and customs, including the need for enabling local laws for jurisdictional enforcements. This sorry scheme would lead to a form of governance that would stand in the quagmire of power-based politics.

To address such a scenario, this chapter presents the following two arguments: first, that international law, despite its noble intent to both establish harmony between states and protect personal liberties, is defective in the sense that governments, in implementing it, prioritize state interests and relations over individual rights; and second, that the Gewirthian paradigm on rights and self-fulfillment in accord with the Principle of Generic Consistency (PGC) would clear up hindrances in resolving real-life conflicts by establishing the conceptual link between international law and the mandatory requirements of reason to integrate respect for human agency.

THE PGC AND SELF-FULFILLMENT

The PGC can be considered as a calculated risk in moral foundational reasoning as it purports to establish a substantive and procedural link between action as the necessary content of morality and generic rights as applied rationally. The argument rises or falls on the consistency of its assumptions and conceptual links, and as experienced, it has received criticisms from various philosophical viewpoints while, at the same time, establishing its own group of defenders. In the academic world, however, such noise signifies the importance of the stakes that are raised, and once the fog clears up and the justifications are established, the PGC would be able to bridge the strongest conceptual foundation yet, not only for rights as a minimalist requirement, but also for self-fulfillment as a prudential ideal. With such a solid ground, the principle's implementation in local and international laws and policies could transcend any criticism of arbitrariness, and any conflict involved could easily be resolved by the proper realignment of priorities. In other words, it would be able to provide an understanding of self-fulfillment that could serve as a moral foundation for both public and private international law.

Alan Gewirth, in *Reason and Morality*, laid the groundwork of the PGC by positing that the necessary content of morality could be found in action and in its generic features of voluntariness and purposiveness under a normative structure whereby evaluative and deontic judgements are rationally affirmed through a dialectically necessary method. Such a process requires the satisfaction of two features that are generic or inherent in all actions, both pertaining to what is substantive and to what is procedural. Purposiveness or well-being refers to the substantive aspects of agency, including the agent's reason for acting and his capacity to effectuate this. Voluntariness or freedom, on the other hand, refers to the procedural aspects of agency expressing an informed and unforced choice of means and ends. As regards well-being, Gewirth differentiates three levels: *basic* when it involves the necessary preconditions of action, such as life or health; *additive* when the conditions surrounding the capacity for agency are qualitatively expanded, such as having access to education or achieving greater self-esteem; and *nonsubtractive* when such conditions remain undiminished, such as not being stolen from or defamed. It is through these distinctions by which right claims to well-being are determined. Holistically, freedom and well-being constitute the necessary conditions of successful action.

Gewirth further explains that since rational agents, even with a minimum of self-awareness, want success in achieving their goals, then they necessarily affirm that their freedom and well-being—as the necessary conditions of successful action—are necessary goods. With this, an agent cannot accept deprivation of freedom and well-being without contradicting himself, leading to the implication that he also must claim a mandatory right to these generic features of action. In other words, the agent's evaluative judgement that the conditions of his agency are necessary goods would lead him to a deontic affirmation—at least for himself at this point—that he necessarily has rights to freedom and well-being.

Such a move from the evaluative to the deontic has been questioned by a lot of philosophers. Yet, Gewirth has argued that denying any kind of right claim to freedom and well-being would lead to an affirmation that other people may interfere with these features, leading to the absurd scenario where the same agent who considered features that are necessarily good for him would also treat these as expendable at the same time.

It seems now, at this point, that Gewirth, in establishing this deontic rights-claim, was able to bridge the gap between the agent and other persons as regards the generic rights to freedom and well-being. Once justified, this rights-claim would always lead to a correlative duty that others ought not to interfere with his freedom and well-being. This affirmation also carries a further reflexive characteristic whereby the person, as an agent, must also accept the duty not to interfere with the other agent's correlative right claim to freedom and well-being. Such reflectivity is enshrined in the logical principle of universalizability (formulated as when a person has a right which is justified by a quality, then all those who possess such a quality must have

128 *Montaña*

such a right), and this has found its way not only into ethics, but also into law, as seen in the application of the principle of equity (where those who are similarly situated must be treated similarly). Thus, with the substantive role of action in moral determination, this logical process (which constitutes the Gewirthian Dialectically Necessary Method as applicable to all agents engaged in action) completes the philosophical foundational link between the individual agent and the universal recognition of the generic rights of freedom and well-being.

With such a foundational and a progressive rationalization from the notion of action and its generic features of freedom and well-being, the nature of private rights, status of states, recognition and the rights of states, and even the existence of the United Nations could be traced back to the necessary content of human morality.

International law, however, cannot simply content itself with protecting the minimalist requirements of agency insofar as its subjects possess aspirations and potentialities towards self-perfection; rather, the individual pursuit for self-fulfillment presents itself as a viable policy directive. This is in line with the Gewirthian argument that while reason could provide the basis for a mandatory respect for the necessary conditions of agency, other forms of moralities would lead to a fundamental justification for self-fulfillment.

In his preface to *Self-Fulfillment*, Gewirth noted that, while there had been philosophical discussions on corresponding topics on self-fulfillment, his analysis effectively differs from these due to a distinction between aspiration-fulfillment and capacity-fulfillment. Aspiration-fulfillment, which refers to a person's realization of his deepest desires, is moderated by reason as he attains capacity-fulfillment, or making the best of himself. When such a perspective is assimilated in international law, the global community would begin to treat its subjects in the light of self-fulfillment not merely as an ideal, but also as a prudential standard through which policy is implemented, setting aside the notion that individuals are mere objects or pawns in the international power play between states.

Historically, the discussion of self-fulfillment in its various forms is as old as the advent of wonder in man. As the ancient philosopher began to reflectively analyse his role in the known universe, the question as to how he could develop his faculties to the fullest had been in the forefront of his interests. The Gewirthian PGC, however, has brought the idea of self-fulfillment to include new perspectives: first, an applicative distinction between aspiration-fulfillment (one that is centred on personal desires) and capacity-fulfillment (one that is centred on the actualization of human potentialities) is made where the agent's exercise of his generic rights to freedom and well-being is effectuated maximally while being subject to constraints; second, aspiration-fulfillment is understood as going beyond the simple notion of desire whereby an intent to achieve or acquire a perceived good is integrally considered; and third, capacity-fulfillment is interpreted in the light of universalist, personalist, and particularist forms of morality whereby the parameters

Gewirthian Fulfilment and International Law 129

of aspirations are evaluated against an objective criterion. In addition to this, the PGC establishes reason as the basis for the justification of a universalist morality, through which particularist and personalist moralities are evaluated, prioritized, and reinforced.

As regards aspirations, Gewirth envisions them as the person's deepest higher-order desires that include a future successful possession of what he wants to achieve. This person further orders these desires in a way that characterizes his maturity and his secure sense of himself. Such a notion ventures close to the philosophical idea of the good life having, in addition, a desire and behavior autonomy that provides the person with the ability to control and shape his life-direction without external or unconscious hindrances. From this point of view, a fulfilled person could thus be equated with one having identified himself with his own autonomy. Hence, placed within the purview of international law, this consideration leads to the question as to whether a person ought to be treated as an object or as a subject of such a law. In the former case, individuals are seen in the light of their being members of their respective states, and thus could only act through its instrumentality. Being a subject, on the other hand, brings into the fore the recognition of individual rights, including the ability to be treated as a proper party for an international claim for damages in cases of right violations. This subject-object dichotomy as regards the treatment of individuals could thus be resolved towards respect for persons as subjects when autonomy—subject to rational limitations—is integrated as a directive into international law.

The Universal Declaration of Human Rights, recognizing the 'inherent dignity and the equal and inalienable rights of all members of the human family',[1] brings down the notion of rights to the level of the individual. This global declaration and acknowledgement of rights is very much in accord with the PGC insofar as they emanate directly from the recipients' generic rights of freedom and well-being, expressing the substantive and procedural requirements of his agency.[2] In other words, the appreciation of dignity and rights ought to be foundationally substantiated by the supreme principle of morality, or it would end up being arbitrarily provided simply as a matter of political, economic, or cultural conventions.[3] For instance, the political implications of policies following the Rawlsian 'difference principle'—where the maximization of resources for the least advantaged is mandated—is considered by Gewirth as leaving the poor in a 'condition of passive recipience as beneficiaries of the wider society's principles of justice, and without a sense of personal responsibility for helping themselves'.[4] With this, Gewirth is trying to relay the idea that when policies are philosophically founded on the PGC and the moralities based on reason, its parameters would go beyond the mere respect for and upliftment of the human condition; rather, these would include autonomy insofar as each agent remains 'a reasonable self, one who is considerate of the generic rights of other persons as well as of his own'.[5]

130 *Montaña*

IMPLICATIONS AND CONSEQUENCES OF NEGLECT

Setting aside the consideration of individual aspiration-fulfillment in the creation of national policies and decisions have resulted in states following pragmatic directives that, historically, have victimized peoples and subjected them to innumerable sufferings. Preventive and preemptive wars, for example, have led to displacements and subjugations of individuals in the absence of actual dangers, thereby treating citizens as pawns in the international chess game between and among states. Its application in the legal world was shown by J. Brunnee and S. Toope when they explained that for positivist international lawyers, 'legal norms can only exist when they are produced through fixed hierarchies, usually state hierarchies', and described that it 'is their formal pedigree that creates legal norms . . . therefore law exists regardless of its link to social norms'.[6] In this way, both political and legal interactive applications between and among states must be seen in the light of individual development avoiding, at the same time, the treatment of the subject citizen as a mere collateral damage of international relations.

There are numerous historical events that amounted to this kind of policy implementation. In 1939, Finland was invaded by Russia as a strategy to protect its own territory, particularly Leningrad, from an anticipated attack by German forces. In 1904, Japan militarily set foot in Korea as a result of its war against another country—Russia. In 1941, even without an actual and direct threat on Japan, it attacked Pearl Harbor as a kind of preventive war to secure oil supplies. The 2003 invasion of Iraq was preemptive, yet one of the primary reasons for engaging in it—the development by the Iraqi government of weapons of mass destruction—turned out to be nonexistent up until now. While states have their strategic interests to protect and international relations to conduct, more often than not, it is the individual citizen who bears the burden of their mistakes, especially after the implementing government leaders have either been deposed or replaced. There is then indeed a need to view the state not only as an entity that implements economic, political, and social policies, but also as a major player in the aspiration-fulfillment of its peoples.

While the fulfillment of aspirations of peoples as a basis for international and local policies may be ideal, its application in real scenarios needs a concurrent clarification in the conceptual relation between aspiration-fulfillment and the kind of universalist morality that generally governs international relations. Gewirth was aware of the various criticisms rallied against aspiration-fulfillment as the sole criterion for policy implementation because it may contradict universalist morality as in the case of tyrants, whose aspirations are for the subjection of peoples. Hence, aspirations cannot simply be considered as a generic criterion of what is good and right. To correct this, Gewirth introduced capacity-fulfillment in order to link self-fulfillment to the universalist morality of the PGC.

Gewirthian Fulfilment and International Law 131

Self-fulfillment as capacity-fulfillment in a person, in the manner envisioned by Gewirth, is basically about his making the best of what is in him to become—a kind of perfectionism whereby what is potential is maximally actualized. In its most effective form, such capacity-fulfillment would also be the object of aspirations. This distinction clarifies that, while the law would be generally unable to satisfy the conflicting aspirations of peoples, it should nonetheless integrate structural modifications to accommodate individual capacity-fulfillment. Such considerations would have long-range implications not only to the significance of international law, but also to its effectiveness.

In a 2000 study on the reproductive rights of refugees and internally displaced persons by F. Girard and W. Waldman, they averred that overall, 'international treaties and recent consensus documents provide a clear mandate for governments, UN agencies and NGOs to meet the reproductive rights of refugees and the internally displaced . . . [H]owever, the policies of UN agencies and NGOs do not always correspond to or fully promote international human rights standards'.[7] These and other similar scenarios show that even if the mandates are clear and comprehensive, actual programme creation and implementation end up being hampered by economic, political, and social policies. In this case, the capacities of these persons to make the best of themselves by raising their own families are not fulfilled due to such failures and inconsistencies on the ground.

In 2015, the United Nations High Commissioner for Refugees criticized the actions by the governments of some Southeast Asian countries for what the International Organization for Migration described as a 'maritime ping-pong' when the boats carrying Rohingya refugees who had fled Myanmar were merely given food and water and then towed away out of their respective jurisdictional waters. Even though starvation was prevented temporarily, pushing them back to the sea would be tantamount to what Fortify Rights considered as a 'death sentence'. While there are already international laws governing these situations, such as the 1951 Convention Relating to the Status of Refugees and the 1954 Convention Relating to the Status of Stateless Persons, the application of these are still dependent on government policies and programmes. Gewirth analogically dealt with this scenario when he gave a hypothetical example whereby Ames, who has a large amount of food, is confronted by Bates, a starving neighbor. Inquiring whether the PGC provides a sufficient ground to justify the necessity for Ames to give food to Bates, he explained that the 'principle prescribes, as a matter of strict duty, that agents refrain from inflicting basic harms on their recipients where such infliction violates the recipients' rights to basic well-being'.[8] In the case of the Rohingya refugees, even with the hypothetical scenario whereby they were given enough food and water to survive for a long time, depriving them of an environment where they can make the best of their capacities would be morally questionable,[9] even if the governments concerned were able to provide the minimum assistance they are required by law to perform.[10]

132   *Montaña*

SELF-FULFILLMENT AND UNIVERSALIST MORALITY

This brings us to the question as to how self-fulfillment—as aspiration- and capacity-fulfillment—relates to the kind of universalist morality that stands as the basis for most international law provisions. Gewirth answered this by explaining that agents, abiding by the minimal requirements of reason, recognize the mandate of the PGC, including the interpersonal moralities that justify the universal realization of aspirations and capacities.

International law, as understood within this foundational Gewirthian paradigm, would be able to serve as a guide in determining the prioritization of policies in cases of conflicts. In 2013, a private company in Canada initiated a 50-container plastic shipment to another private company in the Philippines. It turned out upon inspection that these containers contained solid household waste materials like used adult diapers and kitchen wastes. After two years of protests, with Canada being unable—through its local laws—to force its local importer to ship the wastes back, the Philippines had to contend with sending these materials to its own landfill. Although the Basel Convention on the Control of Transboundary Movements of Hazardous Wastes and their Disposal—signed by both countries—could technically govern the conducts of both governments, legal impediments by local laws obviously impeded the spirit of the convention. In 1999, the same thing happened when 120 container vans containing trash from Japan were also shipped to the Philippines. Way back, the Japanese government intervened and took their garbage; on the other hand, with the Canadian government, up until now when some of the wastes have already been processed, there is still no attempt for such an extra-legal intervention. These instances happen when local laws are not enacted in congruence with international law or when moralities are not integrated in the implementation of policies, whereby individuals end up being unable to fulfill their desire and capacity to live in an environment conducive to their freedom and well-being due to these shortcomings.

These actual, real-life scenarios, despite the existence of signed international documents, expose the paradoxical circumstances where governments arbitrarily choose the extent of their compliance to international law, rendering international provisions and agreements subject to discretions and perceptions. For a government to decide within the limitations of local laws and to distance itself from private transactions—even if such actions creates victims beyond these relations—ideates a form of positivist interpretation that inserts a strict wedge between the source and the merits of laws.[11]

INTERNATIONAL LAW AS REFLECTING THE COMMUNITY OF RIGHTS

Gewirthian philosophy, with its conception of a community of rights that serves as the basis for a healthy and decent society,[12] has created a foundational link between the self and the community despite their conflicting

Gewirthian Fulfilment and International Law 133

interests. This link refers to the adherence of an agent to the PGC as the principle of human rights whereby, as a reasonable self,[13] he recognizes his own right claims to his generic rights and similarly respects the correlative claims of others. This gives rise to a conception of the community as a guardian of these relations, leading to a form of compliance that is not based merely on nationalistic, ethnic, or racial factors. Seen in this light, the coercive power of the law becomes now the motivational component by which people are directed towards reasonableness and mutuality, establishing a democratic political order that protects this scheme both for the elected leaders and the electorate. Hence, as applied to the analogical circumstances given above, governments functioning as instrumentalities would identify the validity of the right claims of parties and decide not merely on the basis of their own protectionist policies but by an obligatory compliance to the demands of a universal respect for freedom and well-being. When this happens, the source of human law eventually could be traced back to reasonable selves, while its merit would comprise the justifications inherent in such correlative respects.

This chapter opines that the substantive requirements of justice could be better served if laws are implemented in line with the PGC. Although this may be ideal but not practical because laws have already been enacted, corrective measures in terms of amendments and, if necessary, provisions for extra-legal adaptations ought to be integrated. This is in accord with the Gewirthian argument that the gap between personal morality and the kind of morality which governs international relations must be bridged, especially in cases when the actions of governments affect the well-being of its recipients.[14] The case of Shcks, as mentioned above, may illustrate Gewirth's point. While the immunity of diplomats from the criminal jurisdiction of the receiving state as granted by the 1961 Vienna Convention on Diplomatic Relations may have been meant to protect them from the undue influences of coercive governments,[15] it is possible that such immunity, even with constraints, may end up obstructing justice by protecting actual criminals. The Philippine Senate, in fact, argued against the decision of the Department of Justice, stating that immunity is not absolute and that local laws, in certain situations, are superior to international law.

Governments, from the perspective of Gewirthian philosophy, must expand the horizons of their decisions by counter-validating legal justifications and implications with an overarching supreme principle that is grounded on the nature of action and its features. In the case of the USS Guardian mentioned above, the resulting environmental damage led to a petition before the Philippine Supreme Court[16] for a Writ of *Kalikasan*—a legal remedy to protect the constitutional right to a 'balanced and healthful ecology'.[17] Stating that the US officers were in the performance of their official military duties, including the fact that the United States is not a signatory to the United Nations Convention on the Law of the Sea, the Supreme Court ruled that the Principle of State Immunity has barred its acquisition of jurisdiction in the case. It, however, reminded the parties that there is an expectation that the US would act in accord with its international responsibility. True enough, being a longtime

134 *Montaña*

ally, the US dismantled the ship to prevent further damage and paid the Philippines 87 million dollars for the rehabilitation of the reefs.

This example raises the question as to whether the very notion of international law possesses the mandate to provide the proper milieu for self-fulfillment to thrive. Gewirth has dealt with this indirectly when he tackled the issue on the role of capacity-fulfillment in the promotion of the good life, especially as regards how a particularist morality could extend from the love of friends and families to a loyalty to broader groups, such as communities or even entire countries. Seen in this way, the loyalty enforced by the PGC stems from a relationship whereby the state maintains a holistic environment that equally and equitably protects the citizens' rights to freedom and well-being while the latter reciprocate through their allegiance. The benefits accruing from this structure, however, are limited by the physical geographical boundaries of countries. Such a limitation is then countered by international law as it attempts to create systems of relationships between states to extend this protection to a universal scale.[18] We can surmise that Gewirth intended to extend the loyalty and allegiance of individuals to the instrumentalities of international law inasmuch as it is protective of the agents' freedom and well-being as well as conducive to self-fulfillment.

ESTABLISHING THE MORAL LINK

The mutual benefits stemming from the web of relationships between individuals, states, and international instrumentalities lead us to the significance of enforcement in human rights protection and to the issue as to whether this includes self-fulfillment. It should be remembered that Gewirth has already established that the notion of self-fulfillment includes the best use of one's veridical capacity—reason. In this sense, reason is considered as instrumental to the full expansion of the self even if not every aspect of self-fulfillment is an object of rights.[19]

However, despite the position that persons cannot positively demand that others maximally fulfill their aspirations and capacities, they nonetheless can negatively demand that they not put obstacles in their way as they pursue self-fulfillment as long as they do not violate the rights of others.[20] Some may extend this interpretation to duties associated with the implementation of international law, leading to the idea that there is no obligation on the part of its agencies and instrumentalities to maximize human aspirations and capacities, except to minimally protect provisional rights.

This chapter argues otherwise, considering that international law would be supportive of systems that enhance individual self-fulfillment if such is understood and applied in the light of three moral elements in Gewirthian philosophy, namely, the idea that enforcement also includes in its function the coordination of efforts for the correlative respect for human rights, the communal application of the negative duty to avoid interference in the

Gewirthian Fulfilment and International Law 135

individual's pursuit of self-fulfillment, and the extension of reciprocal duties in the light of the world-citizen's loyalty to international law.

Traditional ideas on the enforcement of the law centred on correction or retribution against transgressors, thereby being instrumental to restoring balance in the applications of distributive justice. Gewirth, however, included the idea that for societies whose citizens are faithful in respecting each other's rights, there remains the need to coordinate the disparate efforts of individuals towards this end in order to ensure efficiency and effectiveness on a larger scale.[21] This conceptual contribution extends the role of law from a minimalist-corrective structure to a cooperative-developmental one. Self-fulfillment, in its aspirational and capacity-based aspects, could find fruition in a large-scale cooperative and developmental application of international law inasmuch as these are limited by the applications of reasonable allocations of resources and by the traditional enforcement of discipline and societal order.

Negative duties, inasmuch as these prevent actions or conditions that would otherwise cause some form of injury or damage, are correlatives of positive rights. While Gewirth, as mentioned above, has averred that self-fulfillment cannot be demanded, certain indirect justifications—such as the universalization of one's duty to fulfill oneself or of having the right to some form of assistance towards this end—could pave the way for such a right. In the international scene, however, where agencies and instrumentalities are immersed in the complexities of real-life political and economic situations, the demarcation line between the exercise of negative and positive rights eventually becomes blurred. In these cases, inaction may end up being considered as negligence, and the only way even to minimally protect rights is to actually engage in positive action not only to prevent further damage, but also to uplift the conditions of their subjects to a certain level. Once involved in such problems, only policies that not only minimally protect the effective use of freedom and well-being, but also those that establish structural modes of development could be considered as feasible ones. Hence, international law and policies, in order for them to be efficient and effective in the exercise of their mandates, must provide an attitude that considers fulfillment beyond negative rights subject to legal and economic limitations.

The world-citizen's adherence and loyalty to local and international laws creates a reciprocal structure whereby instrumentalities and agencies follow the universalization of the individual duty towards self-fulfillment. This is so since the main purpose of government is coordination and enforcement and, as such, goes beyond the duty to enact policies to prevent discordant behavior; rather, its main task is to establish a system where freedom and well-being could thrive for individuals despite being in a complex web of economic, political, and social relations.

The failure of the League of Nations to prevent World War II has highlighted the realization that mere agreements and conventions between states cannot automatically ensure peace, exacerbated by the whimsical

136 *Montaña*

withdrawals by members whenever their interests are hindered by communal obligations. Any form of political, social, and economic clout emanating from international law is sourced from the strength of commitment by member nations to adhere to a moral obligation for an ideal that goes beyond the notion of enforcement. The justificatory foundations laid out by Gewirthian philosophy—where respect for generic rights are sourced directly from the substantive nature of human action—accords a moral paradigm for international law that would not only provide a minimalist protection for rights, but also an extended obligation towards the self-fulfillment of individuals, realizing a kind of an international version of the Gewirthian community of rights.

NOTES

1. See the Preamble of the *Universal Declaration of Human Rights*.
2. Gewirth explains that the notion that '. . . every agent must hold that he has rights to the necessary conditions of agency, freedom and well-being—entails that action has a deontic as well as an evaluative structure. Through the deontic structure, action encompasses not only the agent's evaluative judgements about the necessary goodness of his having freedom and well-being but also deontic judgements he makes or accepts that he has rights to these generic features of action. I shall hence call them *generic rights*'. (See A. Gewirth, *Reason and Morality* (Chicago: The University of Chicago Press, 1978), p. 64).
3. This is true especially in cases of rebellion, where the demarcation line between insurgency and belligerency is blurred. In a 2001 study by N.G. Quimpo, he averred, 'Since the outbreak of the armed conflict in Mindanao 30 years ago, the people of Mindanao and the entire Filipino nation have yearned for a comprehensive and stable peace in the Southern Philippines and the country as a whole'. This paper referred to the peace agreement between the Philippine government and the Moro National Liberation Front in 1996. Up until now, a new peace accord is being finalized this time with the Moro Islamic Liberation Front, exposing a fundamental flaw in considering that political dissentions could be solved merely by conventions and agreements (see N.G. Quimpo, 'Options in the Pursuit of a Just, Comprehensive, and Stable Peace in the Southern Philippines', *Asian Survey*, 41:2 (2001), pp. 271–89, on p. 273).
4. Here, one could perceive how the PGC as a paradigm interprets policy in terms of a foundational understanding from individual action to state responsibility. Hence, contrary to other political treatises, the suggestions of Gewirthian philosophy is never arbitrary, but is always traced back to the logical implications of action and its features (see A. Gewirth, *The Community of Rights* (Chicago: The University of Chicago Press, 1996), p. 112).
5. This is Gewirth's conclusion as he relates universalist morality with capacity-fulfillment. In relation to personalist morality, he argued that 'if a person is to fulfill herself she must be able to make maximally effective use of her practical capacities of freedom and well-being'. In relation to particularist morality, he then concludes that 'self-fulfillment requires deep interpersonal preferential relations of love, friendship, and familial devotion, as well as various communal loyalties'. With all these modes, Gewirth reminds that such 'will make extensive use of reason as the best of human veridical capacities'. All of these requirements of self-fulfillment expose a progressive movement of

Gewirthian Fulfilment and International Law 137

responsibility from oneself to others, and eventually to one's community and state (see A. Gewirth, *Self-fulfillment* (Princeton: Princeton University Press, 1998), p. 61).

6. J. Brunnee and S. Toope, 'Constructivism and International Law', in J. Dunoff and M. Pollack (eds), *Interdisciplinary Perspectives on International Law and International Relations* (Cambridge: Cambridge University Press, 2013), p. 119.

7. F. Girard and W. Waldman, 'Ensuring the Reproductive Rights of Refugees and Internally Displaced Persons: Legal and Policy Issues', *International Family Planning Perspectives*, 26:4 (2000), pp. 167–73, on p. 172.

8. A. Gewirth, 'Starvation and Human Rights', in A. Gewirth, *Human Rights: Essays on Justification and Applications* (Chicago: The University of Chicago Press, 1982), pp. 197–217, on p. 203.

9. Gewirth explains thus: 'As a right of persons, self-fulfillment requires positive actions by respondents, not only refraining from action, so that the right is teleological as well as deontological' (see Gewirth, *Self-Fulfillment*, p. 216).

10. Cole explains this disparity between acknowledgement and practice: 'A state's legitimacy is increasingly pegged to its support of human rights principles; however, scholars from the world society approach routinely acknowledge that many states endorse human rights principles—for example, by ratifying human rights treaties—without putting those principles into practice'. This may be so because governments have other social, economic, and political factors to consider (see W. Cole, 'Human Rights as Myth and Ceremony? Reevaluating the Effectiveness of Human Rights Treaties, 1981–2007', *American Journal of Sociology*, 117:4 (2012), pp. 1131–71, on p. 1132).

11. Some positivist scholars point to the arbitrariness of morality as the reason why law cannot simply choose merit as its basis. H. L. A. Hart argued in this way: 'To use in the description of the interpretation of laws the suggested terminology of a fusion or inability to separate what is law and ought to be will serve (like earlier stories that judges only find, never make, law) only to conceal the facts, that here if anywhere we live among uncertainties between which we have to choose, and that the existing law imposes only limits on our choice and not the choice itself' (H. L. A. Hart, 'Positivism and the Separation of Law and Morals', *Harvard Law Review*, 71:4 (1958), pp. 593–629, on p. 629). With Gewirthian philosophy, however, this arbitrariness is eliminated by the direct link provided by the PGC to action and its features.

12. Discussing the notion of independence, Gewirth expresses, 'In these ways, in contrast to being passive dependents on the actions of others, persons are helped to become effective agents who, as reasonable selves, respect the rights of other persons as well as their own. They are also enabled thereby to live lives that attain ethical, spiritual, and other cultural values and virtues of additive well-being. The resulting community of rights is a much healthier and far more decent society . . .' (see Gewirth, *The Community of Rights*, p. 352).

13. Gewirth describes this concept: 'Such a self is aware of its own agency needs and rights, and it has a sense of personal responsibility for their fulfillment, but it also takes due account of the agency needs of other persons, respecting their rights as well as one's own and maintaining a certain equitableness or mutuality of consideration between oneself and others, as required by the universality of human rights'. While this may be ideal, such approximation comes close to this description if one's adherence to the PGC is strict (see Gewirth, *The Community of Rights*, p. 93).

14. Gewirth explains thus: 'Since states are not individual persons, there seems to be a gap between a principle of personal morality concerned with relations among individuals and the kind of morality which should govern international relations.

138 *Montaña*

This gap must be bridged if international morality is not to be left completely separated from a general rational moral principle and if the application of moral philosophy to complex social problems is to be given adequate rational guidance'. Here, he emphasizes the notion that international law, despite its acceptance by nations, needs a moral justificatory basis for it to remain stable in its applications (see Gewirth, 'Starvation and Human Rights', p. 206).

15. J. Hickey Jr and A. Fisch presents other reasons for such immunity: 'Proponents of the unilateral removal of immunity from criminal jurisdiction for foreign diplomatic personnel, conferred as a matter of right by international law, argue that there is no theoretical justification for that immunity. The argument rests on the erroneous assumption that the sole justification for diplomatic immunity is to assure that foreign diplomatic personnel function effectively in the receiving state . . . That argument errs for two reasons. First, immunity from receiving state criminal jurisdiction rests not on functional necessity alone, but on a number of theories, each of which is contravened by unilateral removal of criminal jurisdiction immunity. Second, unilateral removal of immunity from criminal jurisdiction does, in any event, inhibit the effective functioning of diplomatic personnel'. In cases of actual guilt, however, we can surmise that the state-to-state representational structure becomes a hindrance to substantive justice (see J. Hickey Jr. and A. Fisch, 'The Case to Preserve Criminal Jurisdiction Immunity Accorded Foreign Diplomatic and Consular Personnel in the United States', *Hastings Law Journal*, 41 (1990), pp. 351–82, on pp. 357–8).

16. See Arigo *et al.* v. Swift *et al.*, G.R. No. 206510 (September 16, 2014).

17. The provision is as follows: 'The State shall protect and advance the right of the people to a balanced and healthful ecology in accord with the rhythm and harmony of nature' (see Article II Section 16 of the 1987 Constitution of the Philippines).

18. Gewirth explains: 'The territorial circumscription of states and their laws is not, then, antithetical to their being justified by the universal principle that all persons' rights to freedom and basic well-being must be equally and impartially secured. That the minimal state secures rights only for persons living within its territory is a practical limitation deriving from the fact that the state's functions must operate in relation to persons who are physically present in a specific physical area. The development of international law, with its provisions for the protection of human rights, provides an important mitigation of this limitation'. The problem here seems to be that international law does not possess the same level of enforcement to its recipients compared to states in relation to their citizens (see Gewirth, *Self-Fulfillment*, pp. 153–4).

19. Gewirth explains: 'More generally, while self-fulfillment as capacity-fulfillment includes that the self has and respects human rights, these rights do not, in turn, extend to the whole of self-fulfillment' (see Gewirth, *Self-Fulfillment*, p. 216).

20. Despite this, Gewirth reminds that 'self-fulfillment is already more than an "ideal" in the sense of a mere hope as posited by the above objection. It is, rather, a direct requirement for the actions of persons toward other persons that they both refrain from hindering and that they provide needed assistance with regard to the proximate necessary preconditions of self-fulfillment'. (See Gewirth, *Self-Fulfillment*, pp. 215–17).

21. Here, we see Gewirth going beyond the traditional notion of enforcement. He explains that such enforcement 'need not take the form of coercive threats for noncompliance; it may instead operate as a coordinating device whereby the disparate efforts of individuals are brought into some sort of harmony' (see Gewirth, *Self-Fulfillment*, p. 196).

WORKS CITED

Arigo et al. v. Swift et al., G.R. No. 206510, September 16, 2014.

Brunnee, J. and Toope, S., 'Constructivism and International Law', in J. Dunoff and M. Pollack (eds.), *Interdisciplinary Perspectives on International Law and International Relations* (Cambridge: Cambridge University Press, 2013), pp. 119–45.

Cole, W., 'Human Rights as Myth and Ceremony? Reevaluating the Effectiveness of Human Rights Treaties, 1981–2007', *American Journal of Sociology*, 117:4 (2012), pp. 1131–71.

Gewirth, A., *Reason and Morality* (Chicago: The University of Chicago Press, 1978).

———, 'Starvation and Human Rights', in A. Gewirth (ed.), *Human Rights: Essays on Justification and Applications* (Chicago: The University of Chicago Press, 1982), pp. 197–217.

———, *The Community of Rights* (Chicago: The University of Chicago Press, 1996).

———, *Self-fulfillment* (Princeton: Princeton University Press, 1998).

Girard, F. and Waldman, W., 'Ensuring the Reproductive Rights of Refugees and Internally Displaced Persons: Legal and Policy Issues', *International Family Planning Perspectives*, 26:4 (2000), pp. 167–73.

Hart, H. L. A., 'Positivism and the Separation of Law and Morals', *Harvard Law Review*, 71:4 (1958), pp. 593–629.

Hickey, J., Jr. and Fisch, A., 'The Case to Preserve Criminal Jurisdiction Immunity Accorded Foreign Diplomatic and Consular Personnel in the United States', *Hastings Law Journal*, 41 (1990), pp. 351–82.

Quimpo, N. G., 'Options in the Pursuit of a Just, Comprehensive, and Stable Peace in the Southern Philippines', *Asian Survey*, 41:2 (2001), pp. 271–89.

The United Nations (1948), *Universal Declaration of Human Rights*.

9 Thomas Piketty and Alan Gewirth
Is a Global Community of Rights Possible in the Twenty-First Century?

Gregory J. Walters and Marie Constance Morley

INTRODUCTION

This chapter offers Gewirthian perspectives on the 2007–2008 global financial crisis. We look at the key agents, agencies, and aftermath of the crisis. We then give a brief exposition of Thomas Piketty's seminal work, *Capital in the Twenty-First Century*, and the fundamental force for divergence of wealth distribution, $r > g$, with particular attention to the prospects of a 'social state' in this century. Finally, we suggest that Alan Gewirth's philosophy is of vital importance in clarifying fundamental problems of inequality and the adverse impacts of the financial sector on human rights. Gewirthian theses concerning mutuality, justice, equality, social contribution, economic redistribution, economic democracy, and political democracy help illuminate the crisis of global capitalism and inequality. Is a global community of rights possible in the twenty-first century? Yes, but human mutuality and the categorical requirements of the Principle of Generic Consistency (PGC), as a principle of reasonableness, are more pressing today than ever in light of increasing global inequality.

Our main objective in this chapter is to suggest that there is untapped potential in Alan Gewirth's theory of human rights that holds current and future importance for political economy. We begin (I) with a brief description of the financial crisis of 2007–2008 that helps to specify important theoretical and structural problems in economics and finance. We then briefly describe (II) how Piketty understands the ratio of capital to income as a tool that could be used to avoid the negative economic events that increase inequality and violate human rights. We identify some of the institutional features of financial markets and social systems that complicate attempts to assign responsibility and produce, too often, ineffective policies that deny the promotion and protection of human rights. Such injustices are the result of interpretations of economic reality that slip into the realm of public policy making to replace the scarcity of normative moral and political philosophy in economics. Where gross inequality prevails, one observes a strong human tendency to blame and shame victims for their poverty or engage in systemic disregard for basic human rights. Gewirthian moral philosophy themes (III) related to social contribution, economic democracy, political democracy, and economic redistribution corroborate and enhance Piketty's macroeconomic measures and contemporary problems with neo-liberal economic theory.

I. THE GLOBAL FINANCIAL CRISIS: AGENTS, AGENCIES, AND AFTERMATH

The 2007–2008 financial crisis exposed limitations in economic theory as well as philosophical problems related to economic and political democracy, especially the problem of inequality. The Great Recession heightened popular awareness of economic uncertainty and fragility. Bankruptcies and market crashes, alongside skyrocketing numbers of US home foreclosures, repeatedly made headlines over a two-year period. Low interest rates, excessive risk taking, cutbacks in corporate capital spending and share buybacks, cheap global credit, and the boom-bust global housing cycle were major roots of the crisis.

As events unfolded, the crash took on the air of an apocalyptic drama, while the American government surrendered to pleas by the banking 'titans'[1] for bailouts to save the global financial system. The crisis arguably began on August 9, 2007, when BNP Paribas, France's largest bank, froze three giant funds that held subprime loans. In mid-September 2007, Northern Rock Bank's failure to sell its securitized mortgages caused a liquidity crisis that led to bank runs. Over the weekend of September 13–14, 2008, inter-business decisions were made, with Bank of America buying up Merrill Lynch and Lehman Brothers filing for bankruptcy. On September 15, 2008, with the public announcement that Lehman Brothers Bank was bankrupt came the 'Monday Meltdown'[2] and the wave of investors' panic.

In Britain, on September 18, 2008, Lloyds of London announced it was taking over the Bank of Scotland, which had carried out a £30 billion merger with the bank in 2001, for a mere £12 billion. The same day, the UK government announced a loss of 32,500 jobs in the previous month, which was the highest loss in 16 years. Economists' January 2008 announcement of tumbling home sales was followed by the March 14, 2008 takeover of Bear Stearns by JP Morgan for '$2-a-share'.[3] Economic instability worsened. By December 2008, the US feds had reduced interest rates close to zero in the hopes of easing the liquidity crisis. Lowered interest rates in Europe followed suit, which provided banks access to the central banks' 'lending of last resort'.[4] In January 2009, Iceland suffered violent protests, with thousands of people marching in the streets with pots and pans to remind their government of the need for workers to have jobs and food. The country had been hard hit by banking fraudsters who deepened the economic harm. The government coalition collapsed. PM Geir Haarde was forced to resign.

142 *Walters and Morley*

Meanwhile on Wall Street, in January 2009, the news media reported that $18.9 billion in bonuses were paid to bankers, brokers, and CEOs in the previous year while their companies lost billions. The titans now took home less money than in 2006, when they got 'bonuses of nearly $36 billion'.[5] On March 27, 2009, the banking titans met with President Obama, who wanted to discuss the crisis and convince them to reduce their pay bonuses. The bankers reassured the president that they would pay back the loans, while incentive compensation was putatively necessary to make certain they could retain employees. In 2012, the United States Department of the Treasury estimated that '$19.2 trillion of household wealth' had been lost.[6] Others estimate there were losses of '$7.4 trillion in stocks and $650 billion of US GDP'.[7] Millions of people suffered poverty and homelessness along with unemployment and workers' lost wages.

There were many factors that contributed to the crisis. Lack of transparency seems to win first place. Subprime mortgage lenders used lax standards. KPMG, Moody, and S&P moved from the business of rating bonds into rating securitized products too complex for average investors to understand. Asset managers often held inaccurate or incomplete information about the quality of underlying assets owned, and a 'flawed risk assessment model'.[8] When the dust settled on the financial crisis, Merrill Lynch had been acquired by Bank of America. Bear Stearns was bought at dollar store prices by JP Morgan Chase. Lehman Brothers was bankrupt. The investment banks Goldman Sachs and Morgan Stanley were converted into bank holding companies. The knock-on effects continue today with legal impunity, especially for Goldman Sachs, who sold toxic mortgages—'crap' and 'junk'—to investors, while at the same time 'making multi-billion-dollar bets for its own firm that the deals would fail'.[9]

II. THOMAS PIKETTY: ECONOMIC DISTRIBUTION, GLOBAL INEQUALITY, AND THE SOCIAL STATE

If Thomas Piketty is correct, then the crisis is no mere accident, nor a result of temporary greed, or even lax regulatory standards. There remains a dangerous disjunction in the flow of wealth between the financial sector and the real economy today. The almost exclusive focus on market stability betrays the role of financialization and deregulation that started in the 1970s with the trickle-down economic policy. Deregulation accelerated under the Ayn Randian watch of Federal Reserve Chair Alan Greenspan, US Secretary Treasurer Robert Rubin, and Larry Summers. Deregulation brought far greater power to the financial sector leading, *inter alia*, to a greater divergence in income and wealth. It is no small merit that Thomas Piketty places the question concerning the distribution of income and wealth back at the heart of economic theory. He helps us better understand the recent financialization process across a number of Western economies and its contribution to terrifying global inequality.

His thesis is straightforward. 'When the rate of return on capital exceeds the rate of growth of output and income . . . capitalism automatically generates arbitrary and unsustainable inequalities that radically undermine the meritocratic values on which democratic societies are based'.[10] He expresses the fundamental force for the *divergence* of wealth distribution as $r > g$, where R signifies the average annual rate of return on capital. The sources of return include profits, dividends, capital gains, interest, rents, royalties, and other income expressed as a percentage of the total value. G stands for the rate of growth of the economy, i.e., the annual increase in income or productivity output. Income is expressed as the sum of income from labour and income from capital. When the return on capital stays above the broader economy's growth rate over time, divergence in the distribution of wealth is almost assured. Wealth accumulated in the past always grows faster than productivity output and labour wages and has little to do with market 'imperfection' or entrepreneurial spirit, and even less with 'common utility'. Because he anticipates a global 4–5 per cent average return on capital, and a growth rate that will not exceed 1–1.5 per cent no matter what global economic policies are adopted, the central structural contradiction of capitalism $(r > g)$ will remain intact. His hope for checking the unlimited growth of global inequality of wealth is a progressive annual tax on capital,[11] which will require serious transformations of global institutions, international cooperation, regional political integration, economic transparency, and democratic control of capital.

Income inequality is expressed in the twofold sense of inequality of income from labor or worker wages and inequality of income from capital. The more unequal the distribution is of both labor income and capital income, the greater becomes the total inequality. Ever since the transformation of feudalism into capitalism, economies have certainly *not* been marked by a regular tendency toward natural equilibrium, as envisioned by classical political economists. Economic history shows powerful forces pushing toward convergence and divergence at different periods and under constantly shifting social, political, and technological factors. In fact, the more perfect the capital market is, the more likely it is that r will be greater than g, which has nothing to do with 'market imperfection'[12] per se, and everything to do with public institutions and taxation and financial policies. Piketty looks at wealth data from the 1800s up to the present day in Britain, France, Germany, and the United States. Inegalitarian spirals of wealth accumulation accelerated from 1880 to 1913, but decelerated from World War I until the early 1970s, when the acceleration of the concentration of capital in the wealthiest ten per cent of the population took off. He acknowledges the existence of an uneasy consensus during the past one hundred years concerning abstract principles of social justice, especially social rights. 'Democratic debate' and even 'political confrontation' must be used to generate practical outcomes to support 'income replacement' and provide for people's social welfare needs or old-age pensions. He invites the reader

144 *Walters and Morley*

to consider philosophical and ethical considerations for a much-needed broader context of understanding to improve economic science.

Piketty asks three guiding questions about the possibility of a 'social state' for this century: First, 'Can we imagine political institutions that might regulate today's global patrimonial capitalism justly as well as efficiently?' Second, 'What is the role of government in the production and distribution of wealth in the twenty-first century?' Third, 'What kind of "social state" is most suitable for the age?'[13]

In response to the first question, he responds with a qualified 'yes'. The primary means will be by way of a global tax on capital that would expose wealth to mechanisms of transparency and accountability. A global tax is even more suitable than the progressive income tax structure that worked after World War II, but the two taxation forms are not mutually exclusive. Economic democracy is also imperative if we are to have effective regulation of international banking systems and international capital flows that avoid currency war trading, with its devastating impact on state economies. Between 1920 and 1980, the share of national income in wealthy countries went to increased spending for 'the social state'. Between 1980 and 2010, taxation stabilized in wealthy countries,[14] but at lower rates. Economic democracy will here need to move much closer to post-World War II social welfare state rates. In the Eurozone, North America, and elsewhere, a tax on corporate profits is imperative to stop companies from artificially assigning their profits to places where taxes are very low on the putative justification of their share of 'marginal utility' to the overall economy.[15]

In response to the second question, he notes that the role of government is greater than ever before, despite extreme calls on the political right for anarchic state abolition, US Federal Reserve abolition, return to a gold standard, or the vitriolic clashes between 'lazy Greeks' and 'Nazi Germans' in light of the recent European financial regulation imposed by the 'Troika' of the European Commission, European Central Bank, and the International Monetary Fund.[16] The fact is that economists of all stripes—whether Monetarists, Keynesians, or Neoclassicists—agree that central banks must be lenders of last resort in order to avoid financial crises and deflationary spirals. The problem is that the Euro came into existence in 2002 without a state. The weakness of central banks everywhere is their ability to decide *who* should receive loans, in what amount, and for what duration. This weakness points to the need for subjecting political and economic controls to moral requirements as regards their sources, limits, and ends or purposes. This is also in line with Gewirth's argument for the community of rights, to be presented below.

Piketty's response to the third question brings us to the heart of the matter in relation to Gewirth's conceptions of economic and political democracy: the importance of economic redistribution and the *logic of rights*. Modern redistribution, Piketty sums up, does not consist of transferring income from the rich to the poor, at least not in so explicit a way. It consists rather of financing public services and replacement incomes that are more or less equal for everyone, especially in the areas of health, education, and pensions. In the latter case, the principle of equality often takes the form of a quasi-proportionality between replacement income and lifetime earnings.[17]

What, then, are the key reform challenges for the twenty-first-century social state? Assuming that total taxes remain roughly the same and public spending stays at 50 per cent of national incomes in Germany, France, Italy, Britain, and Sweden, what programmes will be given priority? Will it be hospitals and adjustments to physician fees and drug costs? Reform of K-12 or higher education? Adjustment of social insurance pension and unemployment benefits? Public debate is essential because the adaptation of social services to public needs is imperative given aging populations and youth unemployment rates. Piketty focuses on higher education and Pay As You Go public pensions systems unfolding in a low-growth environment. Regardless of social origin or the genetic lottery, everyone ought to have equal access to education. But is it in fact the case that university education fosters social mobility? This is an empirical question. His data suggest that there is no intergenerational correlation of education and earned incomes. 'Parents' income', in fact, 'has become an almost perfect predictor of university access'.[18] Thus, meritocratic discourses on education and reality have parted ways. Academics will find happy confirmation from him about the total absence of transparency in university admission procedures. With respect to the future of retirement, baby boomers who contributed up to 1980 are being repaid because growth rates were c.5 per cent, but our global economic situation has changed. Here again, Piketty projects R at 4–5 per cent and G at 1.5 per cent. We underestimate the problem of resources if we think we can move from the PAYGO system to a capitalized system. One of the most important reforms of the social state will be 'to establish a unified retirement scheme based on individual accounts with equal rights for everyone, no matter how complex one's career path'.[19]

What about the social state in the poor and least-developed countries? Because governments take in only 10–15 per cent of national income in Sub-Saharan Africa, South Asia, and India, and 15–20 per cent in Latin America, North Africa, and China, it will be difficult for developing states to do much more than fulfill 'regalian' responsibilities of policing or judicial systems. He expects a vicious circle: poorly functioning public services undermine confidence in the government, which makes it more difficult to raise taxes. Rich countries and international organizations are partly to blame to the extent that, after 1980, developing countries were forced to cut public sectors, leading to a decrease in customs duties via trade liberalization. Nothing could be less certain than the idea of developing countries following the path of the social state in rich countries in the last century.

In contrast to Marx, Piketty is wary of *economic determinism* with respect to inequalities of wealth and income. Economic reductionism is as wrong as is the reduction of inequalities to social or political actors. Economic, social,

146 *Walters and Morley*

military, cultural, and political factors are all relevant aspects of power in the history of inequality. The dynamics of wealth distribution reveal de facto and de jure power that have and do push alternatively toward convergence and divergence, but 'there is no natural, spontaneous process to prevent destabilizing, inegalitarian forces from prevailing permanently'.[20] There is no smoking economic gun, no invisible hand at play. Power is at play, and vested interests in holding on to wealth. The diffusion of knowledge and investment in training and skills are key to inequality reduction both within and between countries. Nevertheless, what he calls the 'rising human capital hypothesis'—that is, that 'production technologies tend over time to require greater skills on the part of workers, that labor's share of income will rise as capital's share falls'—is an optimistic belief.[21] A putative path from technological rationality to economic rationality that will give way, in turn, to democratic rationality, is a suspect belief. Also optimist is the belief that 'class warfare' will automatically give way to 'generational warfare'. While the key force favoring greater equality is the diffusion of knowledge and skills, this force depends largely on educational policies, training, skill acquisition, and the associated institutions.

Acemoglu and Robinson acknowledge how his research, along with that of Emmanuel Saez and Tony Atkinson, has fruitfully used tax return data to reveal striking trends in the income and wealth inequality of the top 1 per cent and top 0.1 per cent of US taxpayers. In his analysis of the reduction of inequality in France, 1910–2010, and the shift from a 'society of rentiers' to a 'society of managers,' Piketty actually notes that the use of income tax returns is *a limited fiscal source* due to de facto tax evasion and exemptions that vary in France and other countries.[22] The authors' research utilizes the economic and political histories of South Africa and Sweden to argue that Piketty's quest for general laws is misguided. By focusing on the share of top incomes, Piketty misses the key determinants of inequality taking place at the middle and bottom of the income distribution. More important, Piketty leaves out the role of evolving societal institutions and politics.[23] Their emphasis on the role of *de facto* and *de jure power* in political and economic institutions bears directly on Gewirth's understanding of the rights to economic and political democracy,[24] and their critique provides a logical segue to Gewirth's political philosophy.

ALAN GEWIRTH: THE COMMUNITY OF RIGHTS, GLOBAL INEQUALITY, AND REASONABLENESS

The central concern of political philosophy, which, properly understood, is a branch of moral philosophy, is the moral evaluation of political power found in laws and government, but it also is concerned with human motivations and character, as well as external acts of power. There can be no separation of politics and morality because political philosophy deals with criteria for bringing political controls under moral control, including the 'source, locus, limits, and ends'[25] of political and economic power. Piketty's critics remind us that no general laws of capitalism can be used to answer the problematic that exists at the root of economic theory. Political and economic institutions are owned and operated by individuals whose agency must be reasonable. There is often a conflict between reasonableness, the PGC, and means-ends rationality, a cost-benefit type reasoning that does not give rightful priority to 'basic needs', or 'when the ends that are made most pressing are not the equal rights of all persons affected'. Instead, the ends are the agent's own self-interest or a particularistic interest of a group or institution, like Goldman Sachs's toxic debt for example, in opposition to the rest of society. The categoricalness of the PGC justifies its necessary truth over 'egoistic and particularistic rationality'.[26]

Gewirth laid the foundations of his theory of human rights by means of a systematic analysis of the rational basis of morality in *Reason and Morality* (1978). Because historical and evolving definitions and objects of rights and their logical extension to normative public policy applications left the problem of epistemic *justification* unresolved, Gewirth's argument for the PGC remains unparalleled. His theory of human rights appropriates a dialectically necessary method leading to a moral principle, a principle of reasonableness, that he calls the Principle of Generic Consistency: '*Act in accord with the generic rights of your recipients as well as of yourself*'.[27] Because in this principle, requiring respect for the freedom and well-being of others is a necessary truth, persons who violate it cease to be rational in terms of the pain of self-contradiction. However, his practical policy proposals are based on more than the PGC alone. In *The Community of Rights* (1996), he extended his fundamental principle of equal and universal human rights to the arena of social and political philosophy, exploring its implications for both social and economic rights. He argues that the ethical requirements logically imposed on individual action hold equally for the supportive state as a community of rights, whose chief function is to maintain and promote the universal human rights to freedom and well-being. Social afflictions such as unemployment, homelessness, and poverty are basic violations of the rights that the supportive state is required to overcome. His work presents a critical alternative to both liberal and communitarian views, and his refutation of the 'adversarial conception' of the relation between community and rights remains compelling.

Gewirth makes it clear that *The Community of Rights* is an effort to close the gap on inequality by tracing the whole of the human being's *economic biography*. He achieves this remarkable task by means of moving from the deprivation focus and the problems of welfare and the right to productive agency and education, including the development of the virtues and capacities and characteristics that lead to caring, social solidarity, and mutuality,[28] to rights to private property, employment, economic democracy, and political democracy. Gewirth seeks the reduction of economic inequalities, but

148   *Walters and Morley*

in numerous dynamic, and not static, ways. As such, the work is a probing diagnosis of the economic state of affairs at the end of twentieth-century America. If the sceptic judges that the community of rights envisioned by Gewirth has foundered in the US and elsewhere, given the reality of the neoliberal 'Market Fundamentalist Model'[29] in place since the 1970s, the idea deserves reconsideration in light of the deprivations and grotesque inequality.

As noted above, Piketty invokes Article I of the *Declaration of the Rights of Man and the Citizen* (1789), that all 'men are born free and remain free and equal in rights', followed by the proposition that 'social distinction can be based only on common utility'.[30] Yet, how does one define 'common utility'? Do moral or human rights actually exist? If so, how far do rights extend, e.g., to a free contractual market relation only, or to education, healthcare, and a pension? Or even to rights to culture, housing, and travel? Persons hold clearly widely divergent views about what constitutes common utility, the common good, the nature of the human being, and what constitutes a reasonable self in relation to a historical and particular community. There is perhaps even more suspicion today about human rights and rights inflation than there was two decades ago. By grounding moral and human rights in the necessary conditions of successful agency, Gewirth manages to give to rights a firm structure that goes a long way to escaping the problems of vagueness, relativity, and inflation that persistently dog rights-claims.

When it comes to inequalities of wealth and power and the resentment and discord that inequality brings, Gewirthian theses concerning social contribution, economic, and political democracy and redistribution are apropos. The PGC's society is a genuine community of rights because it provides mutual assistance to those who are unable to secure basic rights and protect and promote the freedom and well-being of all its members. A genuine community also entails psychological harmony. Members are generally aware of whether or not economic arrangements are just or not. Is there an '"inverse ratio of labor and reward"'[31] today, given the debate over increasing the minimum wage in numerous countries? If persons are indeed nurtured and socialized by their society in some significant ways, and society contributes to effectuating the human rights of its members, then the members of a given society also must recognize and accept obligations to their own communities and society. The nurture we receive from society is a necessary condition of our being successful purposive agents. The titans of the banking industry surely owe more to their community than their hyper-wealth goals have suggested. After all, even money itself is not so much a commodity as it is a 'social relationship of credit and debt'.[32]

The community of rights consists of differing levels or layers. The minimal state protects negative rights to freedom and well-being by criminalizing and punishing acts of killing, enslaving, injuring, and stealing. The democratic state protects positive rights to freedom by guaranteeing every citizen various participatory rights and civil liberties. The supportive state protects positive rights to well-being, providing education, healthcare, and opportunities for earning an income. Civil liberties must be truly effective powers that have 'social, teleological, and tendentious'[33] features related to speaking, publishing, and assembling, and, as such, require vast economic resources for effective political *actions*. The ability of the few super-rich to dominate US politics is surely 'a crisis for a nation that seeks to conduct truly fair elections in which all citizens have an equal opportunity to participate'.[34]

In the community of rights, there is also an institutional embodiment of economic democracy, building on a system of co-determination, producer cooperatives, and 'market socialism'[35] combining the competitive market with social safety networks. This is a very different model from the one in which AIG, the American International Group, could allow itself to receive more than \$170 billion in taxpayer bailout money from the US Treasury and Federal Reserve in 2009. AIG also paid out c. '\$165 million in bonuses to executives', in addition to an earlier '\$121 million paid out to 6,400 employees'.[36] AIG justified the bonuses on the basis of a legal claim right. The bonuses were contractual and legal, and thus could not be cancelled. AIG also appealed to retention pay as justification. For a company that arguably caused one of the biggest financial crises in US history, the arguments appear weak. The irony is that nearly 80 per cent of AIG is now, by necessity, owned by the US government.

With respect to economic redistribution, Piketty places the distributional question concerning income and wealth at the heart of economic theory, and Gewirth places the distributive question at the heart of moral philosophy. Whose interests, other than one's own, should be considered in economic actions?[37] To which persons should goods accruing from such considerations be distributed in personal and institutional actions? Modern redistribution for Piketty doesn't seem to consist of the redirection of income from the rich to the poor directly, but rather by the financing of public services and replacement incomes that are more or less equal for everyone. The mutuality entailed by the PGC certainly entails that the rich, the top 1 per cent or even 0.1 per cent, contribute to the development of the poor, who, in turn, with the development of productive agency, will make contributions to the well-being of others through their work and support a mutualist community. How might redistribution be done? The means include progressive taxation, lump-sum payments in money, or in-kind, progressive taxation, and means-tested benefits. What is important is the mutualist provision for those who are most in need of help in accordance with his 'deprivation focus'.[38] We must distinguish taxes on income, capital, and consumption. Taxes are progressive when the rate is higher for some rather than others because a person earns, owns, or consumes more. Progressive taxation is politically under serious threat today, as Piketty notes, 'because tax competition is allowing entire categories of income to gain exemption from the common rules'.[39] It is scandalous that the wealth of the world has become divided by two, with almost half of global wealth going to the richest 1 per cent, and in the US, since 2009, 'the wealthiest one percent captured 95 percent of post-financial crisis growth . . . while the bottom 90 percent became poorer'.[40]

Gewirth's logic of rights, the PGC, and understanding and application of the generic rights to freedom and well-being are virtually absent from mainstream economic theory. His philosophy is urgently needed as a counterweight to economic models that are used to manage capital and financial markets. Recognition of the generic rights to freedom and well-being, as the very conditions of successful productive agency, would benefit humanity in any substantive philosophical analysis of the systemic structure of financial markets, swaps, and other derivatives products. His notion of professional ethics and the 'separatist thesis' is also useful for critically reflecting on the institutions that run and regulate global finance and capital markets. Professionals monitoring the international finance system use models that often lack a human rights theory. Gewirth's philosophical theory may ultimately be used in the future to develop and support the use of democratically beneficial monetary policies. This includes, for instance, the application of the criterion of 'degrees of needfulness for action' by which rational thought must *assess* the conflict of rights that arise over claims concerning investment goals within the broader economy, or how poor or how rich individuals ought to be. Human dignity pertains equally to all persons by virtue of their being actual or prospective purposive agents and despite varying capacities. All persons have a right, whatever other rights they may have, to 'a fundamental equality of positive consideration for their dignity'.[41]

CONCLUSION

Violations of the generic rights to freedom and well-being, to both the procedural and substantive conditions of action, occurred during the crisis of 2007–2008. Millions of global investors, as purposive economic agents, had their freedom interfered with by lenders, traders, and large financial institutions selling products that they knew were doomed to fail; as such, investors' nonsubtractive and additive well-being were harmed by being misled, lied to, or restricted in their opportunities for acquiring wealth and income. The massive fraud and unprosecuted criminal activity committed during the 2007–2008 period continues.[42]

Piketty's work refutes the neoliberal market fundamentalist policy model that contradicts the PGC and has led to violations of freedom and well-being. Given the global financial crisis of 2007–2008, and the growing global inequality, it is difficult to deny that Piketty's analysis of the ratio of capital to income from 1980 to the present day is important proof of the need for policy and regulatory measures to urgently improve the channelling of wealth from the vast financial markets in derivatives and other financial instruments to the real economy, but it is unlikely that regulation alone will make a difference. Economic decision-making needs to be informed by the human rights of freedom and well-being. It is important in this context to note that well-being includes more than life, food, clothing, and other necessities, but also entails a physically healthy environment. If we destroy the planet, we destroy any condition of possibility for a global community that respects human dignity and human rights. Is a global community of rights possible? Without the reasonableness embodied in the PGC and duly appropriated by reasonable politicians, banking titans, and the wealthiest families with enormous economic power, the future not only of capital inequality divergence, but also of the human global family, is uncertain. We have choices of purposive agency that provide possibilities for greater global social and economic development, interpersonal trust, intergroup cohesion, and mutuality. The 'democratic deficit'[43] in global political and economic institutions must move beyond values of profits and GDP alone. The global institutionalization of mutuality and, indeed, love, understood as the heartfelt concern for the freedom and well-being of all human beings, may well come to pass first and foremost by the ongoing growing pain of human self-contradiction within the global financial sector and the broader economy.

NOTES

1. The titans included Jamie Dimon, CEO of JP Morgan Chase, Lloyd Blank-fein, CEO of Goldman Sachs, Robert Willumstad, CEO of American International Group (AIG), John Thain, CEO of Merrill Lynch, Richard Fuld, CEO of Lehman Brothers, Vikram Pandit, CEO of Citigroup, Robert Diamond, CEO of Barclays Capital, Larry Fink, CEO of BlackRock, Stephen Schwarzmann, CEO of Blackstone Group, John Mack, CEO of Morgan Stanley, and Robert Steel, President and CEO of Wachovia. A. R. Sorkin, *Too Big to Fail: The Inside Story of How Wall Street and Washington Fought to Save the Financial System—and Themselves* (New York: Penguin Books, 2010), p. xiiff.
2. J. D. Sachs, 'How Lehman's Fall Created a Global Panic', *Fortune* (December 15, 2008), p. 1.
3. Sorkin, *Too Big To Fail*, p. 69.
4. European Commission Directorate–General for Economic and Financial Affairs, 'Economic Crisis in Europe: Causes, Consequences and Response', *European Economy* 7 (Luxembourg: Office for Official Publications of the European Communities, 2009), p. 9.
5. B. White, 'What Red Ink? Wall Street Paid Hefty Bonuses', *New York Times* (28 January, 2009), p. 1.
6. U.S. Department of the Treasury, *Financial Crisis Response in Charts* (April 13, 2012), p. 3.
7. W. Sun, J. Stewart and D. Pollard (eds), *Corporate Governance and the Global Financial Crisis* (New York: Cambridge University Press, 2011), pp. 2–3.
8. 'Building models is important not only to value products but to understand the risks being taken and the dangers in the assumptions being made by traders . . . Transparency is an important feature of a financial product. If the cash flows from a product cannot be calculated in a relatively straightforward way, the product should not be traded'. J. Hull, 'The Credit Crisis of 2007 and Its Implications for Risk Management', in M. Pinedo and I. Walter (eds), *Global*

152 *Walters and Morley*

Asset Management: Strategies, Risks, Processes, and Technologies (New York: Palgrave Macmillan, SimCorp StrategyLab), pp. 93–106, on p. 105.

9. P. Martens and R. Martens, 'Brooksley Born: Still Telling the Uncomfortable Truths about Wall Street', *Wall Street on Parade: A Citizen Guide to Wall Street* (May 7, 2015), p. 1.

10. T. Piketty, *Capital in the Twenty-first Century*, A. Goldhammer (trans) (Cambridge, MA and London, UK: The Belknap Press of Harvard University Press, 2014), p. 1. [Hereafter, *Capital*.]

11. Piketty, *Capital*, p. 572, proposes '0.1 or 0.5 percent on fortunes under 1 million euros, 1 percent on fortunes between 1 and 5 million euros, 2 percent between 5 and 10 million euros, and as high as 5 or 10 percent for fortunes of several hundred million or several billion euros'.

12. Piketty, *Capital*, p. 27.

13. Ibid., pp. 471–2.

14. Ibid., p. 476.

15. Ibid., pp. 650–1, n. 33, refers to the case of Google.

16. Ibid., p. 553.

17. Ibid., p. 479.

18. Ibid., p. 485.

19. Ibid., p. 490.

20. Ibid., p. 21.

21. Ibid., p. 22 and p. 246.

22. Ibid., pp. 281–4.

23. Piketty, *Capital*, p. 559, proposes a European 'budgetary parliament' drawing from EU national parliaments in which 'European parliamentary sovereignty would rest on the legitimacy of democratically elected national assemblies'.

24. D. Acemoglu and J. A. Robinson, 'The Rise and Fall of General Laws of Capitalism', *Journal of Economic Perspectives*, 29:1 (Winter 2015), pp. 3–28, on p. 20: 'Political institutions also affect . . . the distribution of de facto political power . . . [which] depends on the extent to which different social and economic groups are organized and how they resolve their collective action problems and how resources influence their ability to do so. De facto and de jure power together determine economic institutions and also the stability and change of political institutions. In turn, economic institutions affect the supply of skills—a crucial determinant of inequality throughout history and even more so today'.

25. A. Gewirth, *Political Philosophy* (London and Toronto: Collier–Macmillan Ltd., 1965), p. 4.

26. A. Gewirth, 'The Rationality of Reasonableness', *Synthese* 57 (1983), pp. 225–47, on p. 244.

27. A. Gewirth, *Reason and Morality* (Chicago and London: University of Chicago Press, 1978), p. 135.

28. A. Gewirth, *The Community of Rights* (Chicago and London: University of Chicago Press, 1996), pp. 136–7.

29. T. I. Palley, 'Making Finance Serve the Real Economy', *State of the World 2014: Governing for Sustainability* (Washington, Covelo and London: Island Press, 2014), pp. 174–80, on p. 176.

30. Piketty, *Capital*, p. 479.

31. Gewirth, *The Community of Rights*, 208, n. 83. Gewirth cites J. S. Mill's, *Principles of Political Economy*, 2.1.3., W. J. Ashley (ed) (London: Longmans Green, 1950), p. 148.

32. J. Ryan-Collins, T. Greenham, R. Werner and A. Jackson, *Where Does Money Come From? A Guide to the UK Monetary and Banking System* (London: New Economics Foundation, 2014), p. 6.

Thomas Piketty and Alan Gewirth 153

33. Gewirth, *The Community of Rights*, p. 337ff.
34. C. Lee, B. Ferguson and D. Earley, *After Citizens United: The Story in the United States* (New York: Brennan Center for Justice at New York University School of Law, October 9, 2014), p. 2.
35. Gewirth, *The Community of Rights*, pp. 259–60.
36. E. L. Andrews and P. Baker, 'A.I.G. Planning Huge Bonuses after $170 Billion Bailout', *New York Times* (March 14, 2009), p. 1.
37. Gewirth, *Political Philosophy*, p. 3.
38. Gewirth, *The Community of Rights*, p. 110.
39. Piketty, *Capital*, p. 497.
40. Oxfam International, *Working for the Few: Political Capture and Economic Inequality*, 178 *Oxfam Briefing Paper* (20 January 2014), p. 3.
41. Gewirth, *The Community of Rights*, p. 73.
42. Citigroup, JP Morgan, Barclays, and RBS pleaded guilty in May 2015 to criminal charges of massive fraud in foreign exchange markets. 'It is time for the Justice Department and the SEC to get serious about enforcing our laws against financial fraud. These agencies don't take big financial institutions to trial . . . Even when financial institutions engage in blatantly criminal activity. Instead, they use what they call deferred prosecution agreements or non-prosecution agreements . . .' (Senator Elisabeth Warren, cited in P. Martens and R. Martens, 'Can the Public Ever Get Justice in New York Courts?', *Wall Street on Parade: A Citizen Guide to Wall Street* (September 9, 2015), p. 1.
43. J. E. Stiglitz, *Making Globalization Work* (New York and London, W.W. Norton & Company, 2007), p. 276.

WORKS CITED

Acemoglu, D. and Robinson, J. A., 'The Rise and Fall of General Laws of Capitalism', *Journal of Economic Perspectives*, 29:1 (Winter 2015), pp. 3–28.

Andrews, E. L. and Baker P., 'A.I.G. Planning Huge Bonuses after $170 Billion Bailout', *New York Times* (March 14, 2009), available at http://www.nytimes.com/2009/03/15/business/15AIG.html?pagewanted=all&_r=0 [accessed 10 September 2015].

European Commission Directorate–General for Economic and Financial Affairs, *Economic Crisis in Europe: Causes, Consequences and Response*', Series European Economy 7 (Luxembourg: Office for Official Publications of the European Communities, 2009).

Gewirth, A. *The Community of Rights* (Chicago and London: University of Chicago Press, 1996).

———, 'Economic Rights', *Philosophical Topics*, XIV/2 (Fall 1986), pp. 169–93.

———, 'The Rationality of Reasonableness', *Synthese*, 57 (1983), pp. 225–47.

———, *Reason and Morality* (Chicago and London: University of Chicago Press, 1978).

———, *Political Philosophy* (London and Toronto: Collier–Macmillan Ltd., 1965).

Hull, J., 'The Credit Crisis of 2007 and Its Implications for Risk Management', in M. Pinedo and I. Walter (eds.), *Global Asset Management: Strategies, Risks, Processes, and Technologies* (New York: Palgrave Macmillan, SimCorp StrategyLab), pp. 93–106.

Lee, C., Ferguson, B. and Earley, D. *After Citizens United: The Story in the United States* (New York: Brennan Center for Justice *at New York University School of Law*, October 9, 2014), available at http://www.brennancenter.org/publication/after-citizens-united-story-states [accessed 10 September 2015].

154 *Walters and Morley*

Martens, P. and Martens, R., 'Brooksley Born: Still Telling the Uncomfortable Truths about Wall Street', *Wall Street on Parade: A Citizen Guide to Wall Street* (May 7, 2015), available at http://wallstreetonparade.com/2015/05/brooksley-born-still-telling-the-uncomfortable-truths-about-wall-street/ [accessed 10 September 2015].

——, 'Can the Public Ever Get Justice in New York Courts?' *Wall Street on Parade: A Citizen Guide to Wall Street*, (September 9, 2015), available at http://wallstreetonparade.com/?s=Can+the+public+ever+get+justice+in+public+courts%3F [accessed 10 September 2015].

Oxfam International, *Working for the Few: Political Capture and Economic Inequality*, 178 Oxfam Briefing Paper (January 20, 2014), available at https://www.oxfam.org/en/research/working-few [accessed 10 September 2015].

Palley, T. I., 'Making Finance Serve the Real Economy', in T. Prugh, M. Renner, and L. Mastny (eds.) *State of the World 2014: Governing for Sustainability* (Washington, Covelo and London: Island Press, 2014), pp. 174–80.

Piketty, T., *Capital in the Twenty–first Century*, Translated by A. Goldhammer (Cambridge, MA and London, UK: The Belknap Press of Harvard University Press, 2014).

Ryan-Collins, J., Greenham, T., Werner, R. and Jackson, A., *Where Does Money Come From? A Guide to the UK Monetary and Banking System* (London: New Economics Foundation, 2014).

Sachs, J. D., 'How Lehman's Fall Created a Global Panic', *Fortune* (December 15, 2008), available at http://archive.fortune.com/2008/12/15/news/economy/monday.meltdown.fortune/index.htm [accessed 10 September 2015].

Sorkin, A. R., *Too Big To Fail: The Inside Story of How Wall Street and Washington Fought to Save the Financial System—and Themselves* (New York: Penguin Books, 2010).

Stiglitz, J. E., *Making Globalization Work* (New York and London: W.W. Norton & Company, 2007).

Sun, W., Stewart, J. and Pollard D. (eds.) *Corporate Governance and the Global Financial Crisis* (New York: Cambridge University Press, 2011).

U.S. Department of the Treasury, *Financial Crisis Response in Charts* (April 13, 2012), available at http://www.treasury.gov/resource-center/data-chart-center/Pages/Financial-Crisis-Response-In-Charts.aspx [accessed 10 September 2015].

White, B. 'What Red Ink? Wall Street Paid Hefty Bonuses', *New York Times* (January 28, 2009), available at http://www.nytimes.com/2009/01/29/business/29bonus.html?_r=0 [accessed 10 September 2015].

Part III
Gewirthian Applications

10 A Gewirthian Framework for Protecting the Basic Human Rights of Lesbian, Gay, Bisexual, and Transgender (LGBT) People

*Vincent J. Samar**

Recognition of LGBT rights in Western Europe, the United States, some South American countries, and South Africa notwithstanding, LGBT persons continue to be subjected to discrimination and, in some places in the world, persecution. The first section of this chapter is meant only to briefly chronicle the reality of how widespread the discrimination and possible persecution that LGBT persons face are in order to establish the need to provide an interpretative framework for human rights to bring such discriminations and persecutions to an end. The focus of the chapter is thus directed toward showing that several of the most basic human rights LGBT people claim—such as the right to privacy, free expression, and equality before the law (including the right to marry members of the same sex)—are supported not only by the United States Constitution and various international law documents, but also by the writings of Alan Gewirth in *Reason and Morality* (1978)[1] and *Self-Fulfillment* (1998).[2] The role of this important set of philosophical writings on human rights by Gewirth is to provide a bridge for establishing a cross-national, rationally based dialogue for how LGBT rights get protected, within an already existing international human rights framework.

Section 1 provides a brief review of the state of the law affecting LGBT people around the world. Section 2 shows how Gewirth's system provides a moral justification of LGBT rights. Section 3 relates that foundation to a set of suggested intermediate foundations for guaranteeing LGBT dignity and autonomy prescribed by Gewirth's framework. Finally, section 4 shows how Gewirth's framework for protecting the human rights of LGBT persons allows for coexistence with narrower cultural and religious views that might be less liberal.

1. THE LEGAL STANDING OF LGBT PEOPLE IN AN INTERNATIONAL CONTEXT

Wikipedia has compiled data regarding same-sex sexual activity, recognition of same-sex relationships, same-sex marriage, adoption by same-sex couples, anti-discrimination laws, and laws concerning gender identity/

158　*Samar*

expression from 197 sources covering five regions of the world: Africa, the Americas, Asia, Europe, and Oceania.[3] The compilation sets out some very different directions regarding criminalization of same-sex sexuality, prohibition versus acceptance of same-sex relationships and marriage, and discrimination and treatment of LGBT people.

For instance, on the African continent, thirty-eight countries make same-sex sexual activities illegal for at least males, with most providing for some imprisonment time (six months to fourteen years to life); four support a death penalty, and four some form of corporal punishment, while twenty-four others, including five territories, have legalized same-sex activity, along with nine having legalized it only for women. South Africa and two territories recognize same-sex marriage. Two territories and South Africa also allow same-sex couples to adopt. Five territories and one country have some form of anti-discrimination law, and two territories and one country allow gender identity change without sterilization, while two territories require sterilization.

In the Americas, eleven countries provide for some kind of imprisonment; none impose death or corporal punishment. Forty-four countries or territories treat adult consensual same-sex activity as legal, but five make it legal for women only. Eighteen afford some recognition of same-sex relationships, while five ban same-sex marriages. Additionally, twelve states allow adoption, twenty-nine have some sort of anti-discrimination statute, and eleven protect change of gender identity without sterilization, while six require sterilization.

On the Asian continent, seventeen countries punish by imprisonment (a few months to life) for same-sex activity, seven afford a possible death sentence, four have corporal punishment, twenty-three do not criminalize adult consensual same-sex sexual activity, while six only do not criminalize it for women. No country, except maybe Taiwan, will recognize civil unions. Israel will recognize foreign same-sex marriages. Same-sex couple adoptions don't appear to be permitted in either country. Six countries also have laws prohibiting some sexual orientation discriminations. Fourteen countries permit some form of alternative gender identity expression.

Europe contrasts the regions discussed above in that no European nation criminalizes adult consensual same-sex sexual behavior, while fifty-nine report it being legal. Probably, decriminalization occurred much earlier if they even had at one time made criminal same-sex sexual activity, like when the Nazis occupied some European countries. Twenty-nine states recognize civil unions or registered partnerships, or recognition is pending. Fourteen states allow same-sex marriage, or allowance is pending. Twenty-five nations allow some form of gay adoption. All but one Central European state seem to have some kind of anti-discrimination law. Among Eastern European states, only three have anti-discrimination laws. All Northern European states have some kind of anti-discrimination law, as do all but two Southern European nations; Vatican City doesn't report. And all but one Western European state and territory have some kind of anti-discrimination law. While gender transition is allowed in all but ten states, ten states require that gender transition be accompanied by sterilization.

Finally, in Oceania, seventeen countries and territories legalize same-sex sexual activities; nine make it illegal, with possible prison sentences of three to fourteen years. Of those that criminalize same-sex conduct, six do not criminalize it for women. Also, six countries recognize same-sex partnership or civil union; five recognize marriages, while Australia bans it by federal statute. Six nations allow same-sex adoptions. Ten countries provide some sort of anti-discrimination protection. Two states allow gender identity expression without sterilization; three require sterilization.

2. ALAN GEWIRTH AND THE MORAL JUSTIFICATION OF LGBT RIGHTS

Gewirth argues that human rights can be rationally derived from the normative structure of human action using what he labels 'the dialectically necessary method'.[4] Since every moral theory by virtue of being prescriptive must presuppose that the persons it addresses are voluntary, purposive human agents (or actors), it follows that the normative structure of human action—as voluntariness and purposiveness—might provide a common ground from which moral and human rights claims are derived, including claims by LGBT people to privacy, free expression, and equality before the law.[5]

Most important is 'that human rights involve requirements or claims of necessary conduct on the part of other persons or groups'; this is because the nature of these claims is to impose correlative duties on the part of others regarding the maintenance or advancement of the right-holder's freedom and well-being to engage in purposeful action.[6] Consequently, it is of the greatest importance, if these rights are to be secured, that the justification (or proof) proceeds by showing what every agent logically must affirm 'on pain of contradiction'.[7] This Gewirth believes he achieves by use of the dialectically necessary method, which he explains more fully in *Reason and Morality*.

According to the dialectically necessary method, 'every agent must hold or accept, at least implicitly, that he has rights to freedom and well-being' from the mere fact that certain objects are the proximate necessary conditions of human action.[8] The method is 'dialectically necessary' in that it proceeds from what all agents logically must claim or accept, on pain of contradiction.[9] The idea of freedom derives from the fact that the action is voluntary, meaning that the agent affirms her own freedom by performing the act.[10] Similarly, the agent affirms her well-being to perform the action as including the capacities that makes the action possible.[11] Freedom and well-being thus are operating respectively as procedural and substantive conditions that the agent affirms by virtue of being an agent, i.e., an author of her own actions.

160   Samar

Put another way, the agent is implying, '*I must have freedom and well-being*' by her very agency. From this, Gewirth says the agent impliedly affirms that she has rights to freedom and well-being.[12]

If the agent were to deny that she has rights to freedom and well-being, she would be forced to deny the correlative duties associated with those rights, at least insofar as those duties are dependent on the existence of the rights. That is, she would have also to deny, '*All other persons ought at least to refrain from removing or interfering with my freedom and well-being*'.[13] But this means she would have to accept that '*it is permissible that other persons interfere with or remove [her] freedom and well-being*'.[14] But this clearly contradicts the agent's earlier justified claim, '*I must have freedom and well-being*' because it is necessary to my being an agent.[15] Hence, the only way to avoid the contradiction is for the agent to accept, from her own point of view, *I have rights to freedom and well-being*.[16]

At this point, Gewirth only argues that the rights-claim being affirmed is a prudential rights-claim; i.e., it is what the agent must accept from her own point of view *qua* agent. To develop this into a moral claim, Gewirth believes that both the agent and all other prospective purposive agents would have to affirm each other's mutual rights to freedom and well-being.[17] Gewirth accomplishes the move from *prudential* to *moral* rights by first noting that the only basis upon which the agent made her rights-claim was that she was a prospective purposive agent.[18] In other words, there was nothing specific about the agent, other than that she was an agent, to ground her claim. But if that were the case, then by operating within the dialectically necessary method, any agent would be in the same position to make the same claim.[19]

Gewirth concludes that every rational agent, from her own point of view, must accept as categorically obligatory the following Principle of Generic Consistency (PGC): '*Act in accord with the generic rights [i.e., the rights to freedom and well-being] of your recipients as well as of yourself.*'[20] Moreover, having arrived at this conclusion from within the dialectically necessary method and realizing that any other agent operating within this same method would have arrived at the same place, she no longer has to affirm the truth of the conclusion just dialectically, but may also affirm it as an assertoric or a necessary moral truth.[21]

Two important further results also arise from Gewirth's analysis. First, the rights claimed will not just be *negative* rights from interference or intrusion, but also *positive* rights to certain benefits or entitlements that lead to self-fulfillment, which other agents also claim.[22] These positive rights, claimed by the agent in particular on the side of well-being, include first, the 'basic goods' 'that are the proximate necessary preconditions of his performance of any and all his actions', viz., life, physical integrity, and mental equilibrium; next, 'nonsubtractive goods', which maintain his current level of purpose-fulfillment, such as not being lied to, cheated, or defrauded; and lastly, 'additive goods', which increase his current level of purpose-fulfillment, e.g., a good education and a decent job with a guaranteed living wage.[23] Second,

A Gewirthian Framework for LGBT Rights 161

a foundation for *human dignity* can be discovered from the fact that human dignity supervenes on claims of human rights.[24]

The latter is illustrated by the fact that from the agent's point of view, the 'locus and source' of

> the worth he attributes to his purposes pertains a fortiori to himself. They are *his* purposes, and they are worth attaining because *he* is worth sustaining and fulfilling, so that he has what for him is a justified sense of his own worth. . . . [H]e pursues his purposes not as an uncontrolled reflex response to stimuli, but, rather, because he has chosen them after reflection on alternatives. Even if he does not always reflect, his choice can and does sometimes at least operate in this way. Every human agent, as such, is capable of this. Hence, the agent is, and regards himself as, an entity that, unlike other natural entities, is not, so far as it acts, subject only to external forces of nature; he can and does make his own decisions on the basis of his own reflective understanding. By virtue of these characteristics of his actions, the agent regards himself as having worth or dignity.[25]

In terms of the more specific rights claimed by, among others, LGBT persons, to privacy, free expression, and equality before the law, Gewirth's justificatory arguments provide a strong foundation.

Since the PGC as a basic moral standard may be too general to decide particular cases, given that no two cases are exactly alike, what the PGC does identify are classes of cases that fit well under its two basic components of freedom and well-being. These classes of cases involve claim rights to privacy, free expression, and equality before the law. Privacy and freedom of expression can be shown to directly relate to the PGC's freedom component and indirectly to its well-being component. Equality before the law directly connects to the PGC's well-being component and indirectly to its freedom component, since without equality before the law, it is doubtful one can gain access to the necessary conditions for action. Thus, the protections found in these classes of cases derive directly from the PGC and, as will be shown more fully below, indirectly by the essential role they play in how the agent comes to regard 'himself as having worth and dignity'.[26]

3. DIGNITY AND AUTONOMY IN GEWIRTH

A. The Legal Standing of Privacy, Free Expression, and Equality

Before showing more specifically how privacy, free expression, and equality are justified in a Gewirthian framework, it is helpful to consider how these intermediate, autonomy-affirming legal rights arise under both the domestic

162 *Samar*

jurisdiction of American courts and under various international documents, which, depending on their language and how international and domestic courts construe them, are either aspirational, or legally binding.

In the American context, the line of cases involving intimate decisions from *Griswold v. Connecticut*[27] to *Roe v. Wade*[28] to *Lawrence v. Texas*[29] establish a privacy/liberty right to form intimate relationships under the due process clause of the Fourteenth Amendment to the US Constitution. In the international law environment, the *Universal Declaration of Human Rights*,[30] along with the *International Covenant on Civil and Political Rights*,[31] provides privacy protections, and the General Assembly Human Rights Council Resolution 17/19 (which ninety-four countries have signed as of this writing) favors adopting an interpretation of the *Universal Declaration* and the *International Covenant* to protect the basic privacy/liberty rights of LGBT people.[32]

Specifically, in American law, the right to privately engage in intimate sexual acts among consenting adults was recognized as applying to gay people in *Lawrence v. Texas*. That case involved 'two adults who, with full and mutual consent from each other, engaged in sexual practices common to a homosexual lifestyle. The [Court acknowledged that the] petitioners are entitled to respect for their private lives'.[33] Similarly, the idea of a private act seems implicit in various international agreements including in the *Universal Declaration* under Article 3, which expresses the aspiration that '[e]veryone has the right to life, liberty, and security of person' and under Article 20–1, which further states, '[e]veryone has the right to freedom of peaceful assembly and association'.[34] Those aspirations are legally binding (subject to how the terms are interpreted by both international and domestic courts) for the countries that signed, without relevant reservation, the *International Covenant on Civil and Political Rights*.

Together, these international provisions seem to carve out an area of personal freedom in which state actors ought to respect the private liberty of their own people, subject only to the rule of law, which ideally would protect, in the first instance, self-regarding actions. Indeed, it is my view that, whether we are speaking domestically or internationally, '*[a]n action is self-regarding (private) with respect to a group of other actors if and only if the consequences of the act impinge in the first instance on the basic interests of the actor and not on the interests of the specified class of actors*'.[35] By 'in the first instance', I mean that *the mere description of the act, without the inclusion of any additional facts or causal theories* should impinge on no one else's interests other than those of the actor.

I use the term 'basic interest' rather than 'interest' alone because I want to stress that an overly broad definition of interest could lead to no action ever being private. A basic interest is one that does not presuppose any conception about facts or social conventions and contrasts with 'derivative interests', which do presuppose some conception about facts or social conventions. The two most general categories of basic interests are freedom

A *Gewirthian Framework for LGBT Rights* 163

and well-being, the same categories of concern that the PGC protects. Under the first are included freedom of thought, worship, expression, and privacy. Under the second, the preservation of one's life and health, including physical integrity and mental equilibrium. These categories contrast with derivative interests where a particular conception of facts or social conventions is involved in defining the interest. For example, one's interest in being allowed to marry combines one's basic interest in freedom with the social convention of marriage. Similarly, one's interest in being 'out' as a gay or transgender person combines a basic interest in well-being along with the factual understanding that one's mental well-being is more likely to be enhanced by being honest about who one is. Consequently, except where one's understanding of the facts can be shown objectively to be in error or the accepted social convention is necessary to prevent temporal harm, a prima facie case for freedom and well-being is established notwithstanding any limitation imposed by the fact or social convention.

Of course, defining an action to be private doesn't by itself afford any value to the action. That is accomplished only if the action is *necessarily* a part of something else that is already valued. Consequently, if autonomy in the sense of self-rule is valued, as would be the case under the freedom component of the PGC, then private actions piggyback onto the value of autonomy insofar as they are the ideal case of an autonomous action where no one else's basic interests are involved. Thus, there are good reasons to believe that if the above cases and documents carve out a normative space where such freedom is valued, they simultaneously define a space where privacy is rationally justified under the freedom component of the PGC. Indeed, if the concern was only about how the classification might restrict freedom and not how restrictive laws also implicate human dignity, the cases might have been more straightforwardly resolved.

On the international front, the *Universal Declaration* provides the following aspirations:

> *Article 6*—Everyone has the right to recognition everywhere as a person before the law.
>
> *Article 7*—All are equal before the law and are entitled without any discrimination to equal protection of the law. All are entitled to protection against any discrimination in violation of this Declaration and against any incitement to such discrimination.
>
> *Article 16*—Men and women of full age, without any limitation due to race, nationality or religion, have the right to marry and to found a family. They are entitled to equal rights as to marriage, during marriage and at its dissolution.[36]

Many other provisions of the *Declaration* also talk about everyone having various rights, but the cited ones provide the general principle of equal protection of the law in the international arena.

164 Samar

In the *International Covenant on Civil and Political Rights*, these aspirations are made legal obligations for the signatory states. Article 26 states: '[T]he law shall prohibit any discrimination and guarantee to all persons equal and effective protection against discrimination on any ground such as race, colour, sex, language, religion, political or other opinion, national or social origin, property, birth or other status'.[37] Most importantly for our purposes here is the inclusion of the phrase 'other status', as this signifies that the provision is not meant to be limited to only the specified grounds mentioned, but rather that the specified grounds mentioned are merely illustrative of the openness of the provision to avoid any form of irrational or irrelevant discrimination.

Similarly, Article 23 provides:

1. The family is the natural and fundamental group unit of society and is entitled to protection by society and the State.
2. The right of men and women of marriageable age to marry and to found a family shall be recognized.
3. No marriage shall be entered into without the free and full consent of the intending spouses.[38]

While the marriage provision does not say who can marry and probably would have been understood by most signatories to refer to opposite-sex relationships, the semantics do not mandate that men should only marry women or that women should only marry men. At the very least, there is a basis for a fuller discussion based on the language, reasons, and sensitive purposes served by these provisions.[39]

Not to be forgotten is why marriage is important, not just to opposite-sex couples but to same-sex couples as well, as this directly implicates human dignity. It is not just for the external benefits marriage provides, such as being able to file a joint tax return, ownership of property in tenancy by the entirety, ease of second parent adoption, and the marital privilege from having to testify in court against one's spouse or being forced to reveal confidential communications between the spouses. In antithesis 'to what most scholars put forth as the bases for marriage—i.e. relational permanency, financial stability, or child-rearing—I want to claim that these are more the external attributes of marriage'.[40] I do not mean to suggest that these are unimportant attributes; rather, like privacy of information and places, they support an internal structure of private relationships that goes deeper than 'the first things to come to mind when society attempts to define marriage beyond its visual trappings'.[41] 'The more internal structure or "real" stuff of the marriage relationship' finds 'its connection to individual human dignity' from the opportunities 'it provides its participants to achieve levels of human self-fulfillment that are wholly unique and otherwise unobtainable'.[42] In this sense, the marriage arrangement plays an essential role in the couple's efforts to further that part of their individual self-fulfillment that

A Gewirthian Framework for LGBT Rights   165

represents a publicly acknowledged mutual commitment to the satisfaction of one another's most personal needs beyond what might be possible via other legal mechanisms.

B. Justifying These Intermediate Rights

Gewirth's idea that dignity is at the foundation of human rights provides a basis for intermediate rights to privacy, freedom of expression, and equality. Included under freedom are the essential civil liberties that allow one to be a self-ruling individual, such as freedom of speech, freedom of the press, right of assembly, right to worship, and right to privacy. These goods follow out of the freedom component of the PGC because they are essential to the doing of any action for any purpose the agent regards as good.

In a strict sense, the right to privacy with the understanding of a private act offered above is that feature of agency that presents the ideal case example of where human dignity is affirmed. Mill's discussion of '[t]he liberty of expressing and publishing opinions' also fits the Gewirthian idea of dignity, even though Mill was not a rights theorist, but a utilitarian.[43] For, as Mill acknowledges, even though expression 'may seem to fall under a different principle, since it belongs to that part of the conduct of an individual which concerns other people; but being almost of as much importance as the liberty of thought itself, and resting in great part on the same reasons, is practically inseparable from it'.[44] What Mill is describing here is as much about the way humans actually come to have and value their own thoughts, often by way of debate and discussion, as it is about who they influence; thus, it fits as much within a Gewirthian perspective for affirming individual dignity as it does in a utilitarian explanation for favouring an especially strong presumption in favour of free expression.

The principle of equality before the law, for Gewirth, serves, at minimum, a static-instrumental role to insure procedural fairness, but need not be confined to just procedural fairness.[45] Here, Gewirth's framework can be seen to provide a bridge between libertarians, who only require individuals to satisfy the needs of the *minimal* state, with very little intrusion on individual freedom, and egalitarian liberals, who see the need for a more robust *supportive* state to guarantee individual equality.[46] The bridge is at the place where freedom itself is threatened if the means to exercise it are held only by a few. That is to say, at the point where voluntariness and purposiveness are being challenged through no fault of the agent, Gewirth's framework provides a language of human dignity that requires maximal liberty for all, rather than just maximizing liberty, which usually only benefits a few.

Gewirth's foundational structure for rights based on the normative structure of human action works here to privilege those additive goods, which are the conditions effecting voluntariness and purposiveness that must be present for there to be any human rights, even in the minimal state. Voluntariness and purposiveness are undercut when people's basic needs for well-being

166 *Samar*

aren't being met because of irrelevant or irrational discrimination. At this point, the theory provides an argument for passage of laws like, in America, the proposed Employment Non-Discrimination Act,[47] guaranteeing in the private sector that LGBT persons will be afforded the basic human dignity to express publically who they are without fear of loss of job, housing, or other forms of public accommodation. The libertarian who wants to continue to claim that employers should have a nonsubtractive right to discriminate would then be forced to explain why voluntariness and purposiveness work to provide this right to freedom, but fail to provide basic rights to well-being for others similarly situated. Recall that it is not just freedom alone that Gewirth's methodology affords a right to, but the combination of freedom and well-being as jointly necessary for human rights to be sustained.

4. PROTECTING THE HUMAN RIGHTS OF ALL PERSONS

In this section, I take up Gewirth's idea of particularist morality as allowed within universal morality[48] to serve as a cultural or religious haven where groups of people with shared values may find opportunity for greater self-fulfillment, even though they may restrict membership to only those of like mind with themselves. Such communities are typically represented by membership in various voluntary associations, whether they are based on religious belief, or personal affinity toward various intellectual, cultural, aesthetic, professional, or political ideas. What they afford their members are opportunities to find deeper levels of human self-fulfillment than might be thought available from membership in the society at large. As a consequence, they fall under the freedom component that the PGC protects, provided they do not at the same time impose their own more particularistic values on others or seek to deny rights to others outside the group. The latter would violate universal morality and be a source of real temporal harm. For example, a religious understanding of marriage may limit those who can marry within the religion to only opposite-sex persons or persons of the same faith, or those who have not been previously married according the tenets of the religion, just as lesbians or gay men might develop alternative forms of intimate relationships other than same-sex marriage or civil unions.[49] Gewirth recognizes the need to protect such voluntary cultural/religious groups when he notes

> the ways in which diverse cultural groups may themselves be treated by the state or the society at large. At issue here is the well-founded contention that members of various groups . . . are markedly inferior to members of other, dominant groups in their effective rights to freedom and well-being, power, wealth, and status. The members of such submerged groups are discriminated against by the dominant political, economic, educational, and other salient institutions of the wider

A Gewirthian Framework for LGBT Rights 167

society. As a result, the persons in question suffer from serious material disadvantages but also from deep feelings of inferiority, envy, and injustice. What the PGC requires here is that cultural pluralism be affirmatively protected: the right to cultural pluralism is an affirmative as well as a negative right. The needs of the members of various subcultures within the dominant culture must be recognized and steps must be taken toward their fulfillment as important parts of capacity-fulfillment.[50]

Protecting cultural/religious groups doesn't mean, however, looking the other way when the group attempts to impose its values on those outside or even those inside who may not be able to consent.[51]

Gewirth considers the example of

> the Hindu practice of suttee, where a widow was required to throw herself on her husband's funeral pyre. Concerning this practice it has been written ". . . A shared cremation absolves sins and guarantees eternal unity between husband and wife, linked to each other as god and goddess through the cycle of future rebirths." Even if given the most benign interpretation of the widow's willingness to commit suicide with this justification, there remains the question of whether her conduct is free and voluntary in the sense that she not only controls her behavior by her unforced choice but has knowledge of relevant circumstances, and is to this extent rational. If one views the religious beliefs in question as having been instilled through a long process of enculturation, with no opportunity provided for their critical (including empirical) assessment, then suttee and similar practices are egregious violations of the human rights to freedom and well-being.[52]

A problem emerges in setting the boundary line for the freedom to act between traditional and universal morality where the two views are likely to differ.

Should the various anti-discrimination laws, which many American states and the federal government have adopted and provisions of various international documents require of their signatories, force private persons to violate their religious beliefs? At least with regard to one American federal statute, the Religious Freedom Restoration Act (RFRA),[53] the US Supreme Court in *Burwell v. Hobby Lobby*[54] said that Congress provided the RFRA to allow an exception from a federal regulation, where the regulation is likely to intrude on religious freedom. The case involved the Department of Health and Human Services' (HHS) employer mandate, under the Affordable Care Act,[55] for companies above the minimal size of twenty employees to provide their female employees with health insurance that would cover contraceptive drugs and methods of birth control some might object to on religious grounds because they prevent 'an already fertilized egg from developing any further by inhibiting its attachment to the uterus'.[56]

168 *Samar*

In that case, the Supreme Court accepted that providing affordable healthcare to women was a compelling interest recognized by the RFRA, which normally would override Congress's grant of additional protection for the free exercise of religion from what the court had previously held the First Amendment to require.[57] However, because the HHS had found a way to allow the government to provide these benefits directly to employees of religiously affiliated not-for-profit corporations, the court found that extending the same treatment to the petitioners (three closely held for-profit corporations) was more consistent with protecting their religious freedom than mandating that these employers provide the benefits through their employee insurance in violation of their faith.[58] Obviously, corporations with many owners, as for example those that are publically traded, may, as a practical matter, not avail themselves of this RFRA exception, unless their boards of directors or officers believe that doing so might improve the company's financial bottom line.[59] Still, the question arises, how will a future court handle a situation where certain types of discrimination in employment, housing, and public accommodations are prohibited and no less intrusive alternative is available as, for example, with applying state or federal anti-discrimination laws to LGBT people or providing insurance benefits to the spouses of same-sex or transgender partners? Will closely held for-profit corporations be exempted from these regulations as well? And what about publically traded corporations, where the majority of the shares are held by a group of individuals who have religious objections to the application of these anti-discrimination laws?

The posed hypothetical does not allow for the religious freedom of employers and the well-being of employees to both be fully served, and so a choice will need to be made. Because Gewirth's system acknowledges that a certain degree of well-being is necessary to the effective operations of human freedom, it provides an avenue for evaluating the rights-claims of employers and employees in such situations. In the posited circumstance, employers would be legally obligated to provide these services, since there is less reason for an employer to perceive herself as operating in violation of her own faith, especially after a final decision is rendered by the Supreme Court as to what the law requires.[60] To allow employers to be able to opt out of anti-discrimination laws would potentially harm the dignity and very likely the basic well-being of employees in ways the employees would be hard-pressed to offset. In effect, the tradeoff here is between an employer's nonsubtractive well-being (in having its goals or purposes reduced where it doesn't even have to accept responsibility for the reduction) and an employee's basic well-being (to the conditions and abilities necessary for agency at all). The latter is clearly more essential, especially where individual dignity is concerned, to the PGC's guarantee of fostering human rights. So, here too we see within the Gewirthian framework a language of rights, which may help resolve a related future controversy involving human rights to religious freedom and LGBT nondiscrimination.

5. CONCLUSION

In this chapter, I have shown the utility of the Gewirthian framework to both clarifying and advancing many rights claimed by LGBT people in the areas of privacy, free expression, and equality. My focus has not been so much to afford conclusive answers to all the questions raised as it has been to show the contribution the framework affords toward guaranteeing the dignity of LGBT persons. In this sense, the framework serves to provide an overarching rational unity to the claims of LGBT persons in these most important areas.

NOTES

* The author would like to thank his friend and colleague, Professor Mark Strasser of Capital University Law School, who was also a doctoral student of Professor Gewirth's, for his very helpful review of and comments on an earlier version of this chapter, along with this book's editor, Professor Per Bauhn, for keeping this chapter within the size constraints.
1. A. Gewirth, *Reason and Morality* (Chicago: University of Chicago Press, 1978).
2. A. Gewirth, *Self-Fulfillment* (Princeton, NJ: Princeton University Press, 1998).
3. https://en.wikipedia.org/wiki/LGBT_rights_by_country_or_territory. *See also* 'Lesbian, Gay, Bisexual and Transgendered Rights Around the World', *The Guardian*, http://www.theguardian.com/world/ng-interactive/2014/may/-sp-gay-rights-world-lesbian-bisexual-transgender. In the United States, same-sex marriage became constitutionally protected in all fifty states, as a matter of equal protection of the law, following the U.S. Supreme Court's decision in *Obergefell v. Hodges*, 135 S. Ct. 2584 (2015).
4. Ibid., p. 46.
5. A. Gewirth, 'Introduction', *Human Rights: Essays on Justification and Applications* (Chicago: University of Chicago Press, 1982), p. 5.
6. Gewirth, 'Introduction', pp. 5–6. Here, Gewirth limits himself to what Wesley Hohfeld called 'claim-rights', which are rights that would logically impose correlative duties upon others. Ibid., p. 2. *See* Wesley Hohfeld, *Fundamental Legal Conceptions*, Walter W. Cooked (ed) (Westport, CT: Greenwood Press, 1946), p. 5.
7. Gewirth, 'Introduction', p. 5.
8. Gewirth, *Reason and Morality*, p. 78.
9. Ibid., pp. 42–7. Gewirth's methodology is distinguishable from other common dialectically 'contingent' methods, such as occurs in Plato's *The Republic*, where Socrates challenges *various* views of justice or morality by showing how they give rise to internal inconsistencies with the beliefs held. See ibid., pp. 43–4.
10. Gewirth, *Reason and Morality*, pp. 52–3.
11. Ibid., pp. 53–4.
12. Ibid., p. 80 (italics added).
13. Ibid., p. 80 (italics added).
14. Ibid., p. 80 (italics added).
15. Ibid., p. 81 (italics added).
16. Ibid., p. 81 (italics added).
17. The phrase 'prospective purposive agent' takes account of obligations agents may owe one another even when not acting because they are asleep or in a temporary coma.

170 Samar

18. Ibid., pp. 104–12.
19. Ibid., pp. 104–12.
20. Ibid., p. 135.
21. Ibid., p. 153.
22. A. Gewirth, *Self-Fulfillment* (Princeton, NJ: Princeton University Press, 1998), p. 85.
23. Gewirth, *Reason and Morality*, pp. 53–4.
24. 'A set of properties A supervenes upon another set B just in case no two things can differ with respect to A-properties without also differing with respect to their B-properties. In slogan form, "there cannot be an A-difference without a B-difference"'. *Stanford Encyclopedia of Philosophy*, http://plato.stanford. edu/entries/supervenience/.
25. Gewirth, *Self-Fulfillment*, p. 169.
26. Ibid., pp. 168–9.
27. 381 US 479 (1965).
28. 410 US 113 (1973) *reaffirmed with modification* in *Planned Parenthood v. Casey*, 505 US 833 (1992).
29. 539 US 558 (2003).
30. *See Universal Declaration of Human Rights*, G.A Res. 217(A)(III), U.N. GAOR, 3rd Sess., 71, U.N. Doc. A/810 (1948).
31. 999 U.N.T.S. 171, 6 I.L.M. 368 (1967).
32. Human Rights Council Res. 17/19, Human Rights, Sexual Orientation and Gender Identity, 17th Sess., May 30–June 17, 2011, U.N. GAOR, 65th Sess., A/HRC/RES/17/19 (July 14, 2011). *Contra* Letter to the President of the Human Rights Council from Zamir Akram, UN Ambassador and Permanent Representative, and Coordinator of the *Organization of Islamic States on Human Rights and Humanitarian Issues*, February 14, 2012, unwatch.org: http://www.unwatch.org/atf/cf/%7B6deb65da-be5b-4cae-8056-8bf0bedf4d17%7D/OIC%20TO%20PRESIDENT.PDF.
33. 539 US at 578.
34. *Universal Declaration*, art. 3.
35. V.J. Samar, *The Right to Privacy: Gays, Lesbians, and the Constitution* (Philadelphia: Temple University Press, 1991), p. 64. For my defencee of self-regarding actions as legally private, see generally ibid., Chapter 3, pp. 83–116.
36. *Universal Declaration*, art.s 2, 7, & 16.
37. *International Covenant on Civil and Political Rights*, art. 26.
38. Ibid., art. 23.
39. For a discussion of how Gewirth's framework might support recognizing marriage under international law, see V.J. Samar, 'Throwing Down the International Gauntlet: Same-Sex Marriage as a Human Right', *Cardozo Public Law, Policy, and Ethics Journal*, 6 (2007), pp. 1–55.
40. See, e.g. M. Strasser, *The Challenge of Same-Sex Marriage: Federalist Principles and Constitutional Protections* (Westport, CT: Praeger Publishers, 1999) (discussing the interests of the state in respect to marriage).
41. V.J. Samar, 'Privacy and Same-Sex Marriage: The Case for Treating Same-Sex Marriage as a Human Right', *Montana Law Review*, 68 (2007), pp. 340–1 (citation to the federal *Defense of Marriage Act* omitted)
42. Ibid. See also Gewirth, *Self-Fulfillment*, p. 143: '[U]nlike baseball teams and other voluntary associations, [marriage] is formed, as reflecting the partners' mutual love, for purposes of deeply intimate union and extensive mutual concern and support for the participants, purposes that enhance the partners' general abilities of agency and thus contribute to their capacity-fulfillment'.
43. See J.S. Mill, *On Liberty* in *Essential Works of John Stuart Mill* (New York: Bantam Classics, 1961), p. 264.

A Gewirthian Framework for LGBT Rights   171

44. Ibid., p. 265.
45. See Gewirth, *Reason and Morality*, pp. 298, 302–4. It is important to see the *PGC's* application to the minimal state as the least that morality requires if the state is unable to provide more services. Since marriage itself is generally not a condition that requires a 'supportive' state, the requirement of equality of the minimal state should include marriage equality.
46. *See* ibid., pp. 304–11.
47. *See Employment Non-Discrimination Act (ENDA) of 2013*, 113 Cong., S. 815 (passed Senate on Nov. 11, 2013 but never being brought to a vote in the House of Representatives the bill expired). In 2015, the *Equality Act* was introduced in the House, which amends the Civil Rights Act of 1964 to add sex, sexual orientation, and gender identity as protected categories. *See* H.R. 3185, 114th Cong. (2015–2016).
48. Particularist morality differs from universal morality in that '[i]n universalist morality it is the interests of all persons equally; in particularist morality it is in the interest of some favored groups as against others' (Gewirth, *Self-Fulfillment*, p. 55).
49. For example, Canon Law 1075 §1 states: 'Only the supreme authority of the Church can authentically declare when the divine law prohibits or invalidates a marriage'. *The Canon Law: Letter & Spirit* (Collegeville, MN: A Michael Glazier Book, 1995). Canon 1085, §2 states: 'Even though the previous marriage is invalid or for any other reason dissolved, it is not thereby lawful to contract another marriage before the nullity or dissolution of the previous one has been established lawfully and with certainty'. Ibid. 'While consummation is not a constitutive element of marriage, it does make a merely ratified marriage indissoluble'. Ibid., Commentary 2072, (citing Cannon Law 1056).
50. Gewirth, *Self-Fulfillment*, p. 155.
51. For a review of Supreme Court decisions on the First Amendment Establishment Clause and where they might be going, see V. J. Samar, 'Religion/State: Where the Separation Lies', *Northern Illinois University Law Review* 33 (2012), pp. 1–63. *See also* Gewirth, *Self-Fulfillment*, pp. 142–5.
52. Gewirth, *Self-Fulfillment*, pp. 203–4 (citing R. A. Shweder, *Thinking Through Cultures* (Cambridge, MA: Harvard University Press, 1991), p. 16).
53. 107 Stat. 1488, 42 US C. §2000bb *et seq.* (1993).
54. 573 US —, 134 S. Ct. 2751 (2014).
55. 42 US C. §300gg-13(a)(4) (2010).
56. 573 at US, 134 S. Ct. at 2762–63.
57. Employment Division, Department of Human Resources of Oregon. v. Smith, 494 U.S. 872 (1990) (where the court determined that Oregon could deny unemployment benefits to a person fired for violating a state prohibition on the use of peyote, even as part of a religious ritual).
58. See 573 US at __, 134 S. Ct. at 2780 (J., Alito, majority opinion), p. 2787 (Kennedy, J., concurring opinion). *Cf.* ibid., p. 2705 (Ginsburg, J., dissenting opinion) (arguing that the majority's view approving some religious claims while deeming others unworthy of accommodation' could be 'perceived as favoring one religion over another,' the very 'risk the Establishment Clause [which is separate from the free exercise clause but also part of the First Amendment] was designed to preclude.').
59. Justice Alito's majority opinion only states as a matter of fact that '[t]hese cases, however, do not involve publicly traded corporations, and it seems unlikely that the sort of corporate giants to which HHS refers will often assert RFRA claims. HHS has not pointed to any example of a publicly traded corporation asserting RFRA rights, and numerous practical restraints would likely prevent that from occurring. For example, the idea that unrelated

172 *Samar*

shareholders—including institutional investors with their own set of stake-holders—would agree to run a corporation under the same religious beliefs seems improbable'. Ibid., p. 2774.

60. For instance, the Supreme Court, in *Pruneyard Shopping Center v. Robins*, 447 U.S. 74 (1980), held that allowing high school students the opportunity to ask patrons at a private shopping center to sign a protest against a UN declaration against Zionism would not be thought by visitors to the cen-tre that this was supported by the owners; whereas to keep the students off the property effectively nullified their First Amendment right to freedom of speech, under the California constitution, since visitors enter the property by automobile.

WORKS CITED

A. Books, Journal, and Internet Articles

The Canon Law: Letter & Spirit (Collegeville, MN: A Michael Glazier Book, 1995).

Gewirth, A., *Reason and Morality* (Chicago: University of Chicago Press, 1978).

———, *Human Rights: Essays on Justification and Applications* (Chicago: Univer-sity of Chicago Press, 1982).

———, *Self-Fulfillment* (Princeton, NJ: Princeton University Press, 1998).

Hohfeld, W., *Fundamental Legal Conceptions*, ed. Walter W. Cooked (Westport, CT: Greenwood Press, 1946).

'Lesbian, Gay, Bisexual and Transgendered Rights Around the World', *The Guardian*, available at http://www.theguardian.com/world/ng-interactive/2014/may/-sp-gay-rights-world-lesbian-bisexual-transgender.

'LGBT Rights by Country', available at https://en.wikipedia.org/wiki/LGBT_rights_by_country_or_territory.

Mill, J. S., *On Liberty* in *Essential Works of John Stuart Mill* (New York: Bantam Classics, 1961).

Samar, V. J., *The Right to Privacy: Gays, Lesbians, and the Constitution* (Philadel-phia: Temple University Press, 1991).

———, 'Privacy and Same-Sex Marriage: The Case for Treating Same-Sex Marriage as a Human Right', *Montana Law Review* 68 (2007), pp. 335–61.

———, 'Throwing Down the International Gauntlet: Same-Sex Marriage as a Human Right', *Cardozo Public Law, Policy, and Ethics Journal* 6 (2007), pp. 1–55.

———, 'Religion/State: Where the Separation Lies', *Northern Illinois University Law Review* 33 (2012), pp. 1–64.

Shweder, R. A., *Thinking Through Cultures* (Cambridge, MA: Harvard University Press, 1991).

Stanford Encyclopedia of Philosophy, available at http://plato.stanford.edu/entries/supervenience/.

Strasser, M., *The Challenge of Same-Sex Marriage: Federalist Principles and Consti-tutional Protections* (Westport, CT: Praeger Publishers, 1999).

B. Cases, Treaties, Statutes, and UN General Assembly Resolution

Burwell v. Hobby Lobby, 573 U.S. —, 134 S. Ct. 2751 (2014).

Employment Division, Department of Human Resources of Oregon. v. Smith, 494 U.S. 872 (1990).

A Gewirthian Framework for LGBT Rights 173

Employment Non-Discrimination Act (ENDA) of 2013, 113 Cong., S. 815. Nov. 11, 2013.

Griswold v. Connecticut, 381 U.S. 479 (1965).

Human Rights Council Res. 17/19, Human Rights, Sexual Orientation and Gender Identity, 17th Sess., May 30-June 17, 2011, U.N. GAOR, 65th Sess., A/HRC/RES/17/19 (July 14, 2011).

International Covenant on Civil and Political Rights, 999 U.N.T.S. 171, 6 I.L.M. 368 (1967).

Lawrence v. Texas, 539 U.S. 558 (2003).

Letter to the President of the Human Rights Council from Zamir Akram, UN Ambassador and Permanent Representative, and Coordinator of the *Organization of Islamic States on Human Rights and Humanitarian Issues* (February 14, 2012), available at unwatch.org: http://www.unwatch.org/atf/cf/%7B6deb65da-be5b-4cae-8056-8bf0bedf4d17%7D/OIC%20TO%20PRESIDENT.PDF.

Patient Protection and Affordable Care Act. 42 U.S. C. §300gg-13(a)(4) (2010).

Planned Parenthood v. Casey. 505 U.S. 833 (1992).

Pruneyard Shopping Center v. Robins. 447 U.S. 74 (1980).

Religious Freedom Restoration Act. 107 Stat. 1488, 42 U.S. C. §2000bb *et seq.* (1993).

Roe v. Wade. 410 U.S. 113 (1973).

Universal Declaration of Human Rights. G.A Res. 217(A)(III), U.N. GAOR, 3rd Sess., 71, U.N. Doc. A/810 (1948).

11 Justifying Mental Health Rights From a Gewirthian Perspective

Phil Bielby

INTRODUCTION

In this chapter, I seek to offer a Gewirthian justification of mental health rights. In particular, I will explore the interrelationship between two themes which feature within Gewirthian ethics and which are central to the human condition. The first of these is the inevitability of human vulnerability. The second of these is the significance of psychological well-being to successful agency. Justifying mental health rights is relevant both to the very idea of these rights as well as evaluating how specific iterations of these rights have been manifested in positive law. In this chapter, my focus will be on the former.

I will develop this argument through four sections. In the first section, I outline the significance of psychological well-being within Gewirth's argument for the Principle of Generic Consistency (hereafter PGC) and highlight its fragility as an element of our agency. In the second section, I introduce Beyleveld and Brownsword's concept of 'vulnerable agency'[1] as a means to understand what all agents share in terms of threats to their psychological well-being. From this, I develop a concept of 'heightened vulnerable agency' in order to understand and identify where vulnerability in terms of threats to psychological well-being is particularly prominent. I argue that heightened vulnerable agency essentially involves amplifications of the factors that give rise to vulnerable agency. In the third section, I use the continuum between vulnerable agency and heightened vulnerable agency to draw a distinction between those mental health rights to psychological well-being common to all agents by virtue of our vulnerable agency and those rights specifically intended to deal with circumstances where an agent develops different or particular needs that follow from experiences surrounding a severe mental health problem (the preferred term I will use for 'mental disorder' or 'mental illness')[2] or an intellectual disability by virtue of heightened vulnerable agency. I will call the former 'general mental health rights' and the latter 'specific mental health rights'. In the fourth and final section, I argue that both types of mental health rights are underpinned by an obligation implicit within the PGC to develop caring dispositions and attitudes. To this end, I

Gewirthian Mental Health Rights 175

outline the role Gewirth's 'reasonable self'[3] and vision of 'a caring society'[4] play in discharging the duties that both general and specific mental health rights create. Lastly, I draw the chapter to a close by considering future research directions for a Gewirthian justification of mental health rights.

1. THE PLACE OF MENTAL HEALTH IN GEWIRTH'S MORAL THEORY

The role of mental health in Gewirth's moral theory is significant both in terms of the central place it occupies and, paradoxically, how little Gewirth has to say about it directly. Gewirth is clear that 'mental equilibrium' is a basic good, and thus necessary for agency.[5] Yet, in both *Reason and Morality* as well as in a concise presentation of the argument for the PGC published shortly afterwards, Gewirth refers to mental equilibrium obliquely:

> Basic goods are the essential preconditions of action, such as life, physical integrity, and mental equilibrium. Thus a person's basic rights—his rights to basic goods—are violated when he is killed, starved, physically incapacitated, terrorized, or subjected to mentally deranging drugs.[6]

Clearly, 'mental equilibrium'—which I will refer to subsequently by the more contemporary expressions 'psychological well-being' and 'mental health'—is implicated within all of these examples of violations of basic rights, though of these, the infliction of terror or involuntary intoxication connect most vividly to violations of psychological well-being. Other remarks elsewhere by Gewirth further suggest the deep relationship psychological well-being has with agency. Although Gewirth accepts that 'previous psychological conditioning' and 'strong emotional factors'[7] are compatible with voluntary action, Gewirth claims that beyond a threshold of 'foolish and uninformed' choices, action is not voluntarily chosen, giving examples of kleptomania and deranged violence as instances of 'severely diminished capacity to be aware of relevant circumstances, alternatives and reasons to select among them'.[8] Later in the book, Gewirth returns to consider individuals whose mental health may compromise their agency by discussing briefly the position of adults with severe mental health problems and intellectual disabilities within the application of the PGC.[9] Gewirth assumes (in my view wrongly)[10] that such individuals approach but do not possess 'full-fledged agency',[11] referring to such individuals in regrettably anachronistic terms as 'the insane and other such mentally deficient persons'.[12]

Subsequently, in *Self-Fulfillment*, Gewirth again refers to psychological well-being implicitly when he discusses the role of 'self-respect and self-esteem' as components of well-being, although he frames them as 'virtues' of 'additive well-being' (the means for developing one's level of capability for successful action)[13] rather than as basic psychological needs of agency.[14]

176 *Bielby*

Nonetheless, they form important conditions of Gewirth's vision of self-fulfilment, where the 'deepest desires or . . . best capacities' of the self are realized.[15] This concept of the self involves an idea of 'a continuing or enduring embodied entity that is aware of itself as a distinct person, can anticipate a future for itself, and that has desires on which it can reflect'.[16] Such a diachronic concept of the self presupposes good mental health over time, much as a right to 'mental equilibrium' articulates an enduring basic psychological well-being claim by any agent. Gewirth also engages with themes of psychological well-being when he considers, albeit sceptically, the idea of a 'right to be loved', though he accepts its importance in the healthy development of children.[17]

What unifies these observations is the idea that psychological well-being, as a crucial dimension of agency, is inherently fragile, much like freedom and other aspects of well-being. Indeed, Gewirth himself accepts that '[t]here is always the possibility of interference with . . . agency and hence of . . . losing the freedom and well-being that agency requires'.[18] And even if psychological well-being is not lost altogether, it can be jeopardized, challenged, and impaired in various ways over one's lifetime, for example, through the experience of depression or dementia. In some cases, such as in congenital intellectual disabilities, challenges to psychological well-being may be experienced from childhood. Common to all such experiences, however, is a complex interplay of social and neurobiological factors arising from the interaction of the individual agent with her immediate and broader socio-cultural environment.[19]

In this way, our agency is inherently vulnerable, and mental health is no less vulnerable than any other of the other 'generic features of action'[20] that Gewirth identifies. This idea of 'vulnerable agency' is developed by Beyleveld and Brownsword in their analysis and application of Gewirth's moral theory.[21] In the next section, I outline this account of vulnerable agency, and propose my own which complements this, 'heightened vulnerable agency'.

2. VULNERABLE AGENCY AND HEIGHTENED VULNERABLE AGENCY

Beyleveld and Brownsword's account of vulnerable agency draws out an understanding of vulnerability embedded in Gewirth's moral theory.[22] For them, agents are vulnerable in three main ways. First, agents are 'insecure' in the sense that they can appreciate that they are able to be harmed because their freedom and well-being may be interfered with against their will.[23] Second, this 'insecurity' also derives from the fact that the pursuit of their own ends will typically involve dependence on others to help supply the means for this.[24] Third, by definition, agents 'have rational capacities that enable them to reflect upon the implications of their bodily

Gewirthian Mental Health Rights 177

and psychological frailties . . . which . . . leads them to suffer existential anxiety'.[25] Although there are parallels elsewhere in Kantian ethics,[26] what distinguishes Beyleveld and Brownsword's approach is that this vulnerability goes beyond providing a context for agency—it goes to the heart of what it means to ascribe the generic rights of agency and thus confer dignity under Gewirth's PGC.[27]

Accordingly, the agent acknowledges the inevitability of her vulnerability during the dialectically necessary argument of the PGC at two stages. First, she does this when accepting that it is possible for others to interfere with her having freedom and well-being although they ought not to, and that their assistance is needed when she alone cannot obtain freedom and well-being (at step 6 of the argument). Second, she does this when implicitly recognizing its universality by ascribing rights to all agents under the logical principle of universalization (at step 8 of the argument).[28] This account of vulnerable agency as inevitable and universally shared resonates with recent accounts of 'universal',[29] 'inherent',[30] 'ontological',[31] or 'baseline'[32] vulnerability. It also highlights the fact that, whilst vulnerability may be able to be managed,[33] it cannot be eradicated, and is compatible with accepting that our vulnerability may have a positive influence, enriching rather than undermining our lives.[34]

From this, it is clear that vulnerable agency is a strongly egalitarian and inclusive principle. Psychological well-being is constitutive of this vulnerability insofar as it is susceptible to the action and inaction of others and to existential angst, as well as our resilience to this. Thus, the starting point for thinking about mental health rights is what *all* agents face in terms of threats to mental health, the premise that no agent enjoys 'perfect' mental health and the constraints we all encounter in terms of resilience to the (in)action of others and our existential predicament. Because this fundamental threat to our psychological well-being is shared universally, it highlights the continuum—rather than divide—between people experiencing a typical level of mental health and people experiencing severe mental health problems or intellectual disability. In other words, vulnerable agency focuses on what unites agents in terms of threats to their mental health, rather than the alleged differences between the mentally 'well' and 'unwell'. Of course, if we are all vulnerable in terms of our freedom and well-being in general and our mental health in particular, it is particularly important that we can understand where vulnerability in terms of psychological well-being is particularly prominent and why.[35] To this end, it is important to draw a distinction between vulnerable agency, which is experienced universally, and what I call 'heightened vulnerable agency', which is experienced contingently.

In doing so, we should recognize at least three senses in which a lack of psychological well-being can heighten the experience of our vulnerable agency. These derive from interactions between the individual agent and her environment as well as from subjective experiences of mental distress.

178 *Bielby*

The first is state action or inaction that violates freedom or any one of the three types of well-being—'basic', 'nonsubtractive', and 'additive'—which Gewirth identifies.[36] Examples of this include inadequate, neglectful, or unduly coercive mental health service provision (including involuntary detention and treatment) or denial of legal capacity or access to justice, all of which can interfere with the freedom we need to exercise our agency. The second is adverse social responses, most obviously prejudice and discrimination, which create stigma and undermine the conditions in which we can choose to act as well as the purposes available to us.[37] The third is first-person experience of mental distress, such as a disrupted or 'challenged' sense of self.[38] In extreme instances, such as in severe schizophrenia, advanced dementia, or profound intellectual disabilities, poor mental health may erode voluntariness and purposivity, though, unlike Gewirth, this does not mean we should *assume* such individuals lack agentive capacities.[39]

It follows from this that the nature and extent of what we are vulnerable to is amplified to varying degrees by the experience of poor mental health. The distinction between the universality of vulnerable agency and the contingency of heightened vulnerable agency turns on this amplification. To be sure, this amplification is not uniform—it varies depending upon how supportive the social environment is and the coping resources and resilience of the individual agent, which is itself a socially influenced, relational quality.[40] It also avoids a tendency to label or stigmatize people experiencing severe mental health problems or intellectual disability by recognizing that the origin of their heightened vulnerability lies in something we all share equally and is something to which we are all susceptible. Careful attention to the manner in which a *particular* agent, rather than a group of agents, experiences heightened vulnerability (e.g., via a disintegrating sense of self in dementia or a predisposition to make reckless choices whilst in a 'manic episode' of bipolar depression) reduces the risk of what Scully refers to as 'ascribed global vulnerability', where the entire life of a person is deemed to be more than usually vulnerable on the basis of a heightened vulnerability in one area of their life.[41] Crucially, if vulnerable agency is seen as universal and inevitable, and heightened vulnerable agency is something we all are likely to experience to some degree at some point in our adult lives, there are no grounds whatsoever for viewing either type of vulnerability as alien, stigmatizing, or necessarily disempowering. Rather, it is from the recognition of the prevalence of this vulnerability that we can seek to refocus social and political institutions upon acceptance and even celebration of this fact rather than a denial of it.[42]

The discussion in this section now leads us to two questions: From an acceptance both of vulnerable agency and heightened vulnerable agency, what kind of mental health rights might Gewirthian ethics justify, and what difference does heightened vulnerable agency make to the rights held? We will explore both questions in the next section.

3. APPLYING THE CONCEPTS OF VULNERABLE AGENCY AND HEIGHTENED VULNERABLE AGENCY TO MENTAL HEALTH RIGHTS

A useful starting point in answering these questions is to be clear about what is meant by mental health rights. Surprisingly, there is very little literature on conceptualizing or even defining these.[43] One approach would be to understand mental health rights as a subset of those rights which 'inhere in the experience of disability',[44] as are present within the UN Convention on the Rights of Persons with Disabilities (hereafter CRPD).[45] Whilst it is true that some mental health rights can also be understood as 'disability rights' under the CRPD, to associate mental health rights with disability rights exclusively supposes that such rights are connected to the experience of heightened vulnerable agency alone, overlooking those mental health rights that all agents share.

The continuum between vulnerable agency and heightened vulnerable agency we have already recognized highlights how some mental health rights are common to all agents by virtue of our vulnerable agency, whereas others are specific to the experience of severe mental health problems or intellectual disability by virtue of heightened vulnerable agency. In light of this, and in keeping with the argument for the PGC in justifying positive as well as negative rights,[46] a more inclusive approach towards conceptualizing mental health rights involves drawing a distinction between those mental health rights that under Gewirth's moral theory would function as positive and negative rights to good psychological health and well-being (constitutive of a general right to health which Gewirth intimates),[47] and those positive and negative rights intended specifically to deal with circumstances where an agent develops different or particular needs that follow from the experience of a severe mental health problem or an intellectual disability.[48] I will call the former 'general mental health rights' and the latter 'specific mental health rights'.

Negative general mental health rights include, amongst other things, a basic right for any agent (irrespective of whether they are experiencing a mental health problem) not to be subject to coercive psychiatric interventions (such as psychotropic drugs) when they have the decisional competence to refuse,[49] and to an environment in which agents are free from persecution and degrading treatment. These also extend to nonsubtractive rights to be free from social exclusion, as well as from emotional manipulation and emotional neglect (which would constitute a basic right for a child, given their relative lack of resilience to this compared to adults).[50] Positive general mental health rights include the provision of appropriate treatment and services in order to maintain good mental health (e.g., counselling and psychotherapy) and education about understanding and promoting good mental health (including 'emotional literacy'),[51] both as part of a child's formal education and throughout life. These rights would also require the state to

180 *Bielby*

properly fund and provide access to mental healthcare on a par with physical healthcare, and a meaningful commitment on behalf of its institutions and wider civil society to respecting 'neurodiversity'—i.e. promoting inclusion and non-discrimination towards agents with 'brain differences', such as people with dyslexia or people on the autistic spectrum.[52] More generally, the right not to be subject to negatively differential treatment on the basis of one's level of mental health would involve the state and civil society organizations supporting programmes to eliminate discrimination and stigma surrounding mental health problems (such as the 'Time to Change' campaign in the UK.)[53] Such measures would collectively serve to maintain, as far as possible, an environment in which the mental health of all agents would be optimally preserved and enhanced, and reduce the risk of vulnerable agency becoming heightened vulnerable agency as far as mental health is concerned.

Specific mental health rights encompass rights for people experiencing mental health problems that raise their experience of mental distress above a typical level. These rights overlap with and are justified in the same way as general mental health rights, but are modified by circumstantial factors contingent on the experience of severe mental health problems and intellectual disability, such as disempowerment (e.g., denial of legal capacity), challenges surrounding access to justice, and susceptibility to exploitation.[54] As such, these rights derive their moral force from what agents with poor mental health all too often confront: prejudicial social environments, liberty-limiting legal frameworks, and the subjective experience of poor mental health itself, together tending to undermine one's ability to pursue and protect one's own needs of agency.[55] These rights involve positive and negative right-claims against the state and others in respect of upholding, amongst other things, civil liberties (e.g., which would heavily constrain liberty deprivation powers),[56] access to specialist mental healthcare, and non-discrimination. Since its introduction in 2006, the CRPD now provides a comprehensive list of such measures that apply to people with severe mental health problems and intellectual disability just to as much to individuals with physical disability.[57]

The distinction between general and specific mental health rights is nonetheless compatible with the egalitarian basis of the PGC on the following three grounds. First, the basis on which these rights is ascribed is the same basis as for all: vulnerable agency. The recognition that some agents are more vulnerable than others does not represent alternative grounds for the ascription of rights, but rather, it acknowledges why some agents are less able than others to secure their own needs of agency. Indeed, there are other examples of individuals who in various ways and to varying degrees experience heightened vulnerability, such as prisoners, asylum seekers, and children, for whom appropriate specific rights are also justifiable. To the extent that the justificatory grounding of rights is the same (i.e. the PGC), there is a clear point of integration between vulnerable agency and heightened vulnerable agency. Second, the continuum between vulnerable agency and heightened vulnerable agency allows specific mental health rights to be conceived of in

Gewirthian Mental Health Rights 181

moral terms as embodying a 'latent universality'. This means they are rights which can be held by all, but are triggered by need or by experiences of using mental health services. As such, they can be thought of as amplifications or reassertions of existing human rights as applied to contextual demands (e.g., disability).[58] Third, the social context in which rights are exercised is fully acknowledged. This is especially important for the context of heightened vulnerability due to severe mental health problems or intellectual disability, given that the rights bearer may be subject to experiences that are not universally shared, such as involuntary detention, denial of legal capacity, or forced medication. For these reasons, this model of mental health rights is also compatible with Mégret's recognition that some disability rights (such as 'the right to "live in the community"') are bespoke or 'new' rights,[59] in the sense that the lived experience of psychosocial disability requires rights that connect with the spirit of rights enjoyed universally but that are responsive to the obstacles that law, policy, and social attitudes (even in supposedly liberal societies) all too often create for people with severe mental health problems and intellectual disabilities.

It is not possible within this chapter to consider the extent to which the rights bestowed by the CRPD would satisfy the specific mental health rights endorsed by the PGC, which is a task for future research. However, insofar as the CRPD provisions have been recognized as compatible with rights-based moral philosophy,[60] there is a *prima facie* alignment between the values of the CRPD and the mental health rights of the PGC. In order to complete this justification of mental health rights, I will now turn my attention in the final section to an overlooked justificatory dimension of mental health rights implicit in the argument for the PGC. This is the idea that mental health rights (like rights in general) involve care in discharging the duties these rights create, comprising an important part of a wider Gewirthian moral obligation to develop caring dispositions and attitudes towards other agents.

4. CARE AND MENTAL HEALTH RIGHTS

Given that much discussion of Gewirthian ethics has turned upon a defence or critique of the argument for the PGC, comparatively less attention has been paid to the attitudes and dispositions that facilitate these rights being upheld. Gewirth goes some way to address this by proposing a concept of the 'reasonable self' who is inclined to abide by the moral prescriptions of the PGC and to cultivate character traits that assist in this.[61] Moreover, Gewirth draws parallels between his rational argument for the existence of human rights and an ethics of care in *The Community of Rights*, where he states explicitly:

> The thesis I present . . . can indeed be viewed as arguing not only for a caring society but also, in a parallel way, for an institutionalization of love . . . embodied in a system of policies motivated by a concern for

182 Bielby

the fulfilment of all persons' needs for dignity, self-respect, and more generally for the necessary conditions of action and generally successful action.[62]

Gewirth goes on to reaffirm this by explaining that an 'institutionalization of love' represents 'a deep concern for the freedom and well-being of all the members of the society'.[63] Unfortunately, as Gewirth does not develop this argument further, it is now for others to consider to what extent care is implicated in the duties the PGC generates. Despite this inchoate reference to care and a lack of association between the PGC and care ethics, I consider that the significance of care to Gewirth's moral theory allows one to read Gewirth's argument for the PGC as a rationalist ethics of care (based upon a rationalist theory of human rights), for reasons I offer below.

Nonetheless, it is perhaps unsurprising that the lack of sustained attention given to care within the PGC has coincided with the development of a relationship between care and rationalist ethics beyond the PGC rather than from within it.[64] Of those that engage with Gewirthian ethics explicitly, Engster develops a moral obligation to care that is tenuously informed by—though is ultimately different from—Gewirth's PGC. Engster's argument offers a rich seam of thinking about why a rationally justified obligation to care is valuable,[65] along with the lines along which a rational justification of caring may be justified.[66] Engster explains his 'principle of consistent dependency',[67] in which we all have an obligation to offer care for others to the extent we can do so,[68] in the following terms:

> *Since all human beings depend upon the care of others for our survival, development, and basic functioning and at least implicitly claim that capable individuals should care for individuals in need when they can do so, we should consistently recognize as morally valid the claims that others make upon us for care when they need it, and should endeavor to provide care to them when we are capable of doing so without significant danger to ourselves, seriously compromising our long-term functioning, or undermining our ability to care for others.* [Emphasis in original] Capable individuals who refuse to honor this principle violate the logical principle of noncontradiction and behave hypocritically.[69]

In one sense, there are clear parallels between this and the argument for the PGC. Engster recognizes a move between a prudential and moral claim right over care in the sense that our need for care is universalized to others in similar need, and that to deny care to others where the costs to ourselves are not great is to contradict the basis on which we all stand in need of care during our lives.[70] These steps in the argument are akin to the move from Stage 2 (prudential rights claim) to Stage 3 (universalized moral rights claim) in the argument for the PGC[71] and the requirement that agents are able to think logically (thus avoiding self-contradiction) about what their action entails.[72]

Gewirthian Mental Health Rights   183

However, Engster's reasons for departing from the PGC seem to overlook the resources available *within* the PGC to support care—even though these resources are not as vivid or as developed as they could have been.

Gewirth's concept of the 'reasonable self',[73] disposed to follow the prescriptions of the PGC, offers a relational standpoint to incline an agent towards a caring outlook in respect of other agents. According to Gewirth, 'the reasonable self recognizes that it has obligations toward others as well as rights against others' and has a 'commitment to social solidarity' that moves beyond an 'adversarial' focus on upholding rights to an ethos of cooperativeness and 'mutuality of consideration'.[74] This outlook also resonates with Gewirth's observation that 'rational autonomy, far from being self-centred, incorporates . . . interconnectedness and concern for others'.[75] Since Gewirth also makes clear that '[t]he argument [for the PGC] takes humans as they actually are . . . the features of human selves that are permitted to enter the argument [are required to] be only those that no agent can consistently reject'[76] and, as we have seen, the vulnerability of all agents and their dependency on others are inexorable features of the human condition,[77] a corollary of the 'reasonable self' is the development of dispositions and attitudes of empathy and compassion. These function to assist agents in being aware as far as possible of when the plight of fellow agents generates positive duties of assistance (as well as receptiveness to situations in which such assistance may be rejected), and how to discharge these duties most sensitively. Such dispositions and attitudes allow agents to take the vulnerability and dependency of others as seriously as possible precisely because the agent must take *her own* vulnerability seriously (at Stage 2 of the argument), recognizing through universalization (at Stage 3 of the argument) the basis of the common need for care to which Engster crucially draws our attention. This fosters a collective approach towards fulfilling agents' rights-claims which is, using Engster's phrase, 'attentive, responsive, and respectful'.[78]

Taken together, we can consider these caring dispositions and attitudes of the 'reasonable self' as individuating the traits of the 'caring society' to which Gewirth refers.[79] In eliciting these latent resources within the PGC to support care, Engster's reasons for seeking to depart from Gewirth in developing a rational theory of caring therefore appear less compelling. Moreover, Engster's claim that 'Gewirth's argument depends upon the willingness of individuals to recognize themselves and others as autonomous agents',[80] which he regards as 'one of the central weaknesses' of the PGC,[81] suggests having overlooked that anyone who acts in pursuit of freely chosen purposes (whatever these are) *is an* autonomous agent under the PGC, irrespective of her willingness to identify herself as such or accept this—indeed, her very reluctance or refusal to do so evinces her agency.[82]

The role of care—as an application of the empathic traits of the 'reasonable self'—becomes all the more important in the context of both general and specific mental health rights. In the context of general mental health rights,

184 *Bielby*

the PGC's support for 'a caring society'[83] requires that all agents contribute to fostering a compassionate social environment in which genuine concern is shown for the mental health of all individuals. This derives from the caringly minded dispositions and attitudes of the 'reasonable self' described above, cultivating respect for and understanding of mental health issues as well as 'self-care' for one's own mental health drawn from the recognition of the universal vulnerability of all. When collectivized, such dispositions and attitudes would be conducive to a culture in which mental health is treated on a par with physical health, negative portrayals of poor mental health are avoided, and educational resources are directed towards understanding and promoting what good mental health involves. They also provide a foundation from which to make progress collectively towards an ideal environment in which the mental health of all agents would be optimally maintained and enhanced, thereby reducing as far as possible the possibility and probability of levels of mental health associated with vulnerable agency deteriorating towards levels associated with heightened vulnerable agency.

In the context of specific mental health rights, where the capacity to secure one's own generic rights is reduced and where the social and legal context may all too often fail to recognize one's rights, such rights need to be all the more robust and thoroughgoing to accommodate these challenges. Accordingly, strategies towards securing the generic rights on behalf of individuals living with the socially mediated experience of severe mental health problems or intellectual disability must promote attempts to help such agents realize their decisional and participative capacities as far as possible. They should also treat the agent in question with respect and sensitivity as a distinct individual with particular wishes, values, and fears rather than as an impersonal member of an overarching group. Encouragingly, steps have already been taken towards this goal in international law during the last decade via the CRPD. In particular, the concept of 'supported decision-making', where autonomy and participation is maximized in situations that involve decision-making about medical treatment, financial affairs, or participation in civil society, has much that is consistent with positive rights under the PGC to freedom and well-being.

Supported decision-making requires, as Arstein-Kerslake puts it, 'an empowering dependency',[84] in which the individual and her supported decision-maker enjoy respect for their moral agency and 'legal personhood', the supported decision-maker does not dominate this dependent relationship or influence the decision reached, and that the practice avoids intrusive regulation within the life of the person to be supported.[85] Certainly, this is an ambitious aim, not least because existing mental health and capacity laws often do not embody such a system of decision-making, which may require a move away from disability-dependent binary divisions such as 'capacity' and incapacity', and conventional 'best interests' assessments.[86] Of course, in the most extreme cases, where any prospects for the individual's

Gewirthian Mental Health Rights 185

participation in their own decision-making have diminished irrevocably (such as in advanced dementia), conventional paternalistic strategies need to be pursued that still ensure that such individuals are treated attentively with respect and sensitivity.[87] Nevertheless, the empowering ethos of the CRPD and the direction in which it leads law reform in signatory states represents a promising congruence with specific (as well as general) mental health rights.

CONCLUSION

In this chapter, I have sought to offer a Gewirthian justification of mental health rights based on an integrated account of vulnerable agency and 'heightened vulnerable agency'. I have attempted to show that mental health rights can be predicated upon our shared vulnerable agency as well as when our vulnerable agency is heightened through the socially mediated experience of severe mental health problems and intellectual disability. From this, I have drawn a distinction between two types of mental health rights under the PGC—'general mental health rights', connected with universal vulnerable agency, and 'specific mental health rights', connected with heightened vulnerable agency. The nature and content of these rights overlap to reflect the continuum between vulnerable agency and heightened vulnerable agency. I then considered how Gewirth's account of the 'reasonable self' and vision of 'a caring society' supports dispositions and attitudes of care in fulfilling mental health rights. In this way, care is a component of articulating and upholding both general mental health rights and specific mental health rights, focusing on promoting good mental health in terms of the former and empowerment in relation to the latter. It also demonstrates why the PGC can be understood as a rationalist ethics of care.

The arguments of this chapter now invite future research questions. The most obvious of these, arguably, is a more detailed consideration of how general and specific mental health rights further a caring vision of the PGC's application. There is also scope for further work to be done (beyond Cavadino's earlier contribution)[88] on the extent to which Gewirthian mental health rights would support a move away from traditional models of detention and treatment for severe mental health problems where an individual's decision-making has not been impaired.[89] Moreover, the PGC's resources to support a rational justification of care outside of the domain of mental health offer numerous possibilities for further investigation. Given that Gewirth had little to say directly on mental health or care, and existing scholarship interfacing Gewirthian ethics and mental health is limited, a Gewirthian justification of mental health rights offers a novel conceptual understanding of these rights that reveals their transformative potential.

186 *Bielby*

NOTES

1. D. Beyleveld and R. Brownsword, *Human Dignity in Bioethics and Biolaw* (Oxford: Oxford University Press, 2001), Chapter 6.
2. Derek Bolton remarks that the term ' "mental health problems" . . . is probably neutral to aetiology' and minimizes stigma. As Bolton acknowledges, it is also an increasingly preferred term across healthcare and public discourse. D. Bolton, *What Is Mental Disorder?* (Oxford: Oxford University Press, 2008), p. 248.
3. A. Gewirth, 'Human Rights and Conceptions of the Self', *Philosophia*, 18 (1988), pp. 129–49.
4. A. Gewirth, *The Community of Rights* (Chicago: The University of Chicago Press, 1996), p. xv.
5. A. Gewirth, *Reason and Morality* (Chicago: The University of Chicago Press, 1978), p. 54.
6. A. Gewirth, 'The Basis and Content of Human Rights', *Georgia Law Review*, 13 (1978–79), pp. 1143–70, on p. 1158.
7. Gewirth, *Reason and Morality*, p. 37.
8. Ibid., pp. 31–2.
9. Ibid., pp. 120–2; pp. 140–2.
10. I discuss this in P. Bielby, *Competence and Vulnerability in Biomedical Research* (Dordrecht: Springer, 2008), Chapters 4 and 5. (Hereafter 'CVBR'.)
11. Ibid., p. 120; pp. 141–2.
12. Ibid., p. 120; pp. 140–2.
13. Gewirth, 'The Basis and Content of Human Rights', p. 1159.
14. A. Gewirth, *Self-Fulfilment* (Princeton, NJ: Princeton University Press, 1998), p. 94.
15. Ibid., p. 13.
16. Ibid., p. 13.
17. Ibid., pp. 150–1.
18. Gewirth, *Reason and Morality*, p. 37.
19. For a discussion, see: P. Bracken and P. Thomas, *Postpsychiatry* (Oxford: Oxford University Press, 2005); and J. Cromby *et al.*, *Psychology, Mental Health and Distress* (Basingstoke: Palgrave, 2013).
20. Gewirth, *Reason and Morality*, p. 25.
21. D. Beyleveld and R. Brownsword, *Human Dignity in Bioethics and Biolaw* (Oxford: Oxford University Press, 2001), Chapter 6.
22. Ibid., p. 115.
23. Ibid., p. 115.
24. Ibid., p. 114. Beyleveld and Brownsword also add to this a capacity to act immorally, though this is not relevant to the present discussion.
25. Ibid., p. 112.
26. P. Formosa, 'The Role of Vulnerability in Kantian Ethics', in C. Mackenzie, *et al.* (eds) *Vulnerability* (New York: Oxford University Press, 2014), pp. 88–109.
27. Beyleveld and Brownsword, *Human Dignity in Bioethics and Biolaw*, p. 112.
28. Here, I am using Beyleveld and Brownsword's concise eight-step presentation of the argument to the PGC, ibid., pp. 73–4.
29. M. A. Fineman, 'The Vulnerable Subject: Anchoring Equality in the Human Condition', *Yale Journal of Law and Feminism*, 20 (2008–09), pp. 1–23, on p. 8.
30. W. Rogers *et al.*, 'Why bioethics needs a concept of vulnerability', *International Journal of Feminist Approaches to Bioethics*, 5:2 (2012), pp. 11–38, on p. 24.
31. Ibid., p. 12.
32. Bielby, *CVBR*, p. 53.

Gewirthian Mental Health Rights 187

33. M. Del Mar, 'Relational Jurisprudence: Vulnerability between Fact and Value', *Recht en Methode in onderzoek en onderwijs*, 2:2 (2012), pp. 63–81, on p. 76.
34. A. Grear, *Redirecting Human Rights* (Basingstoke: Palgrave, 2010), pp. 129–30; and J. Herring, *Caring and the Law* (Oxford: Hart, 2013), p. 55.
35. Bielby, *CVBR*, p. 53.
36. On freedom, see Gewirth, *Reason and Morality*, pp. 31–7; pp. 249–71. On basic, nonsubtractive, and additive well-being, see ibid., pp. 54–9; pp. 210–49.
37. See for a discussion J. Randall *et al.*, 'Stigma and Discrimination: Critical Human Rights Issues for Mental Health', in M. Dudley *et al.* (eds) *Mental Health and Human Rights* (Oxford: Oxford University Press, 2012), pp. 113–24.
38. M. C. Dunn, *et al.*, 'To Empower or to Protect? Constructing the "Vulnerable Adult", in English Law and Public Policy', *Legal Studies*, 28:2 (2008), pp. 234–53, on pp. 245–6; J. Spiers, 'New Perspectives on Vulnerability Using Emic and Etic Approaches', *Journal of Advanced Nursing*, 31:3 (2000), pp. 715–21, on p. 719.
39. Gewirth, *Reason and Morality*, pp. 141–2. I do not have the scope within this chapter to elaborate on the 'precautionary reasoning' approach developed by Beyleveld, Brownsword, and Pattinson to ascribing rights to people whose evidence for agency is questionable, but for a discussion see Bielby, *CVBR*, Chapters 4 and 5 and D. Beyleveld, 'The Principle of Generic Consistency as the Supreme Principle of Human Rights', *Human Rights Review*, 13 (2012), pp. 1–18, on p. 10.
40. See the discussion of resilience in Fineman, 'The Vulnerable Subject', especially pp. 14–15 and Rogers *et al.*, 'Why bioethics needs a concept of vulnerability', especially pp. 12–13, p. 24 and p. 32.
41. J. L. Scully, 'Disability and Vulnerability: On Bodies, Dependence and Power', in C. Mackenzie, *et al.* (eds) *Vulnerability* (New York: Oxford University Press, 2014), pp. 204–21, on p. 209.
42. Fineman, 'The Vulnerable Subject', p. 20.
43. Turner comes close with a vulnerability-grounded model of disability rights, which he extends to intellectual disability and mental health problems, though the idea of 'mental health rights' is not developed. B. S. Turner, *Vulnerability and Human Rights* (University Park, PA: Pennsylvania State University Press, 2006), Chapter 5, especially pp. 103–7.
44. F. Mégret, 'The Disabilities Convention: Human Rights of Persons with Disabilities or Disability Rights?', *Human Rights Quarterly*, 30:2 (2008), pp. 494–516, on p. 498.
45. UN General Assembly, *Convention on the Rights of Persons with Disabilities and Optional Protocol* (New York: UN, 2006), available at: http://www.un.org/disabilities/documents/convention/convoptprot-e.pdf [accessed 28 August 2015].
46. Gewirth, *The Community of Rights*, Chapter 2.
47. Gewirth, *Reason and Morality*, pp. 211–12; Gewirth, *Self-Fulfilment*, p. 195.
48. M. Cavadino, 'A Vindication of the Rights of Psychiatric Patients', *Journal of Law and Society*, 24:2 (1997), pp. 235–51. Of the authors of which I am aware, Cavadino has come closest to developing in this article a Gewirthian theory of mental health rights, though he focuses on the specific context of compulsory detention and treatment for mental disorder, rather than mental health rights more broadly.
49. See for a discussion, ibid., pp. 242–43.
50. For the importance of emotional well-being in developmental terms, see S. Gerhardt, *Why Love Matters* (Hove: Routledge, 2004).
51. See, e.g., D. Spendlove, *Emotional Literacy* (London: Continuum, 2008).

188   *Bielby*

52. See for a discussion T. Armstrong, *Neurodiversity* (Cambridge, MA: Da Capo Press, 2010).
53. See Time to Change, 'Who Are We?' (undated), available at: http://www.time-to-change.org.uk/about-us/what-is-time-to-change [accessed 28 August 2015].
54. For a discussion of this context, see the collection of essays in M. Dudley *et al.* (eds) *Mental Health and Human Rights* as well as E. Flynn, *Disabled Justice?* (Farnham: Ashgate, 2015).
55. This conceptualization of heightened vulnerability is indebted to Mackenzie and Rogers, who understand heightened vulnerability as being less able than usual to safeguard one's own interests. C. Mackenzie and W. Rogers 'Autonomy, Vulnerability and Capacity: A Philosophical Appraisal of the Mental Capacity Act', *International Journal of Law in Context*, 9:1 (2013), pp. 37–52, on p. 52 n. 3.
56. See the discussion in Cavadino, 'A Vindication of the Rights of Psychiatric Patients'.
57. G. Szmukler *et al.*, 'Mental health law and the UN Convention on the rights of persons with disabilities', *International Journal of Law and Psychiatry*, 37 (2014), pp. 245–52, on p. 246.
58. Mégret, 'The Disabilities Convention' on pp. 498–9 and p. 509.
59. Ibid., p. 510.
60. C. Harnacke, 'Disability and Capability: Exploring the Usefulness of Martha Nussbaum's Capabilities Approach for the UN Disability Rights Convention', *Journal of Law, Medicine and Ethics*, 41:4 (2013), pp. 768–80. Harnacke draws on Nussbaum's 'capabilities approach' in this regard, which as she emphasizes, is related to human rights theory. Ibid., p. 771–2. Interestingly, Harnacke gestures towards Gewirth towards the end of the article where she speculates that Gewirth's moral theory (amongst others) may be worth investigating in order to identify a moral theory that can 'underline the requirements of the CRPD and . . . provide normative criteria that can be used to set priorities in practical situations'. Ibid., p. 778.
61. Gewirth, 'Human Rights and Conceptions of the Self'.
62. Gewirth, *The Community of Rights*, xv.
63. Ibid., p. 83.
64. W. Rehg, *Insight and Solidarity* (Berkeley, CA: University of California Press, 1994), Chapter 7; D. Engster, *The Heart of Justice* (Oxford: Oxford University Press, 2007), Chapter 1.
65. Engster, *The Heart of Justice*, p. 49.
66. Ibid., Chapter 1.
67. Ibid., p. 49.
68. Ibid., p. 49.
69. Ibid., p. 49.
70. Ibid., pp. 49–50.
71. Gewirth, *Reason and Morality*, pp. 63–198, D. Beyleveld, *The Dialectical Necessity of Morality* (Chicago: The University of Chicago Press, 1991) Chapter 2, esp. pp. 24–46.
72. Gewirth, *Reason and Morality*, p. 44.
73. Gewirth, 'Human Rights and Conceptions of the Self'.
74. Ibid., pp. 144–5.
75. Gewirth, *The Community of Rights*, p. 117.
76. Ibid., p. 26.
77. Beyleveld and Brownsword, *Human Dignity in Bioethics and Biolaw*, p. 114–5.
78. Engster, *The Heart of Justice*, p. 31.
79. Gewirth, *The Community of Rights*, xv.

Gewirthian Mental Health Rights   189

80. Engster, *The Heart of Justice*, pp. 50–1.
81. Ibid., p. 50.
82. Beyleveld, *The Dialectical Necessity of Morality*, pp. 138–40.
83. Gewirth, *The Community of Rights*, xv.
84. A. Arstein-Kerslake, 'An empowering dependency: exploring support for the exercise of legal capacity', *Scandinavian Journal of Disability Research*, 18:1 (2016), pp. 77–92 on p. 78.
85. Ibid., p. 88.
86. P. Bartlett, 'The United Nations Convention on the Rights of Persons with Disabilities and Mental Health Law', *Modern Law Review*, 75:5 (2012), pp. 752–78, on pp. 762–67.
87. Bielby, *CVBR*, p. 135.
88. Cavadino, 'A Vindication of the Rights of Psychiatric Patients'.
89. For instance, along the lines proposed by Szmukler *et al.*, 'Mental health law and the UN Convention on the rights of persons with disabilities', p. 245.

WORKS CITED

Armstrong, T., *Neurodiversity: Discovering the Extraordinary Gifts of Autism, ADHD, Dyslexia, and Other Brain Differences* (Cambridge, MA: Da Capo Press, 2010).

Arstein-Kerslake, A., 'An Empowering Dependency: Exploring Support for the Exercise of Legal Capacity', *Scandinavian Journal of Disability Research*. 18:1 (2016), pp. 77–92.

Bartlett, P., 'The United Nations Convention on the Rights of Persons with Disabilities and Mental Health Law', *Modern Law Review*, 75:5 (2012), pp. 752–78.

Beyleveld, D., *The Dialectical Necessity of Morality: An Analysis and Defense of Alan Gewirth's Argument to the Principle of Generic Consistency* (Chicago: The University of Chicago Press, 1991).

———, 'The Principle of Generic Consistency as the Supreme Principle of Human Rights', *Human Rights Review*, 13:1 (2012), pp. 1–18.

Beyleveld, D. and Brownsword, R., *Human Dignity in Bioethics and Biolaw* (Oxford: Oxford University Press, 2001).

Bielby, P., *Competence and Vulnerability in Biomedical Research* (Dordrecht: Springer, 2008).

Bolton, D., *What Is Mental Disorder? An Essay in Philosophy, Science, and Values* (Oxford: Oxford University Press, 2008).

Bracken P. and Thomas, P., *Postpsychiatry: Mental Health in a Postmodern World* (Oxford: Oxford University Press, 2005).

Cavadino, M. 'A Vindication of the Rights of Psychiatric Patients', *Journal of Law and Society*, 24:2 (1997), pp. 235–51.

Cromby J., Harper, D. and Reavey, P., *Psychology, Mental Health and Distress* (Basingstoke: Palgrave Macmillan, 2013).

Del Mar, M. 'Relational Jurisprudence: Vulnerability between Fact and Value', *Recht en Methode in onderzoek en onderwijs*, 2:2 (2012), pp. 63–81.

Dunn, M. C., Clare, I. C. H. and Holland, A. J., 'To empower or to protect? Constructing the "Vulnerable Adult" in English Law and Public Policy', *Legal Studies*, 28:2 (2008), pp. 234–53.

Dudley, M., Silove, D., and Gale, F., *Mental Health and Human Rights: Vision, Praxis, and Courage* (Oxford: Oxford University Press, 2012).

Engster, D., *The Heart of Justice: Care Ethics and Political Theory* (Oxford: Oxford University Press, 2007).

Fineman, M. A. 'The Vulnerable Subject: Anchoring Equality in the Human Condition', *Yale Journal of Law and Feminism*, 20, (2008–09), pp. 1–23.

190 Bielby

Flynn, E., *Disabled Justice? Access to Justice and the UN Convention on the Rights of Persons with Disabilities* (Farnham: Ashgate, 2015).

Formosa P. 'The Role of Vulnerability in Kantian Ethics', in C. Mackenzie, W. Rogers and S. Dodds (eds.), *Vulnerability: New Essays in Ethics and Feminist Philosophy* (New York: Oxford University Press, 2014), pp. 88–109.

Gerhardt, S., *Why Love Matters* (Hove: Routledge, 2004).

Gewirth, A., *Reason and Morality* (Chicago: The University of Chicago Press, 1978).

———, 'The Basis and Content of Human Rights', *Georgia Law Review*, 13 (1978–79), pp. 1143–70.

———, 'Human Rights and Conceptions of the Self', *Philosophia*, 18 (1988), pp. 129–49.

———, *The Community of Rights* (Chicago: The University of Chicago Press, 1996).

———, *Self-Fulfilment* (Princeton, NJ: Princeton University Press, 1998).

Grear, A., *Redirecting Human Rights: Facing the Challenge of Corporate Legal Humanity* (Basingstoke: Palgrave Macmillan, 2010).

Harnacke, C., 'Disability and Capability: Exploring the Usefulness of Martha Nussbaum's Capabilities Approach for the UN Disability Rights Convention', *Journal of Law, Medicine and Ethics*, 41:4 (2013), pp. 768–80.

Herring, J., *Caring and the Law* (Oxford: Hart, 2013).

Mackenzie, C. and Rogers, W. 'Autonomy, Vulnerability and Capacity: A Philosophical Appraisal of the Mental Capacity Act', *International Journal of Law in Context*, 9:1 (2013), pp. 37–52.

Mégret, F., 'The Disabilities Convention: Human Rights of Persons with Disabilities or Disability Rights?', *Human Rights Quarterly*, 30:2 (2008), pp. 494–516.

Randall, J., Thornicroft, G., Brohan, E., Kassam, A., Lewis-Holmes, E., and Mehta, N., 'Stigma and Discrimination: Critical Human Rights Issues for Mental Health', in M. Dudley, D. Silove and F. Gale (eds.), *Mental Health and Human Rights: Vision, Praxis, and Courage* (Oxford: Oxford University Press, 2012), pp. 113–24.

Rehg, W., *Insight and Solidarity: The Discourse Ethics of Jürgen Habermas* (Berkeley, CA: University of California Press, 1994).

Rogers, W., Mackenzie, C. and Dodds, S., 'Why Bioethics Needs a Concept of Vulnerability', *International Journal of Feminist Approaches to Bioethics*, 5:2 (2012), pp. 11–38.

Scully, J. L., 'Disability and Vulnerability: On Bodies, Dependence and Power', in C. Mackenzie, W. Rogers and S. Dodds (eds.), *Vulnerability: New Essays in Ethics and Feminist Philosophy* (New York: Oxford University Press, 2014), pp. 204–21.

Spendlove, D., *Emotional Literacy* (London: Continuum, 2008).

Spiers, J., 'New Perspectives on Vulnerability Using Emic and Etic Approaches', *Journal of Advanced Nursing*, 31:3 (2000), pp. 715–21.

Szmukler, G., Daw, R. and Callard, F., 'Mental Health Law and the UN Convention on the Rights of Persons with Disabilities', *International Journal of Law and Psychiatry* (2014), pp. 245–52.

Time to Change, 'Who Are We?' (undated), available at http://www.time-to-change.org.uk/about-us/what-is-time-to-change [accessed 28 August 2015].

Turner, B. S., *Vulnerability and Human Rights* (University Park, PA: The Pennsylvania State University Press, 2006).

United Nations General Assembly, *Convention on the Rights of Persons with Disabilities and Optional Protocol* (New York: United Nations, 2006), available at http://www.un.org/disabilities/documents/convention/convoptprot-e.pdf [accessed 28 August 2015].

12 Gewirthian Philosophy and Young Adults Who Have Down Syndrome

Towards a Human Rights-Based Model of Community Engagement for Young People Living With an Intellectual Disability

Miriam Stevenson

INTRODUCTION

As a post-Kantian philosopher, the fundamental motive of Alan Gewirth was to justify morality employing logic via the concept of human agency and to stress the reciprocity of absolute human rights to freedom and well-being.[1] There are few social groups who have suffered the same human rights violations as people with an intellectual disability; their collective history is one of ritual devaluation and exclusion by and from mainstream society.[2] Over the centuries, such individuals have been subject to incarceration in institutions to receive not only 'care', but also ensure their detention.[3] Denial of basic rights is still problematic and abuses have been (and continue to be) widespread globally in ongoing discourses linked to thinly veiled support for eugenics.[4] Although in most Western countries, the process of de-institutionalization was well underway in the 1990s, people with disabilities in general have been slow to access and enjoy their human rights, and for this reason, the 2008 UN Convention on the Rights of Persons with Disabilities (CRPD) was brought into being. The CRPD did not conceive of any new rights for people with a disability; rather, it reiterated a new commitment to the realization of existing rights. This chapter is specifically concerned with integrating Alan Gewirth's moral position with 'disability rights' through critical reflection on a rights-based research project involving young people who have Down syndrome.

DOWN SYNDROME

The medical model of Down syndrome states that:

> Trisomy 21 (Down syndrome) is observed with a frequency of 1 in 650 live births regardless of geography or ethnic background. This should be reduced with widespread screening.[5]

192 *Stevenson*

This syndrome was originally identified by Down, who was superintendent of the Earlswood Asylum for the 'mentally defective' in Surrey, England from 1858–1868. Down was held to be, for his time, a humanitarian and philanthropist. In 1866, he published a paper describing the Down syndrome 'phenotype', observing a 'Mongolian type of idiocy'.[6] Down syndrome has since been defined as a genetic variation that is typically caused by an extra copy of the twenty-first chromosome. There are three forms of Down syndrome: trisomy 21, translocation, and mosaicism. Trisomy 21 is present in 95% of the population who have Down syndrome. The latter two forms are less common. In Australia and internationally, a combination of tests now exists that can identify Down syndrome in the first trimester of pregnancy.[7] In a recent systematic review, the decision to undergo an induced abortion varied depending on whether prospective parents were from the general population (23%–33% would terminate), pregnant women at increased risk for having a child with Down syndrome (46%–86% would terminate), or women who received a positive diagnosis during the prenatal period (89%–97% terminated). Multiple factors influence women's decision-making following diagnosis, including demographic factors such as religion, maternal age, gestational age, number of existing children, and a history of induced abortion. Psychosocial factors, including perceived parenting burden/reward, quality of life for a child with Down syndrome, attitudes toward and comfort with individuals with disabilities, and support from others also are important influences.[8]

Whilst Down syndrome is acknowledged to be one of the most common causes of intellectual disability, Pueschel, an eminent physician, concluded that some people with Down syndrome are not 'mentally retarded' at all, which reflects the contested nature of disability, even in one of the most taken-for-granted categories/labels of intellectual disability.[9] As a social work practitioner and researcher, my own perspective in relation to Down syndrome is that espoused by the Canadian Down Syndrome Society. It is stressed that Down syndrome is 'not a disease, defect, disorder or medical condition'; rather, it is a naturally occurring chromosomal arrangement. 'Down syndrome has always existed; it is a genetic variation which occurs in all races, geographic areas, socio-economic groups, communities and genders'.[10] Evidently, perceptions of Down syndrome and intellectual disability generally are deeply politicized and contentious. For this reason, non-disabled researchers in the field such as myself must exercise critical self-reflection on each step of the journey, and our methodologies must be well-considered and open to scrutiny. The theoretical and methodological discussion is best contextualized by a description of the project that provides a basis for the application of Gewirthian philosophy.

THE RESEARCH CONTEXT

> [We want] To do stuff in our life like everybody else, like getting a job, moving out, seeing friends, going out, having a relationship and helping others.[11]

Gewirthian Philosophy and Down Syndrome 193

Table 12.1 Action research project aims for the community engagement of young people who have Down syndrome.

i. To bring together a steering group made of young people who have Down syndrome, researchers and workers from the disability sector, family members, and an employed coordinator to action the initiative.
ii. To give young people who have Down syndrome the chance to think and talk about their future and identify personal goals.
iii. To bring together a circle of support around each person involved to support that person in reaching their goals.
iv. To support the circle members through training, facilitation, ongoing contact, and by providing relevant information.
v. To ensure the goals identified by the young person who have Down syndrome remain the focus of the team.
vi. To provide the opportunity for young people involved in the project to give and receive support from each other through regular contact.
vii. To provide the opportunity for team members (champions) to network and problem solve together through regular contact.

The research took place in Australia between 2007 and 2011 and was conducted within and driven by a 3-year participatory action research project funded by a national charity and based within a non-government agency. All project participants were young adults who have Down syndrome, aged 18–25 years. The project was based on consultation with the young people themselves, and its broad aims are given in Table 12.1. The project constituted a journey on which the young people were facilitated to develop Circles of Support designed to promote their community inclusion, independent living skills, and work towards achieving personal goals. The research aimed to learn about the nature and meaning of inclusive social citizenship from the perspective of the young people.

There was an evolutionary vision for the project that was grounded in these practical aims, but the initial project was not 'framed' academically as such. My strategy of inquiry was to make all aspects of the research process as participatory as possible with respect to the co-researchers, to draw on their 'local expertise' and ensure that their 'voices' were heard throughout.

THE SOCIETAL INCLUSION OF PEOPLE WITH INTELLECTUAL DISABILITY: WHAT DOES IT MEAN?

Politically, people with an intellectual disability are largely perceived as an 'excluded' group. The language and politics of 'social inclusion' have therefore been deployed in attempts to integrate them fully into the mainstream society. Subsequently, the CRPD sought to reiterate and reinforce the human rights of disabled people with an emphasis on their inclusion and participation in society. Scholars have identified a number of theoretical and practical

194 *Stevenson*

problems with the concept of 'social inclusion', as it lacks a clear definition and a coherent theoretical 'core'.[12] Largely because of these factors, problems of interpretation can occur at the theoretical, cultural, and political levels. For example, 'social inclusion' limits its scope to those people who are (somewhat arbitrarily) deemed 'excluded'. One imagines a scene of the passive 'excluded' minority being (arbitrarily) 'included' by a benevolent and charitable majority.

Additionally, whilst social inclusion generally alludes to and emphasizes participation in the community and is thereby linked to social citizenship, crucially, there is no *theoretical* linkage to rights, as there is with the status of citizenship. Other questions arise: Do all the problems encountered by people with an intellectual disability relate to 'social exclusion'? Can such problems be solved by 'social inclusion'? If there is no clear definition of social inclusion, how can we know this? It can be argued that social inclusion means different things to different people but, by the same token, inclusion can end up meaning 'everything and nothing at the same time'.[13] Social inclusion as a 'stand-alone' and inexplicit concept lends itself easily to political rhetoric but does not furnish 'the excluded' with any means whatsoever of establishing clear accountability at the level of government. This can mean that the excluded (and their supporters) are constantly in the position of lobbying for 'inclusion'. Crucially, 'social inclusion' does not intrinsically suggest or require that the 'excluded' have a role in defining for themselves how they wish to be included. Some authors favour the term 'participation', as it engenders a more proactive and less passive stance on the part of the 'excluded' individual; however, a similar critique can be applied.[14] Given the arbitrary nature of the concepts of participation and inclusion, a major driving force throughout the research was the need to develop and maintain theoretical and ideological integrity within both the research methodology and discussion of findings.

THE THEORETICAL FRAMEWORK OF THE RESEARCH

Primacy was given to the participatory activity and voices of the young people in the research process. Congruent with this approach, I constructed a theoretical framework of inclusive social citizenship informed by the views of the young people in this study, founded on a platform of Gewirthian philosophy. In developing a theoretical basis for the research, I made meaningful links between the CRPD, the social model of disability, the Emancipatory Disability Research (EDR) paradigm, and Participatory Action Research (PAR) as a basis for activist social work research alongside people with an intellectual disability. Figure 12.1 displays Gewirthian objects of human rights (freedom and well-being) with the social model, EDR, and PAR as conceptual pillars.

The methodology of the research is laid out in detail in my previous works,[15] but here, I summarize each of the key conceptual pillars, describe the research methods, and discuss the key findings.

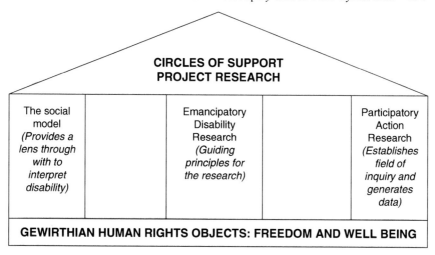

Figure 12.1   The theoretical framework of the research.

THE SOCIAL MODEL OF DISABILITY

Citing a number of studies in support of his argument that responses to impairment are culturally constructed, Oliver used the work of Comte and Marx to explain what happened to disabled people with the development of the capitalist society.[16] Using a materialist perspective, Oliver held that in understanding humanity, we need to understand our relationship with the material environment as it both produces and satisfies human needs. As the complexity of a society increases, so will its limits upon certain human freedoms. The socio-economic structure of society at different points in history influences the types of working practices, living conditions, and the relationships between individuals, groups, and social institutions.

Hence, the social model of disability maintains that 'disability' is socially constructed and it is this, rather than personal impairment, which results in societal disablement. Specifically, the social model of disability defines impairment and disability as a dual classification:

Impairment: lacking part of or all of a limb, or having a defective limb, organism or mechanism of the body;
Disability: the disadvantage or restriction of activity caused by a contemporary social organisation which takes little or no account of people who have physical impairments and thus excludes them from the mainstream of activities.[17]

The social model identifies the difference between impairment and disability such that 'impairment is the functional limitation within the individual

196   *Stevenson*

caused by physical, mental or sensory impairment'. Disability, meanwhile, is the 'loss or limitation of opportunities to take part in the normal life of the community on an equal level with others due to environmental and social barriers'.[18] The social model is now generally considered to be inclusive of people with an intellectual disability and impacts the use of language and terminology.

EMANCIPATORY RESEARCH

In reframing how non-disabled researchers should engage with people living with a disability, Oliver alluded to the need for a consistent and emancipatory form of PAR.[19] In 1991, the principles of EDR were formed following seminars attended by progressive disabled academics who set out to challenge the traditional academic research paradigms, many of which excluded (and continue to exclude) disabled people from the research process. EDR emphasizes the control and involvement of disabled people in research, researcher accountability, practical outcomes, methodological transparency, and the discussion of individual lived experience within environmental and cultural contexts.[20] The social model of disability is central to EDR, as it describes the economic, environmental, and cultural barriers encountered by disabled people and their families.

The PAR methodology was particularly congruent with the Circles of Support project, which was crafted as action research in close collaboration with young people who have Down syndrome. The overall aim was practical: to respond and adapt to the wishes and requirements of the young people and their families and identify the support processes that were useful to them in working to achieve their life goals. Traditionally, Participatory Action Research progresses through a number of cycles.[21] Carr and Kemmis described their own brand of action research as 'emancipatory action research', and this provided an important theoretical consistency within my research framework.[22] Their epistemological position is heavily drawn from Habermas, who aimed to synthesize the classical concern for praxis (wise and prudent action) with the logic and theoretical rigour of rationalist philosophy.[23] In 2005, Kemmis and McTaggart reiterated the intentionally emancipatory nature of PAR:

> Participatory action research is emancipatory. Participatory action research aims to help people recover and release themselves from the constraints of irrational, unproductive, unjust and unsatisfying social structures that limit their self- determination and social development.[24]

PAR is also a *process* whereby people become skilled in research through the process of conducting research, and it is iterative and non-linear.[25] It unfolds in accordance with the development of each project as new understandings and opportunities arise. This also allows for diverse engagement strategies, new activities, and new questions to emerge and be addressed in the course of the project. All these features are necessary if researchers are to challenge barriers and work creatively to solve problems. Arguably, if we want to move 'outside of the prison' of traditional research paradigms, we cannot operate by their incarcerating rules.

DATA COLLECTION AND ANALYSIS

Following ethics approval, research interviews using semi-structured interview questionnaires were conducted throughout the course of the project. The interviews were based on the lived experience of the project activities and outcomes of the young people, their parents and carers, and the project staff. The eventuating 22 interviews were transcribed and the data was analysed using thematic networks to devise basic, organizing, and global themes.[26] In line with the principles of the emancipatory research paradigm, various young people who have Down syndrome participated as co-researchers in formulating the interview questions, conducting the interviews, and the analysis of the data and the dissemination of the findings.

RESEARCH FINDINGS

The findings illustrated the numerous concerns, interests, and aspirations of the young people as citizens, which subsequently contributed to theorizing in respect of social inclusion and social citizenship. The findings from the project staff and parents also helped to illustrate what processes and practices within the project they found enabling and supportive in assisting the young people to achieve their life goals. A further outcome of the research was the identification of some aspects of social oppression using the lens of the social model, particularly from the views expressed by parents.

The study demonstrated that a flexible and responsive approach to research with people with an intellectual disability can facilitate high levels of engagement in research practices that are traditionally regarded as the domain of university-based academics. In turn, the fruits of this engagement demonstrate that people with an intellectual disability and their families have a strong contribution to make both to the development of disability service models and, correspondingly, to the theory and practice of social citizenship. Part of the nature of PAR is the need to develop the theoretical framework to embrace and consider the broader societal issues. In the remainder of this chapter, I discuss the theoretical implications of a Gewirthian approach to social inclusion and social citizenship.

198 *Stevenson*

THE APPLICATION OF A GEWIRTHIAN HUMAN RIGHTS THEORY

Gewirth used deductive logic to identify two broad absolute human rights, those of 'freedom and well-being', and from this, he established the Principle of Generic Consistency (PGC). These are terms which are open to much interpretation (necessarily so), but provide a foundation for the discussion of human rights theory and social citizenship. So, in developing a model of disability rights, what are its key elements? Firstly, Gewirth's post-Kantian theory of human rights forms an important core. Gewirth argued that human action is the basis of human rights:

> . . . for it is with actions that all moralities or moral precepts deal, directly or indirectly. All moral precepts tell human beings how they ought to act, especially toward one another, whether within or outside of institutions; or, as in the case of the virtues, they tell what kind of person one ought to be . . .[27]

The context of action also has necessity, as:

> [all] human beings are actual, prospective or potential agents. No human being can evade the context of action, except perhaps by committing suicide; and even then the steps he takes for this purpose are themselves actions.[28]

Gewirth then goes on to argue that 'purposiveness' or 'intentionality' are required by the agent in that the agent acts to achieve some desired end. Additionally, in order to have agency, humans need the freedom or 'voluntariness' to act on their intentions. 'Freedom', for example, can include access to relevant information, being facilitated to consider all possible alternative actions, and being able to plan strategies to achieve the goal without unjustified interference. Agents also need well-being to achieve their goals. These include the entire individual and social/community factors impacting the individual, for example, their physical and mental health, education, living conditions, emotional and social support, and so forth. Gewirth incorporates all these elements under the concept of 'well-being'.[29]

THE RELATIONSHIP BETWEEN GEWIRTH, DISABILITY, AND THE SOCIAL MODEL

Gewirth held that human rights exist to ensure the conditions necessary for freedom and well-being. This places a political imperative on the provision of environments and services that enable purposive human action and allow individuals who may need support to 'effectively pursue and sustain their own purposes without being subjected to domination and harms from others', hence nurturing the concept of self-determination for all regardless of impairment.[30]

Likewise, the constituent components of 'well-being' will, of course, shift and change according to the characteristics, circumstances, culture, and historical position of the individual. One powerful assertion of Gewirth's thesis is that absolute human rights are not culturally relative. From this we affirm that cultural traditions that discriminate and inhibit the freedom and well-being of some humans on the grounds of race, gender, or religion (or other variables, such as physical or intellectual impairment) cannot be permitted to restrict the application of human rights. With regard to disability, there is an important link with the materialist perspective. Gewirth draws on the work of Marx to explain 'historical variability' in that the 'number and extent of [the worker's] wants, as also the modes of satisfying them, are themselves the product of historical development'.[31] Importantly, this renders Gewirth's thesis of human action as the basis of human rights compatible with the social model of disability, which is also developed from a Marxian materialist perspective. Gewirth's theory is also one of 'practical intent' in that he places the necessary features of freedom and well-being at the heart of state and organizational governance.[32] Disablement can therefore be said to be social oppression, namely structural and attitudinal factors that impinge upon the freedom and well-being of people with impairments, whatever the nature or context of that impairment. The social model is notably non-specific about historical context or the exact nature of what we might term 'disability' for precisely this reason.

LINKING GEWIRTHIAN THEORY WITH HUMAN RIGHTS AND SOCIAL CITIZENSHIP

Ward and Birgden developed a model of rights that charts a movement from absolute rights using the justificatory theory of Gewirth through to pragmatic human rights objects and thence through to policies.[33] They drew upon the work of other human rights authors, including Li,[34] Orend,[35] and Rescher,[36] to argue that there are corresponding duties to respect the stated rights.[37] Ward and Birgden thereby made theoretical links between Gewirth's justificatory theory and the various conventions on human rights. Later, Ward and Stewart applied this model of human rights to people with an intellectual disability.[38] The cogently argued theoretical structure created by Ward and Birgden has great value with respect to the findings of the Circles of Support research when coupled with the observations of Beckett with respect to citizenship and the constituents of engaged citizenship.[39]

Problems with defining citizenship and social citizenship have been identified by a number of scholars; yet it remains an important, if contested, notion on a number of levels.[40] In accordance with the human rights theory

200 *Stevenson*

developed here, Gewirth straightforwardly argued that a citizen is a 'rights bearing agent'. Quoting Aristotle, Gewirth argued that:

> ... to be fully human is to be a member of a *polis*, a *civitas*, a political community, and thus to be a citizen, a *civis*: "man is by nature a political animal".[41]

If we accept this argument, then human rights are inseparable from all civil and political rights. This notion of citizenship demands an integration of human rights with issues of 'governance', defined as the act or process of governing (derived ultimately from the Greek term *kubernesis,* meaning 'steering'). Governments are therefore concerned with law making, the policies, services and professional practices that flow from such laws, and their impact upon social groups. In 2006, Beckett opined that a universally agreed set of non-culturally specific human rights is unlikely, but she did concede that 'individuals would still remain the "citizens" of a state', and hence issues of governance are matters that disability scholars need to engage with. Arguably, we therefore need to continue to engage with human rights theory and citizenship in an integrated, dynamic, and practical way. Beckett also identified social citizenship, that is, the exercise of one's rights as a citizen in their social context, as a 'process' rather than a fixed status, as people are diverse, dynamic entities within diverse and shifting environments.[42] So, what processes constituted social citizenship for participants or co-researchers?

THE CONTRIBUTION OF YOUNG PEOPLE WITH DOWN SYNDROME TO A THEORY OF SOCIAL CITIZENSHIP

Returning to the action research project, four global themes had emerged from an analysis of the data from and by the young people. Their concerns as citizens were explicit in the following global themes, which emerged from out analysis of the data: (i) engagement with human connection; (ii) the need for continuing personal development; (iii) the importance of community contribution; and (iv) the dignity of risk. Positioned together, these themes capture some of the processes of social citizenship (Figure 12.2) that were important to the young participants and co-researchers in this research. The four global themes are made up of organizing themes, and together they form a dynamic matrix of citizenship processes. Most importantly, these processes were identified by the young people themselves through active participation in this research project which, in itself, is a citizenship practice.

It is important to emphasize that the four global themes as illustrated in Figure 12.2 do not comprise an exhaustive list of the constituent elements of social citizenship for the research group. It must also be noted that these are dynamic processes, intertwined, shifting, and changing and specific to each person and their circumstances. Brought together, however,

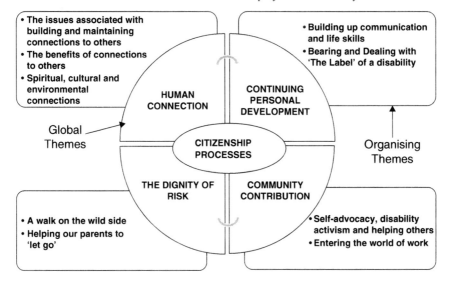

Figure 12.2 Global themes and organizing themes as dynamic and interconnected citizenship processes.

these themes can model some of the processes of social citizenship that the informants and co-researchers held to be of significance. When a young person is positively engaging in these processes or addressing concerns within these domains, this can be interpreted as a positive and active manifestation of human rights and therefore active social citizenship. These processes can now be embedded into a rights-based model of social citizenship, to extend its meaning and practical application.

INTEGRATING SOCIAL CITIZENSHIP PROCESSES IDENTIFIED BY THE CO-RESEARCHERS INTO A HUMAN RIGHTS FRAMEWORK

Taken together, the global themes can be interpreted as social citizenship processes and can be integrated into a framework building on the absolute rights of Gewirth; this framework is illustrated in Figure 12.3.

The importance of this model is that the social citizenship processes defined by the young people have an explicit theoretical core consisting of:

(i) Freedom and well-being as the necessary conditions of human agency, as defined by Gewirth and identified as core human rights objects;
(ii) Human Rights Conventions (for example, the 1948 UN Declaration of Human Rights and the 2008 Convention on the Rights of Persons with Disabilities);

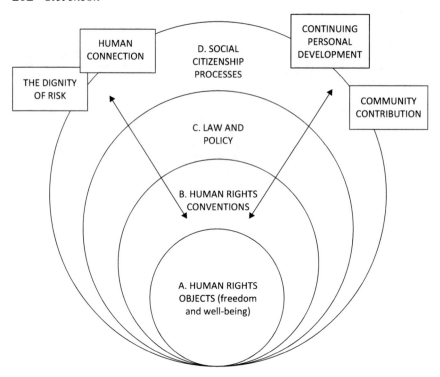

Figure 12.3 Framework of social citizenship theory for young people involved in the research.

(iii) Human Rights Conventions that form the basis of law and policy; and
(iv) Representative practices and areas of engagement of social citizenship.

Gewirthian theory provides for human rights to be placed at the heart of social citizenship by basing them on agency which itself is a precondition as well as a core element of social citizenship. It is this engagement in social citizenship processes by the young people that forms both the active *expression of their human rights* and simultaneously helps to protect human rights and ensure the achievement of the objects of freedom and well-being. In other words, a dynamic and reciprocal process occurs between all the elements of this model, with high integration between the layers. For example, in contributing to the community via the self-advocacy movement, the collective voices of these young people have the potential to influence law and policy, and in turn, law and policy can be formulated to help support these practices. Policy makers, lawmakers, practitioners, and the young people are engaged in a wider 'community of support', which drives participatory (even emancipatory) action.

Gewirthian Philosophy and Down Syndrome 203

CITIZEN ENGAGEMENT

One of the perennial challenges facing social workers, social work agencies, and policy makers is the translation of theory into strategy and thence into practice. Human rights awareness, flexibility, and responsiveness have been emphasized as hallmarks of both the research process and theoretical considerations thus far. However, effective leadership in the provision of services for people with an intellectual disability calls for this approach to be incorporated into a social citizenship paradigm that requires vision, energy, and a sense of direction. Commensurate with the practical and participatory thrust of the research and the EDR emphasis on producing research findings of practical benefit to disabled people, it is appropriate to discuss the final practice model that emerged from the research. The model illustrated in Figure 12.4 consists of five domains of practice that can be said to assist the promotion of social citizenship alongside young people with Down syndrome/an intellectual disability. For this reason, I have renamed the practice model, initially conceived of as a Circle of Support Project at the beginning of this research, the Citizen Engagement Model.

Within my analysis, I identified some of the processes within the project that families and staff identified as positive under a global theme named 'enabling concepts and practices'. The basic themes that emerged in the analysis around positive conceptual thinking and critique of the psycho-medical model of intellectual disability included: a conscious human rights approach to practice, and a belief in human potential and the need to challenge pervasive assumptions of incompetency made by both professionals and laypeople, which are created by the labelling of people with an intellectual disability, which is itself a (flawed) social construct.[43] This powerful label can subsequently place limitations on the aspirations society has for people with an intellectual disability, and correspondingly, on the goals they are allowed to have for themselves.[44] The practices and processes within the Circles of Support Project that parents and staff found to be positive included: staff energy and innovativeness, working with the young person in the context of the family, responding flexibly to the family, developing circles of support, encouraging connections with community organizations, gaining opportunities for those young people who were interested to become researchers and educators, and connecting the young people with each other (via workshops). So how can these enabling processes be incorporated into a new model of support?

FROM THEORY TO PRACTICE: THE CITIZEN ENGAGEMENT MODEL

The Citizen Engagement Model (CEM) is underpinned by an understanding of the history of the oppression of people with an intellectual disability and an awareness of the powerful discourses that can continue to perpetrate their oppression. This understanding is critical, to all oppressed groups,

204 Stevenson

in analysing their continuing oppression and in avoiding the repetition of past mistakes. For example, we could not begin to work alongside Australian Aboriginal people without first having some understanding of the mechanisms and impact of colonialism. To counter oppression, a commitment to universal human rights, grounded in the core values of 'freedom and well-being', is essential. The lens of the social model of disability is employed within the CEM as a strategic tool to identify both disablement and enablement. As such, it serves as a vector for the realization of human rights. The social model is used to reframe the experiences of people with an intellectual disability and their families, evoking a paradigm shift away from deficit-focused and individualized models of disability towards inclusive citizenship with rights to enabling forms of support. Moving from theory, I will now discuss the practice domains of the CEM (Figure 12.4), which will need to be considered by those with an interest in the human rights of people with an intellectual disability.

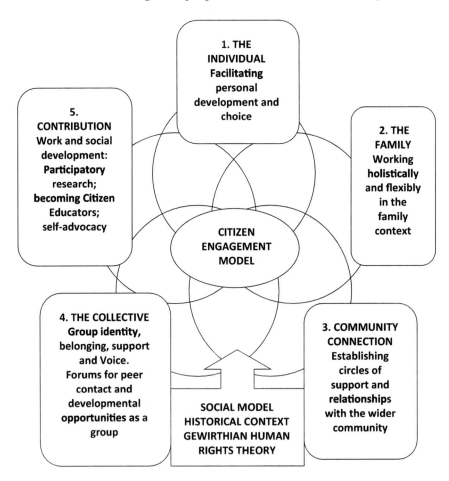

Figure 12.4 The foundation and practice domains of the Citizen Engagement Model.

1. The Individual: Facilitating Personal Choice and Development

This domain of practice draws on the global research themes of 'continuing personal development' and the 'dignity of risk'. Exactly what a participant perceives as personal development is a matter for them to decide. For example, 'personal development' could mean learning a new skill, learning more about oneself, taking a course, or having a new experience. This practice domain reflects Gewirth's concept of 'additive well-being',[45] and new experiences entail a degree of 'risk taking' that needs to be countenanced and discussed by the individual, their family, and the practitioner supporting the family. To some extent, the paternalistic veto on some experiences can be an unintentional disablement via assumptions that the young person does not have the ability to learn how to be safe because of their impairment. Any 'risk', skill, or support assessment processes need to be participatory, avoidant of labelling, and fluid.

2. The Family: Working Holistically and Flexibly

This was an approach emphasized by the young people themselves and the parents and staff as vital. The research established that young adults living with an intellectual disability generally need various kinds of enhanced support in organizing and living their lives. Most of this support is traditionally provided by the family: Often, a parent or parents will have the role/s of being a main support person. Outreach work is a key feature of practice; engagement takes place in the home or community environment.

As well as support with the practical rigours of their role, parents often benefit from emotional support and the opportunity to talk through complex issues. These can include areas such as the need to support their sons and daughters' developing adult rights and freedoms together with any concerns about their safety and well-being. This work is key, as often there are practical and emotional issues to be explored and addressed by families before (and during) the process of working towards a young person's life goals. Again, a flexible and holistic approach that respectfully acknowledges and embraces family circumstances is a cornerstone of the CEM.

3. Community Connection: Establishing Circles of Support and Relationships With the Wider Community

This domain of practice was drawn directly from the analysis of data from the young people. The circle concept needs to be available for implementation, be flexible and adaptable, remain 'dogma free', and be chiefly responsive to the needs and circumstances of families. For example, some young people and their families may not wish to have a 'circle of support' in terms of a regular meeting with people sitting in a room together. They may feel

206 Stevenson

they have a sufficient support network without needing anything more formal, or they may wish to have an 'inner circle' with family and identify 'satellite' members. Circles can vary in membership, disband and reconnect if need be, with the agenda of the participant and family circumstances. Even the deployment of the idea of a circle of support within families can stimulate some valuable thinking, discussion, and awareness which can be utilized at any time. Connecting with the community also engages the project workers proactively and creatively in the generation of opportunities for engagement and involvement in the wider community.

4. The Collective: Group Identity, Voice, Belonging, and Peer Support

This domain of practice reflects the importance of the collective. Monthly workshops in the Circle of Support Project were shown to fulfill a number of functions meeting the emotional, developmental, and self-advocacy needs of the young people, although other collective activities can be beneficial, with the concepts of group identity, the 'voice' of the young people, belonging, and peer support as objectives. Importantly, the individual and the group are not polarized; rather, the group decides together the content and direction of the workshops.

5. Contribution: Working in the Community and Participating in Social Development

This domain of practice is wide-ranging. Young people with an intellectual disability can contribute to society in a number of ways via enabling them to offer help and support to those at home, working either voluntarily or in paid employment in the community. At the political level they can participate in research (as did some co-researchers in this study), or become 'citizen educators' or participants in governance and decision-making forums. The primary message here is that everyone has a right to make a contribution to society, and that contribution can take many forms.

All the identified areas in the CEM have the potential to overlap and relate to each other. Participants in the CEM exercise self-determination and choose which areas they wish to engage in. They can move in and out of the different areas according to their wishes, needs, and individual circumstances. It may be, for example, that even if a participant is not living with their family or does not even have (or wish to have) contact with their family, they can be facilitated to participate in the other areas.

Together, these five domains of practice help to both 'unpack' and apply the notion of inclusive social citizenship at a local level as exemplified by the young people living with Down syndrome in the Circle of Support Project. Locating the notion of 'inclusion' within a well-buttressed Gewirthian human rights and social citizenship framework rather than as a free-floating

Gewirthian Philosophy and Down Syndrome   207

notion in its current vague, under-theorized state strengthens its theoretical integrity and political efficacy.

CONCLUSION

Social work activity is grounded in the promotion of human rights.[46] Legislation, policy, and practice need to explicitly and coherently support this approach. We can (and arguably must) engage within a Gewirthian community of rights, working flexibly to respond to the needs of individuals, families, and communities, locally and globally, whose citizenship rights have been limited or denied. A community engagement model provides a guiding framework. No discourse of diversity is adequate without a corresponding acknowledgement of our common humanity as prospective purposive agents. We are all of equal human value. We all share the same rights. Let us work alongside each other to realize and enjoy them.

NOTES

1. A. Gewirth, *The Community of Rights* (Chicago, USA: The University of Chicago Press, 1996) and *Reason and Morality* (Chicago: The University of Chicago Press, 1978).
2. M. Stevenson, 'Flexible and Responsive Research: Developing Rights-Based Emancipatory Disability Research. Methodology in Collaboration with Young Adults with Down Syndrome', *Australian Social Work*, 63 (2010), pp. 35–50.
3. J. Walmsley, 'Women and the Mental Deficiency Act of 1913: Citizenship, Sexuality and Regulation', *Issue British Journal of Learning Disabilities British Journal of Learning Disabilities*, 28 (2000), pp. 65–70.
4. M. Stevenson, 'Voices for Change: Exploring Aspects of Social Citizenship alongside Young Adults Who Have Down syndrome' (PhD dissertation, University of Sydney, 2012), pp. 35–9.
5. P. Kumar and M. Clark, *Kumar and Clark's Clinical Medicine*, eighth edition (Saunders Elsevier, 2012), p. 37.
6. J.L. Down, 'Observations on an Ethnic Classification of Idiots', *London Hospital Report*, 3 (1866), p. 260.
7. T. Huang, A. Dennis, W.S. Meschino, S. Rashid, E. Mak-Tam and H. Cuckle, 'First Trimester Screening for Down Syndrome Using Nuchal Translucency, Maternal Serum Pregnancy-Associated Plasma Protein a, Free-B Human Chorionic Gonadotrophin, Placental Growth Factor, and A-Fetoprotein', *Prenatal Diagnosis*, 35 (2015), pp. 709–16.
8. J.L. Natoli, D.L. Ackerman, S. McDermott and J.G. Edwards, 'Prenatal Diagnosis of Down Syndrome: A Systematic Review of Termination Rates (1995–2011)', *Prenatal Diagnosis*, 32 (2012), pp. 142–53.
9. S. Pueschel, 'What Is Down Syndrome?', Down Syndrome: Health Issues (1992), available at: http://www.ds-health.com/pueschel.htm [accessed 7th September 2010].
10. Canadian Down Syndrome Society, 'Your Child with Down Syndrome', available at: http://www.cdss.ca/images/pdf/brochures/english/your_child_with_down_syndrome_english.pdf [accessed 31 August 2015].

208   *Stevenson*

11. This was the summarizing statement derived from the preliminary consultation with young adults who have Down syndrome prior to the initiation of the Circle of Support Project in 2007.
12. L. Buckmaster and M. Thomas, *Social Inclusion and Social Citizenship: Towards a Truly Inclusive Society* (Australian Parliamentary Library, 2009).
13. A. C. Armstrong, D. Armstrong, and A. Spandagou, *Inclusive Education: International Policy and Practice* (London: Sage, 2010), p. 31.
14. H. Steinert, 'Participation and Social Exclusion: A Conceptual Framework', in H. Steinert and A. Pilgram (eds), *Welfare Policy from Below* (2003), pp. 45–60.
15. M. Stevenson, 'Flexible and Responsive Research: Developing Rights-Based Emancipatory Disability Research Methodology in Collaboration with Young Adults with Down syndrome', *Australian Social Work*, 63 (2010), pp. 35–50. Also M. Stevenson, 'Participatory Data Analysis alongside Co-researchers who have Down syndrome', *Journal of Applied Research in Intellectual Disabilities*, 27:1 (2014), pp. 23–33.
16. M. Oliver, *The Politics of Disablement* (New York: St. Martin's Press, 1990).
17. Union of Physically Impaired Against Segregation UPIAS, *The Fundamental Principles of Disability* (1976), pp. 3–4.
18. M. Oliver, 'Defining Impairment and Disability: Issues at Stake', in C. Barnes and G. Mercer (eds), *Exploring the Divide: Illness and Disability* (Leeds: Disability Press, 1996), p. 31.
19. M. Oliver, 'Emancipatory Research: A Vehicle for Social Transformation or Social Development', *Using Emancipatory Methodologies in Disability Research Seminar, Dublin* (Dublin: Centre for Disability Studies University College of Dublin, 2002), available at: http://disability-studies.leeds.ac.uk/files/library/Oliver-Mikes-paper.pdf [accessed 20 August 2015].
20. C. Barnes, ' "Emancipatory Disability Research": Project or Process', *Journal of Research in Special Educational Needs*, 2 (2002).
21. B. Dick, 'Action Research: Action *and* Research' (A paper prepared for the seminar 'Doing Good Action Research', held at Southern Cross University, 2002).
22. W. Carr and S. Kemmis, *Becoming Critical: Education, Knowledge and Action* (London: Falmer Press, 1986), p. 136.
23. J. Habermas, *Knowledge and Human Interests* (London: Heinemann, 1972) and *The Theory of Communicative Action: Vol. 1. Reason and the Rationalization of Society*, T. McCarthy (trans) (Boston, MA: Beacon, 1981).
24. S. Kemmis and R. McTaggart, 'Participatory Action Research: Communicative Action in the Public Sphere', in N. K. Denzin and Y. S. Lincoln (eds), *Sage Handbook of Qualitative Research* (California: Sage Publications, 2005), p. 567.
25. P. Freire, 'Creating Alternative Research Methods: Learning to Do It by Doing It', in B. Hall, A. Gillette and R. Tandon (eds), *Creating Knowledge: A Monopoly* (New Delhi: Society for Participatory Research in Asia, 1982), pp. 29–37.
26. J. Attride-Stirling, 'Thematic Networks: An Analytic Tool for Qualitative Research', *Qualitative Research* 1 (2001), pp. 385–405.
27. Gewirth, *The Community of Rights*, p. 13.
28. Ibid., p. 13.
29. Ibid., p. 13.
30. A. Gewirth, *Human Rights: Essays on Justification and Applications* (Chicago, IL: University of Chicago Press, 1982), p. 5.
31. K. Marx, *Capital*, vol 1, (Chicago: Charles H. Kerr & Co., 1909 [1867]), p. 190.
32. Gewirth, *The Community of Rights*, Chapters 4–6.
33. T. Ward and A. Birgden, 'Human Rights and Correctional Clinical Practice', *Aggression and Violent Behavior*, 12 (2007), pp. 628–43.

Gewirthian Philosophy and Down Syndrome 209

34. A. Li, *Ethics, Human Rights, and Culture* (Basingstoke, UK: Palgrave Macmillan, 2006).
35. B. Orend, *Human Rights: Concept and Context* (Ontario, Canada: Broadview Press, 2002).
36. N. Rescher, *A System of Pragmatic Idealism*, Volume II: *The Validity of Values* (Princeton, NJ: Princeton University Press, 1993).
37. T. Ward and A. Birgden, 'Human Rights and Correctional Clinical Practice'.
38. T. Ward and C. Stewart, 'Putting Human Rights into Practice with People with an Intellectual Disability', *Journal of Developmental and Physical Disabilities*, 20 (2008), pp. 297–311.
39. A. E. Beckett, *Citizenship and Vulnerability: Disability and Issues of Social and Political Engagement* (Basingstoke: Palgrave Macmillan, 2006).
40. Buckmaster and Thomas, 'Social Inclusion and Social Citizenship: Towards a Truly Inclusive Society'.
41. Gewirth, *The Community of Rights*, pp. 68–69.
42. A. E. Beckett, *Citizenship and Vulnerability: Disability and Issues of Social and Political Engagement* (Basingstoke: Palgrave Macmillan., 2006), p. 195.
43. S. J. Gould, *The Mismeasure of Man* (London: Penguin Books, 1996).
44. S. Aspis, 'Self-Advocacy for People with Learning Difficulties: Does It Have a Future?', *Disability and Society*, 12 (1997), pp. 647–54.
45. A. Gewirth, *Self-Fulfillment* (Princeton, NJ: Princeton University Press, 1998), p. 123.
46. United Nations, *Human Rights and Social Work: A Training Manual.* (Geneva: UN Centre for Human Rights with IFSW and IASSW, 1994).

WORKS CITED

Armstrong, A. C., Armstrong, D. and Spandagou, A., *Inclusive Education: International Policy and Practice* (London: Sage, 2010).

Aspis, S., 'Self-Advocacy for People with Learning Difficulties: Does It Have a Future?', *Disability and Society*, 12 (1997), pp. 647–54.

Attride-Stirling, J., 'Thematic Networks: An Analytic Tool for Qualitative Research', *Qualitative Research*, 1 (2001), pp. 385–405.

Barnes, C., '"Emancipatory Disability Research": Project or Process', *Journal of Research in Special Educational Needs*, 2:1 (2002), pp. 233–44.

Beckett, A. E., *Citizenship and Vulnerability: Disability and Issues of Social and Political Engagement.* (Basingstoke: Palgrave Macmillan, 2006).

Buckmaster, L. and Thomas M., *Social Inclusion and Social Citizenship: Towards a Truly Inclusive Society* (Australian Parliamentary Library, 2009).

Canadian Down Syndrome Society, 'Your Child with Down Syndrome', available at http://www.cdss.ca/images/pdf/brochures/english/your_child_with_down_syndrome_english.pdf [accessed 31 August 2015].

Carr, W. and Kemmis, S., *Becoming Critical: Education, Knowledge and Action* (London: Falmer Press, 1986).

Dick, B., 'Action Research: Action and Research', (A paper prepared for the seminar 'Doing Good Action Research', held at Southern Cross University 2002).

Down, J. M., 'Observations on an Ethnic Classification of Idiots', *London Hospital Report*, 3 (1866), pp. 259–62.

Freire, P., 'Creating Alternative Research Methods: Learning to Do It by Doing It', in B. Hall, A. Gillette and R. Tandon (eds.), *Creating Knowledge: A Monopoly* (New Delhi: Society for Participatory Research in Asia, 1982), pp. 29–37.

Gewirth, A., *Reason and Morality* (Chicago: The University of Chicago Press, 1978).

210 Stevenson

———, *Human Rights: Essays on Justification and Applications* (Chicago: The University of Chicago Press, 1982).

———, *The Community of Rights* (Chicago: The University of Chicago Press, 1996).

———, *Self-Fulfillment* (Princeton, NJ: Princeton University Press, 1998).

Gould, S. J., *The Mismeasure of Man* (London: Penguin Books, 1996).

Habermas, J., *Knowledge and Human Interests* (London: Heinemann, 1972).

———, *The Theory of Communicative Action: Vol. 1. Reason and the Rationalization of Society* (Boston, MA: Beacon, 1981).

Huang, T., Dennis, A., Meschino, W. S., Rashid, S., Mak-Tam, E. and Cuckle, H., 'First Trimester Screening for Down Syndrome Using Nuchal Translucency, Maternal Serum Pregnancy-Associated Plasma Protein a, Free-B Human Chorionic Gonadotrophin, Placental Growth Factor, and A-Fetoprotein', *Prenatal Diagnosis*, 35 (2015), pp. 709–16.

Kemmis, S. and McTaggart, R., 'Participatory Action Research: Communicative Action in the Public Sphere', in N. K. Denzin and Y. S. Lincoln (eds.), *Sage Handbook of Qualitative Research* (Thousand Oaks, CA: Sage Publications, 2005).

Kumar, P. and Clark, M., *Kumar and Clark's Clinical Medicine*, 8th edition (Edinburgh: Saunders, 2012).

Li, A., *Ethics, Human Rights, and Culture* (Basingstoke, UK: Palgrave Macmillan, 2006).

Marx, K., *Capital*, Volume 1 (Chicago: Charles H. Kerr & Co., 1909 [1867]).

Natoli, J. L., Ackerman, D. L., McDermott, S. and Edwards, J. G., 'Prenatal Diagnosis of Down Syndrome: A Systematic Review of Termination Rates (1995–2011)', *Prenatal Diagnosis*, 32 (2012), pp. 142–53.

Oliver, M., *The Politics of Disablement* (New York: St. Martin's Press, 1990).

———, 'Defining Impairment and Disability: Issues at Stake', in C. Barnes and G. Mercer (eds.), *Exploring the Divide: Illness and Disability* (Leeds: Disability Press, 1996), p. 31.

———, 'Emancipatory Research: A Vehicle for Social Transformation or Social Development', in *Using Emancipatory Methodologies in Disability Research Seminar, Dublin* (Dublin: Centre for Disability Studies University College of Dublin, 2002), available at http://disability-studies.leeds.ac.uk/files/library/Oliver-Mikes-paper.pdf [accessed 20 August 2015].

Orend, B., *Human Rights: Concept and Context* (Ontario, Canada: Broadview Press, 2002).

Pueschel, S., 'What Is Down Syndrome?' Down Syndrome: Health Issues, (1992), available at http://www.ds-health.com/pueschel.htm [accessed 20 August 2015].

Rescher, N., *A System of Pragmatic Idealism*, Volume II: *The Validity of Values* (Princeton, NJ: Princeton University Press, 1993).

Steinert, H., 'Participation and Social Exclusion: A Conceptual Framework', in H. Steinert and A. Pilgram (eds.), *Welfare Policy from Below* (Aldershot: Ashgate, 2003), pp. 45–60.

Stevenson, M., 'Flexible and Responsive Research: Developing Rights-Based Emancipatory Disability Research Methodology in Collaboration with Young Adults with Down syndrome', *Australian Social Work*, 63 (2010), pp. 35–50.

———, 'Voices for Change: Exploring Aspects of Social Citizenship alongside Young Adults who have Down syndrome' (PhD dissertation, University of Sydney, 2012), pp. 35–9.

———, 'Participatory Data Analysis alongside Co-researchers Who Have Down Syndrome', *Journal of Applied Research in Intellectual Disabilities*, 27:1 (2014), pp. 23–33.

Union of Physically Impaired Against Segregation (UPIAS), *The Fundamental Principles of Disability*, (1976), pp. 3–4.

United Nations, *Human Rights and Social Work: A Training Manual* (Geneva: UN Centre for Human Rights with IFSW and IASSW, 1994).

Walmsley, J., 'Women and the Mental Deficiency Act of 1913: Citizenship, Sexuality and Regulation', *Issue British Journal of Learning Disabilities British Journal of Learning Disabilities*, 28 (2000), pp. 65–70.

Ward, T. and Birgden, A., 'Human Rights and Correctional Clinical Practice', *Aggression and Violent Behavior*, 12 (2007), pp. 628–43.

Ward, T. and Stewart, C., 'Putting Human Rights into Practice with People with an Intellectual Disability', *Journal of Developmental and Physical Disabilities*, 20 (2008), pp. 297–311.

13 The Gewirthian Duty to Rescue

Per Bauhn

In his argument for a duty to rescue, Alan Gewirth introduces the case of Carr and Davis:

> Suppose Carr, who is an excellent swimmer, is lolling in the sun on a deserted beach. On the edge of the beach near him is his motorboat, to which is attached a long, stout rope. Suddenly he becomes aware that another person, whom I shall call Davis, is struggling in the water some yards away. Carr knows that the water is about thirty feet deep at that point. Davis shouts for help; he is obviously in immediate danger of drowning. Carr sees that he could easily save Davis by swimming out to him, or at least by throwing him the rope from his boat. But Carr simply doesn't want to bother even though he is aware that Davis will probably drown unless he rescues him. Davis drowns.[1]

Two features of this story are essential to the way in which Gewirth wants to justify the duty to rescue. First, Carr's intervention is presented as being a *necessary* condition of saving Davis's life. Second, Carr can intervene at *comparably little cost* to himself. However, the story of Carr and Davis leaves important questions unanswered.

For one thing, the causal significance of Carr's passivity is made obvious by the fact that he is the only person around who can rescue Davis (the beach is 'deserted'). But what if another potential rescuer had been present? Then it would not be *necessary* for Carr to intervene—but nor would it be *necessary* for the other potential rescuer to intervene, given the presence of Carr. So who has the duty to rescue in a situation in which we have two or more potential rescuers, and in which the duty to rescue is based on the necessity of a particular agent's intervention?

Moreover, if the story of Carr and Davis is intended to tell us that we have a duty to rescue when we can do so at comparably little cost to ourselves, it is not very informative, as Carr obviously would not risk *anything* if he were to rescue Davis. In Gewirth's example, Carr risks neither his health nor his property. Although he is an excellent swimmer, he does not even have to dive into the water to rescue Davis—it is enough if he throws him a rope

The Gewirthian Duty to Rescue   213

from his boat. So how are we to decide what kind of sacrifices a rescuer is supposed to accept for herself?

In what follows, we are going to shed some light on these unclear aspects of the Gewirthian duty to rescue with the help of arguments developed by Gewirth himself. However, in the process, we will also develop and modify these arguments to make them apply to cases not discussed by Gewirth himself, and in which questions of fairness concerning the distribution of burdens among potential rescuers need to be resolved.

THE RIGHTS TO FREEDOM AND WELL-BEING

According to Gewirth's argument, all moral duties are derived directly or indirectly from a supreme principle of morality, the Principle of Generic Consistency (PGC). This principle prescribes that you should '[a]ct in accord with the generic rights of your recipients as well as of yourself'.[2] The generic rights are the rights to freedom and well-being, the necessary goods of action, without which human action would be either impossible or at least predictably difficult and unsuccessful.

Freedom denotes the agent's occurrent as well as dispositional control of her behaviour in accordance with her informed and unforced choice, while well-being denotes various capacities for successful agency. *Basic well-being* thus involves the preconditions of action in general, such as life, health, physical integrity, and mental equilibrium. *Nonsubtractive well-being*, on the other hand, involves the ability to maintain the capacity one has for individual actions by, for instance, being able to protect oneself against attacks on one's reputation or interferences with one's property. *Additive well-being*, finally, involves the ability to expand the capacity one has for individual actions by, for instance, having access to education and the means of earning an income, but also by possessing capacity-expanding virtues, such as prudence, temperance, and courage.

Now, since agents, *qua* agents, necessarily want to be successful in their actions, in the sense that they want to realize the ends for which they act, every rational agent is logically compelled to hold that she *must* have the necessary goods of action, since she cannot be a successful agent without them. This 'must' is not just an expression of the agent's recognition of her needs as an agent, but also carries an at least implicit prescriptive force in relation to all other agents. The agent, at least implicitly, declares that she cannot accept any interference with her possession of freedom and well-being from other agents. This is what is involved in the agent's claiming *rights* to freedom and well-being. On the other hand, every agent must also accept that all other agents are equally justified in claiming rights to freedom and well-being, for the simple reason that it is just as true for them as it is for her that they cannot do without the necessary goods of action. Hence, every agent must accept that she and all other agents have rights to freedom

214   *Bauhn*

and well-being and that, in her transactions with other persons, she has to respect these same rights of her recipients, as prescribed by the PGC.

That an agent's rights to freedom and well-being will entail *negative* duties on the part of all other agents should not cause much surprise. For instance, if an agent has rights to life and property, then all other agents will have corresponding duties to refrain from killing and robbing her. But what about *positive* duties? Such duties typically involve various actions of assistance, help, and support. But how could an agent's demand that other agents *should not interfere* with her having freedom and well-being translate into a request that they *should help* her to have freedom and well-being?

INACTION AS INTERFERENCE WITH RIGHTS

Gewirth's reply is that an agent's intentional refusal to help her recipient will, under certain conditions, constitute an interference with the latter's possession of freedom and well-being. Central to his argument is his distinction between *nonaction* and *inaction*. While nonaction is simply the absence of any action (as when the agent is asleep or unconscious), inaction is a particular kind of action, namely a deliberate passivity on the part of the agent, whereby she intentionally refrains from some action.[3]

Contrary to a criticism of Gewirth's argument, voiced by Eric Mack, that '[t]he power to avert or not is not the power to cause whatever is not averted',[4] there is reason to believe that the choice *not* to do something can indeed be as productive of significant results as the choice to *do* something. We can here think of the 1944 Warsaw uprising against the Germans, and Stalin's decision not to let the advancing Russian Red Army help the Polish Resistance:

> The uprising was crushed. The Russians made no attempt to come to its aid. It was convenient for them that the non-communist Polish Resistance should be destroyed by the Germans, so that it would present no challenge to Russian authority in liberated Poland.[5]

Hence, when an agent intentionally refuses to help her recipient in a situation in which the agent's help would be necessary to protect the recipient from a loss of well-being, this can be construed as a case of the agent *interfering* with her recipient's well-being, and hence as being in contradiction of the PGC:

> Such interference involves not that one turns an antecedent well-being into ill-being, but rather that one prevents the other person from attaining well-being through means that are under one's proximate control. One's refusal to help inflicts harm on the other person not necessarily by making his situation worse . . ., but by permitting the existing harm to continue when it could have been stopped.[6]

Commenting on the example of Carr and Davis, Gewirth observes that Carr's 'intentional failure to come to Davis's rescue is a necessary and sufficient

The Gewirthian Duty to Rescue 215

condition of the drowning', since 'Davis would not have drowned had Carr come to his rescue; and in the circumstances as described, given Carr's failure to come to Davis's rescue, Davis's drowning necessarily followed'.[7]

But what if Carr is in the company of Bates, and it is true of both Bates and Carr individually that each one of them is capable of rescuing Davis at no cost to themselves? Then Carr could claim that his inaction at least cannot be a *sufficient* condition of Davis's drowning, since Bates too could have saved Davis. And Bates could make a similar claim regarding *his* inaction and Davis's drowning, since Carr too could have saved Davis. However, if both Bates and Carr choose to remain inactive and leave Davis to drown, then the inaction of Bates is a necessary condition of Davis's drowning and so is the inaction of Carr, while their *collective* inaction is both a necessary and sufficient condition of Davis's drowning. In such a case, it would only be reasonable to blame both Bates and Carr for Davis's death.

However, the case of multiple potential rescuers could be made much more complicated if it is expanded to include the problem about how to distribute sacrifices among them. So far we have only discussed a case in which a rescue operation could be carried out without any costs to the rescuers. But what if there are such costs? How are these costs to be distributed among the rescuers?

DOING ONE'S FAIR SHARE

This problem has been addressed by Liam Murphy. According to him, in a situation in which there are many potential rescuers and also many rescuees, we have a reason to make sure not only that the rescuees have their rights protected, but also that there is a fair distribution of burdens among the rescuers. In Murphy's words, '[w]e should do our fair share, which can amount to a great sacrifice in certain circumstances; what we cannot be required to do is other people's shares as well as our own'.[8] However, this fair share principle might conflict with other relevant moral considerations.

Consider a case in which we have two potential rescuers, Bates and Carr, and two rescuees, Davis and Evans. It is true of both Bates and Carr that each one of them can, individually and at no cost to himself, rescue both Davis and Evans. A fair distribution of the duty to rescue would be that Bates rescues Davis (or Evans) while Carr rescues Evans (or Davis). But what if Bates simply refuses to do anything? Does this mean that Carr is entitled to invoke an argument about fairness, claiming that his duty is only to rescue one of the rescuees, either Davis or Evans, but not both? An unqualified fair share principle would indeed have this outcome. However, this is not what Murphy intends with his argument. Murphy's fair share principle, the *Cooperative Principle*, states that

> the sacrifice each agent is required to make is limited to the level of sacrifice that would be optimal if the situation were one of full compliance;

216 Bauhn

of the actions that require no more than this level of sacrifice, agents are required to perform the action that makes the outcome best.[9]

Now, since it is possible for Carr to save both Davis and Evans at no cost to himself, he does not have to make any sacrifices at all, and hence, the argument about fair shares is not available to him.

On the other hand, what if things had been different, and Carr would indeed have to make sacrifices, not in order to save either Davis or Evans, but in order to save both of them? Then Carr might well have been morally entitled to save only one rescuee. The responsibility for the death of the rescuee not saved by Carr would then be assigned to Bates. However, much depends here on what we mean by 'sacrifice'.

Of course, any rescuer would have to spend some time and effort as she tries to rescue someone, and this time and effort she cannot spend on any other activity, at least not at the same time as she is involved in her rescue operation. If having to give up alternative activities for the sake of rescuing a person in danger is a sacrifice, then every rescuer is making a sacrifice (even if the alternative activity is just taking a nap or continuing to watch the sunset).

But from the point of view of agency and the rights of agents, which constitute the foundation for the Gewirthian duty to rescue, the concept of a sacrifice cannot be made to refer to just any insignificant interference with our lives. From the point of view of agency, a *sacrifice* in any objectively relevant sense should instead refer to the loss of a necessary good of action. For an agent to lose, for instance, her health, her physical integrity, her reputation, or her income, would indeed be for her to lose goods that are necessary to her being a successful agent. Maybe her loss of these goods will not incapacitate her totally, but she will at least suffer a decreased efficiency as regards either her capacity for agency in general or her capacity to be successful in particular actions. Any agent who accepts for herself a major or minor loss of the necessary goods of action is thereby also making a major or minor sacrifice in a sense that would hold objectively for all agents. And it is when it comes to this kind of sacrifices that potential rescuers can insist on a fair distribution of the burdens involved in a rescue operation.

THE COMBINED COMPARABLE COST CONDITION

Gewirth approaches the topic of sacrifices in rescue situations in his discussion of *comparable costs*. Talking about the sacrifices imposed on the rescuing agent by the duty to rescue, Gewirth argues that

> [b]y "comparable cost" [it] is meant that he is not required to risk his own life or other basic goods in order to save another person's life or other basic goods, and similarly with the other components of the necessary goods of action.[10]

The Gewirthian Duty to Rescue 217

Gewirth's comparable cost condition addresses the issue of what the rescuing agent stands to lose by involving herself in a rescue operation as compared to what the rescuee stands to lose if there is no rescue operation. But the condition is not clear about how to interpret the formulation 'or other basic goods'. Does it mean that a rescuer has to risk *neither* her life, *nor* her other basic goods, for the sake of saving a rescuee's life? Or does it mean that although she does not have to risk her life for the sake of saving the rescuee's life, she should be prepared to risk her *other* basic goods for this end? Moreover, the comparable cost condition does not address the issue of how to distribute the costs and risks of a rescue operation among a plurality of potential rescuers.

In order to deal with these problems, we will expand the original comparable cost condition. The expanded comparable cost condition combines a more precise understanding of what the original condition says about comparable costs with a requirement that sacrifices should be fairly distributed among rescuers. We will call this expanded condition the *Combined Comparable Cost Condition* (CCCC).

The CCCC hence prescribes that while a potential rescuer is indeed required to risk her nonsubtractive or additive well-being for the sake of protecting a rescuee's basic well-being, she is not required to risk *any* aspect of her basic well-being for the sake of protecting *any* aspect of a rescuee's basic well-being, nor is she required to make sacrifices of her nonsubtractive or additive well-being that go beyond what is *necessary and fair*, given the presence of other potential rescuers.

Two things need to be clarified regarding the CCCC and its relation to the Gewirthian duty to rescue. First, we need to be clear about how to understand the formulation concerning comparable costs, that a potential rescuer is not required to risk *any* aspect of her basic well-being for the sake of protecting *any* aspect of a rescuee's basic well-being. Second, we need to be clear about how the fair share requirement applies to rescue situations. Let us begin by clarifying how the CCCC understands comparable costs.

THE LEVEL-BASED INTERPRETATION OF COMPARABLE COSTS

Gewirth's original formulation of the comparable cost condition admits two possible interpretations.

The *strictly symmetrical interpretation* prescribes that a rescuer should not risk her life for the sake of protecting a rescuee's life, or risk a broken arm or leg for the sake of protecting a rescuee from breaking an arm or a leg, or risk being infected with a severe illness for the sake of protecting a rescuee from being infected with such an illness, and so on. However, in this interpretation, a rescuer *should* risk non-fatal injuries, such as a broken arm or a broken leg, for the sake of protecting a rescuee's life. In fact, a rescuer

218   *Bauhn*

should risk even permanent disability and a life in a wheelchair if this is necessary to save another person's life, since any loss short of a loss of life would be considered a less than comparable cost when a rescuee's life is at stake. Gewirth opens for such an interpretation by pointing to a hierarchy not only between different levels of well-being (making basic well-being more important than nonsubtractive and additive well-being), but also *within* the level of basic well-being itself, 'headed by life and then including various other physical and mental goods, some more indispensable than others for action and purpose-fulfillment'.[11]

On the other hand, according to the *level-based interpretation* of Gewirth's comparable cost condition, the hierarchy holds only between levels of well-being, so that while a rescuer should indeed be prepared to sacrifice some of her property (nonsubtractive well-being) or to forgo an attractive business deal (additive well-being) for the sake of saving a rescuee's life, she is not morally obligated to risk even a broken arm or a bout of pneumonia or any other threat to her basic well-being, not even for the sake of saving a rescuee's life. Here Gewirth's reference to 'life or other basic goods' is understood in an inclusive way, so that the rescuer should sacrifice *neither* her life *nor* any other basic good of hers for the sake of protecting *any* basic good (including life) of another person.

There is some evidence that Gewirth intends such a level-based interpretation of his comparable cost condition. Discussing *basic harms*, that is, violations of basic well-being, he seems to consider the infliction of physical injury as comparable to killing in terms of moral impermissibility: 'Basic harms thus include killing, maiming, and other sorts of physical injury, such as depriving of food, clothing, and shelter . . . All such basic harms are prohibited by the PGC'.[12] Moreover, in a later work, Gewirth rejects the idea that it would be justified to remove one of a healthy person's kidneys or eyes in order to preserve the life or sight of another person. Referring to the *criterion of degrees of needfulness for action* (which prescribes that, in the case of a conflict of rights, precedence should be given to the right whose object is more needed for successful action), Gewirth observes that there are limits to the application of this criterion:

> These limits are especially set by the physical integrity which is an essential part of basic well-being. The policies cited above, removing healthy persons' kidneys or eyes to prevent the death or blindness of other persons, are attacks on the former persons' physical integrity. As such, they pose serious threats to their continued agency. Persons can indeed survive with one kidney or one eye; but, apart from their voluntary consent, the criterion of degrees of needfulness cannot justify such inflictions of basic harms.[13]

If the PGC prohibits the infliction of physical injury even for the sake of saving another person's life, then, presumably, no rescuer should be morally

The Gewirthian Duty to Rescue 219

obligated to sacrifice her own physical integrity for the sake of saving a rescuee's life either. After all, no rational agent could consistently accept being deprived of the most basic conditions of her agency, and agency requires more than just being alive. When Gewirth defines basic well-being as including the *preconditions* of agency, he points to the fact that agency in general, and not only individual actions, becomes either completely impossible or more difficult to realize without basic well-being. For instance, when an agent has her arms or legs broken, it can be safely assumed that it is not only individual actions that will become more difficult for her, but action in general, given the pain and the loss of strength and mobility that normally accompany these kinds of injury.

In what follows, we will assume that comparable costs should be understood along the lines of the level-based interpretation. Hence, according to the CCCC, no potential rescuer is morally obligated to suffer any loss of basic well-being, not even for the sake of saving a rescuee's life. Exceptions to this rule would include agents who, for one reason or another, have accepted special responsibilities for the safety of others. Policemen and soldiers belong to this category, but so do parents, when their children are in danger. But in the absence of such special responsibilities, no agent has a moral duty to risk any part of her basic well-being, not even for the sake of saving another person's life.

SAVING LIVES AND BREAKING BONES

What we have said so far does not mean that there is no qualitative difference between being killed and having one's arm broken. If an agent has to choose between saving one person from being killed and saving another person from having her arm broken, the agent should indeed choose to save the person who risks being killed. To this extent, we should recognize the existence of a hierarchy of goods within the level of basic well-being. But it is also important to note that in a case like this, the agent cannot be described as being morally responsible for the physical injury suffered by the person who has her arm broken. The physical injury is not caused by a *morally unjustified inaction*, as in the case of Carr refusing to rescue Davis. Instead, it is caused by a *morally justified action*, namely the action of saving a person who is about to be killed, which makes it impossible for the agent also to prevent the accident which results in another person having her arm broken. (We assume here that the agent does not stand in any special relationship to the person who risks having her arm broken, as that would justify a different prioritization on her part. For instance, a parent would be justified in giving priority to protecting her child from having her arm broken over saving a stranger's life. This would be consistent with the 'preferential familial rights and duties' justified by the PGC.)[14]

Would an agent be morally justified in *breaking* an innocent person's arm in the course of a rescue operation? Well, it depends. Assume, for instance,

220   *Bauhn*

that a terrorist has locked up a child, Alice, in a room with a bomb that is about to go off within minutes. The terrorist has tied another child, Bella, to the door of this room in such a way that you can only open the door by breaking Bella's arm. And when the bomb goes off, it will kill Bella too. Would you be morally justified in breaking Bella's arm in order to be able to enter the room, defuse the bomb, and so save the lives of both Alice and Bella? In this case the answer would be yes, since the breaking of Bella's arm is necessary not only to save Alice's life, but also to save Bella's life. Hence, from Bella's point of view, instead of *depriving* her of basic well-being, you are *minimizing* her loss of basic well-being, and this would certainly be morally justified.

But now consider a different case, in which the terrorist holds Alice hostage and threatens to kill her unless you abduct Bella from her home and break her arm. Should you give in to the terrorist's demand? Here the answer must be no. The fact that the terrorist threatens to inflict basic harm on Alice is no valid excuse for you to inflict basic harm on Bella. Here there is no necessary causal connection between saving Bella's life and breaking her arm. Bella *is* already safe, that is, unless *you* choose to interfere with her basic well-being. Nor is there any necessary causal connection between Bella's loss of basic well-being and Alice's loss of basic well-being, that is, unless *you* choose to cooperate with the terrorist in creating such a connection. If you refuse to break Bella's arm, the terrorist is still free not to kill Alice. It is not as if your refusal to break Bella's arm forces him to kill Alice. If the terrorist chooses to kill Alice, this will be his responsibility and his alone. (In an important article, Gewirth has shown how the *Principle of the Intervening Action* can deal with cases like this.[15] Between your inaction of refusing to break Bella's arm and the outcome which consists in Alice's death, there intervenes the terrorist's action of killing Alice, which is the necessary and sufficient condition of her death. This is why we should consider the terrorist's action rather than your inaction as the cause of Alice's death, and why we should hold the terrorist and him alone responsible for her death.)

QUALITATIVE, NOT QUANTITATIVE, COMPARISONS

It is important in this context to note that the PGC as well as the level-based interpretation of the comparable cost condition focus on *qualitative* comparisons, not on *quantitative* ones. That is, we compare what levels of well-being are at stake for rescuer and rescuee respectively, but we do not compare the number of rescuees that can be saved with the number of rescuers that might get killed or injured trying to save them. It is not as if one rescuer's loss of basic well-being can be outweighed by the prospect of saving many rescuees' lives. David Cummiskey once argued that while the equality of rights prescribed by the PGC could make it understandable that one person's needs should not be sacrificed for the sake of protecting another

The Gewirthian Duty to Rescue 221

person's equally important needs, '[i]t is simply not as plausible to claim that my essential needs are not outweighed by the equal essential needs of many others'.[16]

But this objection ignores the fact that the rights which every agent must claim against all other agents have their foundation in the individual agent's need for the necessary goods of action, not in any utilitarian strategy to maximize good outcomes regardless of their distribution. From any individual agent's perspective, it would indeed be reasonable to sacrifice a less important necessary good of action for the sake of protecting a more important necessary good of action. However, when it comes to the level of basic well-being, there is no more important necessary good of action (although dispositional freedom might be at least equally important, since no agency can take place unless the agent has an at least dispositional control of her behaviour in accordance with her unforced choice). From the perspective of the individual agent, the mere fact that many other persons would benefit from a sacrifice of her basic well-being has no bearing whatsoever on her right to these other persons' non-interference with her basic well-being. Hence, except for cases in which agents have acquired special responsibilities that require of them that they expose themselves to physical risks (for instance, by contracting themselves to work as bodyguards), no agent can be justifiably required to risk her possession of basic well-being.

A FAIR DISTRIBUTION OF SACRIFICES

To sum up our argument so far, we will assume that when the CCCC says of the rescuing agent that 'she is not required to risk any aspect of her basic well-being for the sake of protecting any aspect of a rescuee's basic well-being', this should be understood along the lines of the level-based interpretation of comparable costs. Hence, in the case of the two potential rescuers Bates and Carr above, if Bates's inaction leaves it to Carr to save both Davis and Evans, and Carr can save Davis at no cost to his basic well-being, but can save both Davis and Evans only at the cost of breaking his arm, then his duty is only to save Davis. For Carr to save both Davis and Evans under these circumstances would be supererogatory. If Carr chooses to rescue only Davis and Evans dies, then Carr has done his duty and Bates is to be blamed for Evans's death, provided that Bates could have saved Evans at no cost to his basic well-being.

Let us now turn to the second part of the CCCC, which prescribes that no individual potential rescuer is required 'to make sacrifices of her non-subtractive or additive well-being that go beyond what is necessary and fair, given the presence of other potential rescuers'. Imagine the following case. Bates and Carr can together rescue Davis and Evans from drowning without either Bates or Carr having to lose anything. However, if Bates refuses to participate in the rescue operation, then Carr must spend a lot of

222 *Bauhn*

extra time rescuing both Davis and Evans on his own. As a consequence, Carr will be late for work and for this he will be fired, which will leave him without income for the foreseeable future. Hence, Carr will suffer a loss of both nonsubtractive well-being (his present purchasing power) and additive well-being (his capacity to save money for the future).

Now, if Carr had been the only one capable of rescuing both Davis and Evans, the CCCC would indeed have required of him that he should sacrifice his nonsubtractive and additive well-being for the sake of protecting Davis's and Evans's basic well-being. However, given the presence of Bates, such a sacrifice is not necessary. Hence, the CCCC requires of Carr only that he rescues either Davis or Evans, but not both. Hence, if either Davis or Evans is left to drown as Carr rushes off to work after having rescued one of them, then Bates is to be blamed for this, since it is Bates's inaction, not Carr's rushing off to work, that should be singled out as the morally significant factor in the drowning.

SOCIAL DUTIES

The requirement of the CCCC concerning a fair distribution of sacrifices among potential rescuers will also have social implications. Imagine a case in which Bates approaches Carr and asks him to pay for an operation that Bates's wife urgently needs. Unless Carr pays for the operation, Bates says, Mrs. Bates will die. Carr has the necessary money, but he has intended it for his daughter's college fees. So now Carr is asked to make a choice, either to save Mrs. Bates's life (basic well-being) or to provide his daughter with an education (additive well-being). If we were only to consider this case from the original Gewirthian comparable cost condition, we might well think that Carr would have a moral duty to sacrifice his daughter's education for the sake of saving Mrs. Bates's life.

However, according to the CCCC, a potential rescuer is not required to make sacrifices of her nonsubtractive or additive well-being that go beyond what is necessary and fair, given the presence of other potential rescuers. What Mr. and Mrs. Bates need is money, but not necessarily *Carr's* money. And assuming that Carr has no prior moral obligation to provide for the Bates family, there is no reason to assume that Carr and Carr alone should foot the bill for Mrs. Bates's medical care.

On the other hand, Mrs. Bates has a right to basic well-being, which would include a right to have life-saving medical care, when such medical care can be provided without conflicting with anybody else's right to basic well-being. (For instance, if the operation needed by Mrs. Bates were of such an exceptional and expensive type that it could only be given at the cost of depriving some other patient of her equally needed medical care, then Mrs. Bates would not have a right to her operation.) So if Carr is not personally morally responsible for realizing Mrs. Bates's right to basic well-being, then who is?

The answer is that it is the political community of which both the Bates couple and Carr are members that is responsible for establishing and maintaining an institutional structure that can secure equal rights to freedom and well-being for all its members. Carr, being an individual member and citizen of this political community, has a duty to contribute to this institutional structure as a taxpayer and in accordance with his means, and the same holds for each and every other individual member. In the case under discussion, such an institutional structure would imply some kind of an insurance system, according to which hospitals are paid for their services by the state and hence do not charge their individual patients, such as Mrs. Bates, for their necessary medical care.

Why is Mrs. Bates's need for an operation something that should be taken care of by the political community and not by Carr? After all, Carr *has* the money necessary to pay for Mrs. Bates's operation (although he would prefer to spend it on his daughter's education).

The reason is that, unlike the original case of Carr and Davis, the case of Carr and Mrs. Bates refers to a *social* problem. Mr. and Mrs. Bates ask for Carr's help because the political community of which they are all members is so organized that people who cannot afford it are left without medical care. This is a case of *social injustice*, since it contradicts the equality of generic rights prescribed by the PGC. The solution to such a problem is a reform of the political community, making necessary medical care available to all of its members, regardless of their ability to pay for it. The cost for such a reform should be shouldered by all citizens in accordance with their ability to contribute, rather than being randomly assigned to individual citizens.

This is in line with how the PGC justifies progressively more developed forms of a political community. The political application of the PGC begins by justifying the minimal state, which secures equal negative rights to freedom and well-being as non-interference with each and every member's life and property, and goes on to justify the democratic state, which secures equal positive rights to freedom, and finally justifies the supportive state, which secures equal positive rights to well-being.[17]

Moreover, the problem under discussion is social in another respect, as poverty typically is something that afflicts *groups* of people rather than just random individuals. Groups exposed to poverty in a political community with no institutional structure to protect them typically include the unemployed and uneducated, those who work for low wages, people with health problems, old people, and so on. Hence, Mrs. Bates is unlikely to be the only person in this political community who cannot afford a life-saving operation.

But typically, there are also in every political community *groups* of people who are reasonably well-off and who are capable of contributing to an institutional structure that would secure equal rights to well-being for all members. These groups include healthy, well-educated, well-paid professionals, but also people who own successful companies or large stocks of

224 *Bauhn*

shares in such companies, as well as people who by means of large inheritances or clever speculation have created fortunes for themselves. Hence, Carr is unlikely to be the only person in his political community who is capable of contributing to an institutional structure that would provide not only Mrs. Bates, but every other poor member of the community with needed medical care.

Social justice involves not only that rights are distributed in a fair manner, but also that duties are so distributed. However, to assign the duty to provide the means for Mrs. Bates's operation to Carr alone would be unfair both as regards the designated recipient and as regards the designated agent of this provision. Given that there are many other persons in Mrs. Bates's predicament, why should Carr give his money only to her? And given that there are many other persons who could contribute to Mrs. Bates's operation, why should Carr alone pay for it?

One powerful argument for a social solution to social problems is that this is the only way of being fair to both providers and those being provided for. Gewirth, in his argument for the supportive state, also notes that 'the benefits of these arrangements must be equitably and impartially distributed to the persons who need them' and that 'the duty to contribute to such arrangements through taxes must also be equitably distributed to all the persons who have the required economic resources, in proportion to their ability'.[18] The PGC thus prescribes a 'reciprocal universality', according to which 'there must be a mutual sharing of the benefits of rights and the burdens of duties'.[19]

Another aspect to be considered here is the special responsibility that citizens have for each other, at least when they are members of a democratic political community. As always, with freedom comes responsibility, and with political freedom comes political responsibility. As citizens of a democracy, we have a responsibility for the institutional structures that we create for ourselves and which determine the conditions of social life for ourselves as well as for our fellow citizens. As Anna Stilz has pointed out, 'the fact that my acts contribute to the public coercion of other people through the state also gives rise to important responsibilities to these other people'.[20] Consequently, it is a moral and political duty for each and every citizen to promote and contribute to institutional structures that protect each and every citizen's rights to freedom and well-being.

Hence, the case of Carr and Mrs. Bates differs from Gewirth's original case of Carr and Davis. In the case of Carr and Davis, it is a question of a physical intervention that only Carr is capable of, and as Carr does not stand to risk any aspect of his own basic well-being in rescuing Davis, then Carr, and Carr alone, has the duty to rescue Davis. In the case of Carr and Mrs. Bates, it is a question of social justice, and Carr's duty is to contribute his fair share of support for an institutional structure that can provide not only Mrs. Bates, but everyone in her predicament with medical care, in accordance with the equal rights to basic well-being prescribed by the PGC. However,

The Gewirthian Duty to Rescue   225

the social justice case of Mrs. Bates and Carr shares one feature with the case of Bates and Carr as potential rescuers of Davis and Evans, namely, that it involves a plurality of providers of help. Hence, the CCCC and its requirement of a fair distribution of sacrifices among contributors and rescuers can be applied to both types of case.

CONCLUSION

We have been able to modify and develop the Gewirthian duty to rescue without disconnecting it from the justificatory framework once provided by Gewirth himself. The duty to rescue can now accommodate cases in which there is more than one potential rescuer. Given the level-based interpretation of comparable costs, agents are not required to sacrifice any part of their basic well-being in a rescue operation, which is consistent with the significance that all agents must attach to the very preconditions of their agency. And consistent with the requirement of the PGC that relations between agents should be based on justice, we have introduced the Combined Comparable Cost Condition, which prescribes that there should be a fair distribution of sacrifices of nonsubtractive and additive well-being among rescuers. Moreover, with the help of the CCCC, we have also been able to clarify the distinction between individual duties of rescue and social duties of support for institutional frameworks protective of agents' rights.

NOTES

1. A. Gewirth, *Reason and Morality* (Chicago, IL: University of Chicago Press, 1978), pp. 217–8.
2. Ibid., p. 135.
3. Ibid., p. 219.
4. E. Mack, 'Deontologism, Negative Causation, and the Duty to Rescue', in E. Regis Jr. (ed), *Gewirth's Ethical Rationalism* (Chicago, IL: University of Chicago Press, 1984), pp. 147–66, on p. 162.
5. R. Norman, *Ethics, Killing and War* (Cambridge: Cambridge University Press, 1995), p. 81.
6. Gewirth, *Reason and Morality*, p. 224.
7. Ibid., p. 220.
8. L. B. Murphy, 'The Demands of Beneficence', *Philosophy and Public Affairs*, 22:4 (1993), pp. 267–92, on p. 278.
9. Murphy, 'The Demands of Beneficence', p. 280.
10. Gewirth, *Reason and Morality*, p. 218.
11. Ibid., p. 63.
12. Ibid., p. 212.
13. A. Gewirth, *The Community of Rights* (Chicago, IL: University of Chicago Press, 1996), p. 51.
14. Gewirth, *Reason and Morality*, p. 288.
15. A. Gewirth, 'Are There Any Absolute Rights?', *Philosophical Quarterly*, 31:122 (1981), pp. 1–16, on pp. 12–14.

226 *Bauhn*

16. D. Cummiskey, 'Gewirth's Kantian Consequentialism', in M. Boylan (ed), *Gewirth* (Lanham, MD: Rowman & Littlefield, 1999), pp. 125–39, on p. 137.
17. Gewirth, *Reason and Morality*, pp. 290–327.
18. Ibid., p. 315.
19. A. Gewirth, *Self-Fulfillment* (Princeton, NJ: Princeton University Press, 1998), p. 214.
20. A. Stilz, *Liberal Loyalty* (Princeton, NJ: Princeton University Press, 2009), p. 201.

WORKS CITED

Cummiskey, D., 'Gewirth's Kantian Consequentialism', in M. Boylan (ed.), *Gewirth* (Lanham, MD: Rowman & Littlefield, 1999), pp. 125–39.

Gewirth, A., *Reason and Morality* (Chicago, IL: University of Chicago Press, 1978).

———, 'Are There Any Absolute Rights?', *Philosophical Quarterly*, 31:122 (1981), pp. 1–16.

———, *The Community of Rights* (Chicago, IL: University of Chicago Press, 1996).

———, *Self-Fulfillment* (Princeton, NJ: Princeton University Press, 1998).

Mack, E., 'Deontologism, Negative Causation, and the Duty to Rescue', in E. Regis Jr. (ed.), *Gewirth's Ethical Rationalism* (Chicago, IL: University of Chicago Press, 1984), pp. 147–66.

Murphy, L. B., 'The Demands of Beneficence', *Philosophy and Public Affairs*, 22:4 (1993), pp. 267–92.

Norman, R., *Ethics, Killing and War* (Cambridge: Cambridge University Press, 1995).

Stilz, A., *Liberal Loyalty* (Princeton, NJ: Princeton University Press, 2009).

Contributors

Per Bauhn is a Professor of Practical Philosophy at Linnaeus University, Sweden. He has previously applied Alan Gewirth's moral theory to problems relating to political terrorism and nationalism (*Ethical Aspects of Political Terrorism*, 1989, and *Nationalism and Morality*, 1995, both Lund University Press). He has also applied a Gewirthian approach to the virtue of courage (*The Value of Courage*, Nordic Academic Press, 2003). Professor Bauhn has published several articles in international philosophical journals on the duty to rescue.

Deryck Beyleveld is a Professor of Law and Bioethics at Durham Law School, Durham University, and a Professor of Moral Philosophy and Applied Ethics at the University of Utrecht. He is the author of *The Dialectical Necessity of Morality: An Analysis and Defense of Alan Gewirth's Argument to the Principle of Generic Consistency* and (with Roger Brownsword) of three monographs applying Gewirthian theory, *Law as a Moral Judgment, Human Dignity in Bioethics and Biolaw* and *Consent in the Law*. He is also the author or co-author of numerous articles defending Gewirth's moral theory and applying it to a wide range of topics.

Dr. Phil Bielby is a Lecturer in the Law School and a Research Associate of the Institute of Applied Ethics at the University of Hull, UK. He is the author of *Competence and Vulnerability in Biomedical Research* (Springer, 2008), which applied a Gewirthian framework in theorizing the ethical grounds for making judgements about the decisional competence of cognitively vulnerable people to consent to biomedical research. He has also published a number of journal articles and book chapters in the area of bioethics and medical law, particularly in relation to mental health and mental capacity law and ethics. His current research focuses on conceptualizing mental health vulnerability in legal theory, as well as how rights theory and care ethics may be reconciled.

Michael Boylan is a professor of Philosophy and the Chair of the Philosophy Department at Marymount University in Arlington, Virginia, USA. Boylan

228   *Contributors*

was a student of Alan Gewirth at the University of Chicago. In Boylan's own writings, he has published 29 books and over 130 articles. He has been an invited speaker at major universities in 15 countries covering 5 continents. His 2004 book, *A Just Society*, was the subject of a book of critical essays by 14 authors from 8 countries, entitled *Morality and Justice: Reading Boylan's A Just Society*. Most recently, he published *Natural Human Rights: A Theory* (Cambridge University Press, 2014). He has served on government policy committees, been a fellow at the Center for American Progress, and has been a presenter at the Brookings Institution. Presently, he is at work establishing a bioethics center in Chile.

Dr. Stephen A. Brown is a Senior Lecturer in sociology at the University of Brighton. His research interests are in class and stratification, the concept of power, the philosophy of social science, and the works of Marx and Weber. He completed a DPhil on 'Alan Gewirth and the Political Community' at the University of Sussex in 2002.

Christoph Hübenthal is a Professor of Systematic Theology at Radboud University Nijmegen (The Netherlands). His current research focuses on public theology as an apologetically inspired form of social ethics. One of the application areas of such a public theology is the field of sports. In 2012, he co-edited *Sport and Christianity: A Sign of the Times in the Light of Faith*.

Dr. Robert A. Montaña is a Professor of Philosophy and an Associate Researcher on Corporate Social Responsibility at the University of Santo Tomas in Manila, the Philippines. He wrote a dissertation on the possibility of utilizing the foundational paradigms of Alan Gewirth's Principle of Generic Consistency as an apologetic response against critics. He is the author of *Thomistic Ethics: A Beacon in the Contemporary Moral Landscape*, and has written and delivered papers in theoretical and applied ethics.

Marie Constance Morley is a PhD Candidate in Conflict Studies, Faculty of Human Sciences, at St. Paul University, Ottawa, Canada. Morley has worked in the mental health care sector and did her MA in public ethics thesis on the living conditions of people suffering mental illness using Alan Gewirth's theory of human rights as her philosophical framework.

Vincent J. Samar is an Adjunct Professor of Law at the Illinois Institute of Technology, Chicago-Kent College of Law and an Adjunct Professor of Philosophy at both Loyola University Chicago and Oakton Community College. He is the author of *Justifying Judgment: Practicing Law and Philosophy* (University Press of Kansas, 1998), *The Right to Privacy: Gays, Lesbians and the Constitution* (Temple University Press, 1991),

Contributors 229

and editor of *New York Times, 20th Century in Review: Gay Rights Movement* (2001). He has also published numerous articles and review articles on matters of law, philosophy, same-sex marriage, gay rights, and human rights. Samar holds a PhD in philosophy from the University of Chicago, an LLM from Harvard Law School, and joint JD/MPA degrees from Syracuse University. Samar also teaches 'Sexual Orientation and the Law' at IIT: Chicago-Kent College of Law.

Edward Spence (Honors, First Class, and PhD, University of Sydney) teaches philosophy, including moral philosophy and ethics, as well as applied ethics, in the School of Communication and Creative Industries, Charles Sturt University, Australia. He is a senior research fellow at the ARC Special Research Centre for Applied Philosophy and Public Ethics in Australia, and Research Fellow at the 3TU Centre for Ethics and Technology, Den Haag, the Netherlands. He is the author of several books, including *Advertising Ethics* (2005), *Corruption and Anti-Corruption: A Philosophical Approach* (2005), *Ethics Within Reason: A Neo-Gewirthian Approach* (2006), *Media, Markets, and Morals, New Ethics for Digital Media,* (forthcoming), and *The Good Life in a Technological Age* (edited volume, 2012). He is also the author of numerous refereed papers in national and international journals. He is the founder and producer of the *Theatre of Philosophy* project, whose aim is the introduction of philosophy to the general public through drama and audience participation. Several of Edward's philosophy plays have been performed at arts and cultural festivals throughout Australia and the US.

Dr. Miriam Stevenson has worked as a lecturer, researcher and practitioner in the social work field for almost thirty years. As a qualified social worker in the UK she practiced in a broad number of fields including statutory Children and Families and Disability Services (Transition). She completed her MA in Socio-Legal Studies in 1998 (Sheffield, UK). In Australia, she completed her PhD research at the University of Sydney using a Participatory Action Research framework to explore aspects of social citizenship alongside young adults who have Down syndrome. She has a strong interest in social justice with a focus on the inclusion and empowerment of marginalized citizens via participatory research production. Her specific interests are in applied human rights philosophy in social work practice, restorative justice, intellectual disability and the well-being of young people in out of home care.

Dr. Shu-Mei Tang is a Professor and Chairman of Financial and Economical Law at Asia University (Taiwan). For the past few years, Dr. Tang has been working on projects regarding bioinformatics, privacy issues, biobank, regenerative medicine, and face recognition in eBusiness. She has published over thirty articles in peer-reviewed professional journals

230 *Contributors*

and books and currently is the chief editor for the peer-reviewed journal *Bio-Industry Technology Management Review*. Dr. Tang's research interests now focus on issues such as human dignity, informed consent, human subject research, privacy, and intellectual property rights.

Stuart Toddington (BA Hons Warwick, MA., PhD Sheffield) was the Chair of Jurisprudence at The University of Westminster and (currently) is the Chair at the University of Huddersfield. He has lectured in Europe, the US, and Pakistan, and is the author of several internationally acclaimed books and numerous jurisprudential, philosophical and sociological articles on the relationship between moral theory, natural law, and social science. These include: *Rationality, Social Action and Moral Judgment* (Edinburgh U.P); with H. P. Olsen, *Law in its Own Right* (Hart Publishers); and with HP Olsen, *Architectures of Justice*. He is the director of clinical research and the co-founder of the Legal Advice Centre in Huddersfield, and also writes widely on social justice and legal education.

Gregory J. Walters, PhD, is a Professor of Philosophy on the Faculty of Human Sciences and Philosophy at Saint Paul University/Université Saint-Paul, Ottawa, Canada. He is the author and editor of numerous works, including an application of Alan Gewirth's philosophy to the information age revolution, entitled *Human Rights in an Information Age: A Philosophical Analysis* (University of Toronto Press, 2001), with a foreword by Alan Gewirth.

Dr. Shang-Yung Yen is a Professor at the Graduate Institute of Management of Technology at Feng Chia University (Taiwan). He has been working on projects regarding the bioethical issues of biobank, regenerative medicine, xenotransplantation, and nanotechnology. Dr. Yen's research interests focus on issues such as human dignity, informed consent, human subject research, ethical, legal and social implications issues, and genomic medical research.

Index

abortion 167–8, 192
accountability 144, 194, 196
adoption 157–9, 164
agency 3–7, 14, 24–5, 81–6, 89–93, 149, 191, 198, 202, 219; and sacrifice 216, 221–2; approach to morality 47; and self-fulfilment 126–9; and virtue 35–42; generic conditions of 4–5, 13, 15, 19–21, 25; in Confucianism 115–17; justification 54; productive 103–4, 147, 149–50; vulnerable 174–81
agent(s) 2–7, 35–6, 96, 102, 127, 159–61, 174, 176–7, 198, 213–14, 216; as citizen 200; interests of 81, 162; prospective purposive 5, 48, 81–6, 113, 119, 160, 169n17
anthropology (Kant) 14–15, 26n21
anti-discrimination 157–8, 163–8
Aristotle 51, 53–5, 200
aspiration-fulfilment 128, 130
assertoric validity 18
autonomy 115, 117, 120–1, 123–4, 129, 157, 161, 165, 183–4

Bacon, Sir Francis 73
Benedict XVI 100
benevolence 114, 116, 118, 122
Burwell v. Hobby Lobby 167–8, 171nn58–9

capabilities approach 188n60
capacity-fulfilment 128, 131, 134
capitalism 140ff; and natural equilibrium 143; no general laws of 146–7, 152n24

care ethics 181–5
caring society (Gewirth) 175, 181, 183–5
categorical imperative 13, 15–18, 20–1, 23–4, 27, 113
Catholic Social Thought (CST) 97–101, 103–7
circularity (vicious or virtuous) 66, 68
citizen engagement model (CEM) 203–6
civil liberties 148–9
civil unions 158, 166
class warfare 146
Combined Comparable Cost Condition (CCCC) 217–25; social implications of 222–5
common good 98, 103–6, 148
community; and psychological harmony 148; historical and particular 148; of rights 6, 144, 146–51
comparable cost condition 216–17; level-based interpretation of 218; strictly symmetrical interpretation of 217–18
compassion 183–4
Confucius and Confucianism 111, 114–23
Cooperative Principle 215–16
corporal punishment 158
counselling and psychotherapy 179

degrees of needfulness for action, criterion of 5, 150, 218
dependence 176, 182–4
deprivation focus 147, 149, 153n38
dialectically necessary method 5, 68, 102, 104, 113, 122, 159–60
dialectical necessity 13–25
Difference Principle (Rawls) 129

232 Index

dignity 98, 101–5, 150, 157, 161, 164–5, 177, 182; supervenes on rights 160–1, 169
disability 191–201, 203–6; intellectual 175–6, 178, 181, 191–4, 196–7, 199, 203–6; rights 179, 181, 187n44; social model of 194–6, 199, 204
Down syndrome 191–3, 196–7, 200, 203, 206
Durkheim, Émile 84
duty, -ies; negative and positive 214; perfect to self 21; social 222–5; to rescue 131, 212–25

economic biography 147
economic democracy 140–1, 144, 147, 149
economic redistribution 140–2, 144, 150
economic science 142, 144, 150
education 145, 147, 149; and social mobility 145; and the supportive state 149
egalitarian liberalism 165
emancipatory disability research (EDR) 194–6, 203
empathy 183
end in itself 15, 19, 21
environmental damage 132
evangelization 106–7
equality 140–1, 146, 165; and diffusion of knowledge 146; before the law 128, 157, 159, 161, 163, 165, 169n3
evil 115, 122

fact–value distinction 64, 69, 76
faculties of mind 15, 23, 26n16, 27n38
Fichte, Johann Gottlieb 24
Formula of Humanity 13, 15, 19–21
Formula of Universal Law 14, 16–19, 21
freedom 4, 6, 38, 52, 54, 63, 69, 82–5, 90–2, 99, 102–3, 113, 127, 147, 150, 159–60, 162, 166–8, 176–8, 198, 213
free will 13–14, 17, 19, 21–4, 26, 28; reciprocal to morality 22

gender identity 157–8
gender transition 158–9
genetic lottery 145

Gewirth, Alan; and Catholic social thought 101–7; and Confucian philosophy 111–21; and critical sociological theory 85–93; and economic democracy 146–50; and international law 125–36; and LGBT rights 159–69; and mental health rights 174–85; and social citizenship 198–202; and stoic philosophy 30–43; life of 1–2; moral theory of 3–7, 13–25, 30–1, 35–43, 48–55, 63–72
God 14, 22–4, 26, 28
Golden Rule 119–20, 123
goods; additive 102, 127; basic 102, 107, 127, 175; necessary 4; non-substractive 102, 107, 127; types of 160
Greatest Happiness Principle 113
Griswold v. Connecticut 162

Habermas, Jürgen 84, 93, 105, 196
heightened vulnerability 178, 180–1, 188n55
heightened vulnerable agency 174, 176–81, 184, 185
homo noumenon 22–3, 27
homo phaenomenon 22–3, 27
Hsun Tzu 117, 122–4
humanity 111, 114, 116
Hume, David 16, 63–5, 71–5
Hume's Law 3, 5, 64, 67, 72, 75

immortality 14, 22–4
inaction 214
income 142–3, 145–6, 150, 152n17
inequality 140; and resentment 148; background factors 145–6; global 142, 146–50; of income 143; social 140
internalism 16
international law; as a community of rights 132; legal framework of 125; nature of 125; positivist interpretation of 126; subject–object dichotomy in 129
is–ought problem 63, 66–9, 71

Jen 114–20, 122
John Paul II 98
justice 140: social 143
justification 147

Index 233

Kant, Immanuel 13–25, 47, 51–2, 54–5, 67, 73–4, 113
Korsgaard, Christine 21

Lawrence v. Texas 162
Leo XIII 98–9
libertarians 165–6
liberty, maximal vs. minimal 165
love 151, 181–2
Lukes, Steven 81, 86–93

markets 143, 148, 150, 152n12
market socialism 149, 153n35
marriage 157–8, 162–4, 166; and self-fulfillment 164–5; and the minimal state 171n45; as a unique voluntary association 170n42; Canon Law restrictions concerning 171n49; external vs. internal attributes of 164
Marx, Karl 84, 92, 145, 195, 199
meaning; in life 6; of life 106–7
Mencius 115, 117–18, 122–4
mental equilibrium (Gewirth) 175–6
mental health problems, people with 175, 177–81, 184–5, 186n2
migrants 131
Mill, John Stuart 165
minimal state 165
Morality; particularist vs. universalist 166, 171n48; supreme principle of 13, 25–6; universalist 132
moral law 14, 17–18, 20–4; natural 23; *ratio cognoscendi* for 18, 22; *ratio essendi* for 14, 18–19, 21–4
moral realism 101–2, 105
mutuality 140, 147–9, 151, 152n28

natural law theory 97, 99–101, 105–6
neurodiversity 180
non-contradiction, law or principle of 47–56

participatory action research (PAR) 193–7
phenomenology 25
Piketty, Thomas 140–51
political democracy 140–1; and economic democracy 144; and inequalities of wealth and power 148
poverty 140, 142, 147
power; and economic and political democracy 146; and wealth

143; *de facto* and *de jure* 146; sociological conception of 85–9
power of judgement 14–18, 23–4, 26–8; maxim of 14, 18, 22, 24, 28; reflective 22
precautionary reasoning 187n39
Principle of Generic Consistency (PGC) 5, 13–15, 19, 20–1, 24–5, 28, 48, 101–6, 112–14, 113, 116, 119, 120–1, 126, 140, 147, 160–1, 213
Principle of Hypothetical Imperatives 13–15, 20–1, 23, 25
Principle of the Intervening Action 220
Principle of Reasonableness 140
purposiveness of nature 26

rationality; as economic and technological 146; as means–end 147; as reasonableness 147
rational nature 15, 19
reason; as veridical capacity 134; fact of 14, 17; faculty of 26; harmony of 14, 26; maxim of 13–25; priority of practical 22, 24; supreme principle of practical 16, 19, 21, 25; unity of 24
reasonableness 69, 84, 146–50
reasonable self 129, 148, 175, 181, 183–5
reflective understanding 160
Rerum Novarum 98–9
resilience 177–9, 187n40
right(s); basic 175, 179; equal 145, 148, 152n19; human 102, 104–7, 148, 159–60, 191, 193–5, 198–204, 206; mental health 174–5, 177–81, 183–5, 187n48; negative 160, 179–80; nonsubtractive 179; of Man and the Citizen, Declaration of 148; positive 160, 179–80, 183–4; prudential vs. moral 160; social 143; to assembly and association 162; to cultural pluralism 167; to economic democracy 147; to education 147–8; to employment 6, 147; to freedom and well-being 147, 150, 213; to freedom of expression 157, 159, 161, 165, 169; to healthcare 148; to housing 148; to life 162; to love 176; to pension 148; to political democracy 147; to privacy 157,

234 Index

159, 161, 165, 169; to private property 147; to productive agency 147; to security 162; Universal Declaration of 129, 162–3
Roe v. Wade 162

same-sex relationships 157–8, 166
self, concept of the 183
self-destruction 23
self-fulfillment 6, 126, 128, 132, 135, 160, 166
self-referring 'ought' 15, 20–1
sensus communis 15–16, 18
Separatist Thesis (Gewirth) 150
sexual conduct 162
social citizenship 193–4, 197–8, 200–3, 206
social contribution, 140, 141, 148
social inclusion 193–4, 197
solidarity 98, 103–6, 147
state; democratic 6, 148, 223; minimal 5–6, 148, 165, 223; social (Piketty) 140, 142–5; supportive 6, 101–4, 145, 148–9, 165, 223
sterilization 158–9
subsidiarity 98, 103–6
summum bonum 22–3, 28
supported decision-making 184–5
synthetic *a priori* 13–14, 26

theonomy 99–101, 105
Tian 116, 118–20
transcendental philosophy 13, 15, 21–6, 28
truth, theories of 76

truth-value 66–7, 72, 75–6
Tsze-Kung 117–18, 122

understanding; agential self- 14, 16, 18, 24; common human 14–15, 24; faculty of 26; maxim of 14, 18, 22, 24, 28
universal generalization 50–2, 54
universalizability 119, 127
utilitarianism 165

verificationism 64
Vienna Circle 64
virtue(s) 103, 113–16, 118–19, 122–3
vulnerability 174, 176–8, 183–4, 187n43
vulnerable agency 174, 176–8, 185

war, preemptive and preventive 130
Weber, Max 81, 83–4, 92–3
well-being 4, 6, 33, 38, 53–4, 63, 65, 69, 82–5, 90–2, 102–5, 113, 127, 147, 150, 159–60, 163, 165–8, 174–9, 198–9, 213; additive 4, 6, 113, 150, 160, 175, 178, 205, 213, 222; basic 4, 6, 113, 131, 160, 168, 175–6, 178, 213, 218–19, 221, 225; hierarchy of levels of 218–9; nonsubtractive 4, 6, 113, 150, 160, 166, 178, 213, 222; psychological 174–8
Williams, Bernard 23, 83–5
Writ of *Kalikasan* 125, 133

Yuann/Yuh 114–21